WHITE LIES
WHITE
POWER

The Fight Against
White Supremacy and
Reactionary Violence

Michael Novick

Common Courage Press   Monroe, Maine

Library of Congress
Cataloging-in-Publication Data
Novick, Michael
White lies/white power: the fight against white
supremacy and reactionary violence/
Michael Novick.
p. cm.
ISBN 1-56751-051-5 (cloth).
ISBN 1-56751-050-7 (pbk.)
1. Racism--United States.
2. United States--Race relations.
I. Title.
E184.A1N58 1995
305.8'00973--dc20   94-44051
CIP

Common Courage Press
P.O. Box 702
Monroe, ME 04951
207-525-0900 fax: 207-525-3068
First Printing

Advance Praise for *White Lies • White Power*

Race and racism are central to American politics. Michael Novick provides a vigorous and insightful analysis that helps us understand the ideology of white supremacy and its centrality to contemporary political debates.

—Manning Marable

What does racism and white supremacy have to do with rising violence and our country's drift to the right? Michael Novick offers brilliant, detailed analysis about the role white supremacy plays in the attacks on women's rights, on gays and lesbians, on immigrants, and on other people of color. This work is especially powerful because Novick looks at the history of white supremacy and follows that history to the present, dissecting the evolution of the Ku Klux Klan from crude lynchers to media-savvy but equally crude provocateurs. This solution-oriented work uses all the "c" words that have receded in institutional analysis—capitalism, colonialism, cooptation. Hard-hitting, insightful, refreshing.

—Julianne Malveaux
Pacifica Radio

White Lies/White Power argues powerfully that white supremacy in the U.S. is not a marginal activity by extremists but implicit and complicit with institutionalized liberal democracy and a corporate state willing to use political repression to block dissent, especially in the face of the complacent and comatose mainstream human relations and civil rights community.

—Chip Berlet
Political Research Associates

A PART Book
People Against Racist Terror
P.O. Box 1990
Burbank, CA 91507
310-288-5003

Turning the Tide, a Journal of Anti-Racist
Activism, Research and Education, is available quar-
terly. Sample copies are four dollars, subscriptions
are $15 a year for individuals in the U.S., $25 for
institutions or for foreign subscriptions.

Contents

Acknowledgments

This book is dedicated to my parents, Ben and Charlotte, who taught me the importance of telling the truth; to Avon, who taught me to trust myself enough to accept love; to Lucas, Sasha, and Charles, who taught me to have confidence in the future; and to the memories of Black Panther Fred Hampton and gay liberationist Michael Silverstein, who taught me that we all live on borrowed time.

Although the views and perspectives expressed here are my own, I would like to acknowledge the personal and political guidance, encouragement and support I have received over the years from a number of activists and researchers too numerous to mention individually, but including Kamal Hassan and other participants in the New Afrikan independence movement, Priscilla Falcon, Ricardo Romero and others in the Mexicano liberation struggle, Alejandrina Torres, Jose Lopez and other members of the Puerto Rican independence movement, members of the John Brown Anti-Klan committee and Prairie Fire, Loretta Ross of the Center for Democratic Renewal and that group's former research director, Leonard Zeskind, and such contributors to *Turning the Tide* as Judy Miller, Dan Yurman, and Tom Burghardt.

Problems and Solutions

D uring the 1960s, the Black Panther Party had a slogan, "You're either part of the problem or you're part of the solution." This was an update on the old union question, "Which side are you on?" It was, in some ways, an improvement: more dynamic, more open-ended, and more active. It recognizes that contradictions run through individuals, not simply between them, but that we can put ourselves behind making the world, and ourselves, better. It potentially recognizes that nobody has a monopoly on truth or the whole answer, but that everyone has a contribution to make.

It puts forward the hope that together, we can overcome the problems that face us. It is an invitation and a challenge to people, not simply to take a stand or choose a side, but to help change the balance between the forces of repression and those of liberation. Applied in a positive way, it tends towards inclusion, broadening the definition of friends and minimizing those who are enemies (which is the opposite of what many on the left tended, and still tend, to do).

This book is an invitation to readers to take part in the struggle, to be part of the solution. "Participatory democracy" was one of the first radicalizing notions of the '60s New Left, a rejection of corporate liberalism and authoritarianism. Today, with such "liberals" again in power, people who want to combat racism need to examine the nature of the problem confronting us, and the elements and parameters of possible solutions. It is not enough to recite a litany of things we are against, but also necessary to define what we are for. Such an analysis of problems and solutions must be unflinching, if it is to be helpful.

Problems

In order to find viable solutions, we must first clearly understand the true nature of the problem. One of the appeals of the racist right forces on the march today is that they offer simplistic solutions for the problems of our society by providing scapegoats—Blacks, immigrants, Jews, gays. They draw adherents because many of the liberal solutions of the past have not only been inadequate, but have proven to be part of the problem. In the '50s and '60s, many identified the problem of racism simply as "segregation." But the solution, "integration," had the unforeseen consequence of destroying most of the independent economic and social institutions in the Black community. In the '70s and '80s, the problem was seen as rooted in economic discrimination, but neither the liberal solution of "affirmative action," nor the conservative solution of "color-blindness" has had much impact in improving matters. In the '90s, racism has been reduced to the problem of hate crimes, of which any racial or ethnic group might be the victim at the hands of any other. But the solution, preaching "tolerance," doesn't begin to scratch the surface of the causes of violence.

So what are the fundamental problems, and how can we solve them?

Supremacists

Supremacists are unquestionably a big part of the problem. Klan-types, neo-nazis, and other open advocates of white power should not be ignored, dismissed, or taken lightly. They have the power to inflict damage on Blacks, Latinos, Asians, Native Americans, Jews, lesbians and gay men, and others whom they define as the enemy. They have a strategy, pursued through a wide variety of tactics, to promote a genocidal race war in this country, as a way to reimpose naked white power. Whether they seek to enter and influence the mainstream, like David Duke, or espouse openly racist revolutionism, like Tom Metzger, they share fundamental philosophical underpinnings and a vision of the society they want to create, a society that is the exact opposite of human liberation.

People of good will have a gut reaction of revulsion to the neo-nazis, but are divided about how to deal with them. Some say it's wrong to make a fuss about the neo-nazis, that it only gives them the attention they want. But this assumes that organized racists are only a fringe group, when in fact they are a phenomenon with a historical and material foundation. The white supremacists will not go away if we ignore them; they will fester and take root, like a bad case of athlete's foot, poisoning those they organize. Because they promote terrorism, they pose a threat to all liberatory social move-

7

ments. They are succeeding in influencing broad sectors of the population around various issues.

Much of this volume chronicles and exposes the efforts of racists and neo-nazis to hide their full agenda while they attract new adherents and broaden their base. They do this through high school and college organizing against affirmative action, through efforts to infiltrate the anti-intervention movement, through involvement in promoting anti-immigrant hysteria and violence. A similar pattern exists in the anti-abortion movement, where Klan- and nazi-influenced figures have led the way to bombings and murder. The anti-gay movement is helping forge an alliance between Christian rightists and Christian Identity racists. The racists are seeking to influence the environmental movement. Thus, involvement in any of the pressing social and political issues of our time necessarily involves confronting the supremacists.

State Power

But it's not sufficient simply to focus our fire on opposing the open racists. State power is also part of the problem we confront. It's true that the U.S. state has abandoned the openly white-supremacist laws and procedures that were common until the civil rights period. Except for the die-hard neo-nazi Afrikaners, even the South Africans, the world bastion of nakedly racist white rule, have abandoned open apartheid as the means to maintain white privileges. Israel, the most recently established settler-colonial state, has sought a rapprochement with the Palestinians. But it would be foolish to believe that the repressive states have truly reformed themselves. The white supremacists in the U.S., the

A.W.B. nazis in South Africa, the militant Jewish settlers in the West Bank, are rooted in the state apparatus and the colonial relations of their societies, and enjoy protection as long as they fulfill the interests of the state and the ruling elite.

This is a world-wide problem. In Italy, neo-fascists have won a position in the governing coalition that runs the state apparatus. In Germany, racist forces influence national policy on refugees and immigrants. In Russia, chauvinist and anti-Semitic politics have succeeded in winning a substantial following within the new, post-Soviet parliament. In Canada, white racist infiltration of the armed forces has been exposed. But it's more than a question of simply a few open racists within the state; the problem is that nation-states grew up in the context of racially justified conquest and colonialism.

Some of those who seek to oppose the white supremacists have turned to the police and other repressive apparatus of the state to achieve their goal. This is wrong. Anti-racists must not rely on the state to combat racists. To do so, when the state grows out of the same conditions of oppression that produce the supremacists, would be a fatal error. Police brutality, police spying and counter-insurgency operations, and military psychological warfare programs are all a key part of the problem we must confront. These are not simply aberrations; they are part of the essential nature of the system.

Society

Finally, while dealing with the state is also necessary, it is not sufficient if we are to address the full scope of the problem. Society itself is the third leg of the stool. The state grows out of and is an enforcement mechanism for the political and economic relations within the society as a whole. The supremacists are rooted in and shaped by the overall social structure which incorporates all of us.

The social formation which has sprung up in this country is based on white supremacy and colonialism, slavery and the conquest of land. It will continue to reproduce the resultant problems of racism, within new generations of individuals, new economic stratifications, and new forms of the state apparatus, until the society as a whole is transformed. This requires a social and cultural struggle of great magnitude and duration, not simply a rumble with some supremacists or even a war against the state.

Society exists within all of us and we exist within a society that has been shaped by centuries of exploitation and oppression. Systematic sexism, racism, and other forms of hierarchy shape our world unless and until we challenge them. Many young people today say, "Why bore me with all that history of racism? I'm not guilty of that or responsible for that." That's true—but we are all responsible for understanding the history that has shaped the present; we are all involved in the history that is being made today; and we are all responsible to help shape a different, and more just, future.

Solutions

Which brings us to the question of solutions. Are the problems insoluble? Some people seem to have given in to despair. Many of those who saw socialism as the solution have been disoriented since the collapse of the state socialist regimes of Eastern Europe. Some of those who saw socialism, at least as it existed, as part of the problem, have been no more capable of grasping the historic moment presented by the end of the cold war power blocs. Will more open racism, sexism, and homophobia replace anti-communism as the ideological cement among the supremacists, the state, and society? What can we do to prevent that outcome, and to take the initiative? There are a number of elements of the solution that present themselves.

Self-Esteem

Self-esteem is a critical element of a liberatory, anti-racist movement. The supremacists claim nowadays that they do not hate others, they only love white people; but those who truly love and respect themselves cannot hate and oppress others. The tremendous challenge posed to the system by the truce among Black "gangs", is evidence that the self-esteem of young Black men and women, the refusal to self-destruct, is a potent weapon against the system. The self-esteem of women is targeted by patriarchal society at an early age. In fact, overturning racist and patriarchal social relationships is a key to enhancing the self-esteem and self-respect of all children and young people, so that the character deformations that create hatred and power-hunger will not be produced. The proverb, "Love your neighbor as yourself" is impossible to follow if you do not love yourself. This is work we all need to do, and to support each other in doing. Self-esteem requires self-knowledge and a knowledge of the truth; thus, we see the importance of the scholars of Afro-centrism, of

11

women's studies, and of other techniques for uncovering suppressed history.

Self-Determination

Self-determination is another crucial element of making social change, and of challenging the state and the supremacists. The peoples whose identities have been defined by the oppressors must be able to define and defend themselves. The African Frantz Fanon wrote more than a generation ago of the psychology of decolonization, as the colonized people must break the power that the colonizer maintains over their minds. Because racism is rooted in colonialism and empire, it can only be ended by physical and mental decolonization.

But it is also true that European peoples, whose identity has been defined for half a millennium as colonizers, must also decolonize their own thinking, and create an identity not based on supposed superiority over a racially defined "other." The power relations between men and women must be similarly reexamined and re-defined, as women choose their own destinies and desires. We see gay men and lesbians today redefining on their own terms what it means to be "queer." The sovereignty struggle of native and indigenous people, whether in Hawaii, Australia, Puerto Rico, Palestine, or throughout the Americas, will redefine also the history and nature of the people who have colonized them. We must embrace these redefinitions, and abandon the supremacist identity that is based on the oppression and colonization of others.

Solidarity

Solidarity becomes critical at this juncture. It is not enough to say "I'm o.k., you're o.k." The mentality of "you do your thing and I'll do mine", will not build a new consciousness or a new world. We must be prepared to take up each other's struggles and causes. The supremacists have often reserved their worst venom for those they call "nigger lovers" or "race traitors." To create a new identity and reality, we must actively build new relationships of mutual support, based on respect for self-determination.

It is particularly the responsibility of whites to support Black liberation, of men to support women's liberation, of straights to support gay liberation, of Jews to support Palestinian liberation, of non-indigenous people to support native sovereignty, of Europeans to support African liberation, of Christians to oppose anti-Semitism. Only in this way can we uproot the deeply ingrained and historically determined identification with oppressors.

Furthermore, these struggles must be taken up not from a sense of noblesse oblige, as some sort of left version of the white man's burden. Solidarity is a reciprocal human obligation to be fully human. People fighting oppression want not cheerleaders or supporters, but allies in fighting the state, the system, and the shock troops. The vital contribution that members of oppressing groups have to make is to break the false solidarity of identifying with the oppressor, by identifying instead with the cause of humanity and liberation.

Spirituality

Spirituality, perhaps surprisingly to some, is another element that should be seen as crucial to anti-racist social transformation. I'm not talking about organized religion, necessarily; although as Malcolm X pointed out, through Islam he discovered the equality and unity of people of all races and nations. Jews and Christians too, Buddhists and followers of many other religions can also be found among all the nations of humanity. Religions have commonly put forward ethical principles of love for one's fellows that are more important than their rituals or superstitions. A religion that truly practiced what it preached would not be the basis for as much hatred and repression as so many have been. "Love your neighbor as yourself" is still a vital ethical rule with a revolutionary potential to transform society.

But by spirituality I also mean a reverence for all life, not only humans, and for the planetary and cosmic system that sustains it, a tapestry greater than any individual and yet manifest within every individual. Without this sense of the natural order within which our current society exists, we cannot hope to create a better society, less at odds and more in harmony with that order.

Struggle

Struggle is also a necessary component of the solution. Power concedes nothing without a struggle, said Frederick Douglass, a great Black abolitionist and revolutionary. If you want change without struggle, he said, it's like wanting rain without thunder and lightning. That struggle may be moral, it may be physical, or it may be both moral and physical, Douglass said, but it must be a struggle.

This remains as true today as in the struggle to

14

abolish slavery. As we solidarize with each other, as we seek harmony with the global biosphere, we will inevitably confront those who seek to maintain all the problems—the supremacists, the state, the systems that maintain society as it is and has been. And so we must be prepared for unrelenting struggle. Self-respect, spirituality, solidarity are weapons we can use. We must build a culture of resistance, sustained through our daily lives and interactions, that enables us to carry that struggle forward to victory. Such struggle takes place not only between social groups and forces, but within individuals.

Self-Defense

A key principle of such struggle is the right to self-defense. Life in general does not easily or voluntarily extinguish itself, and though human life is particularly capable of controlling itself self-consciously, there is no need for a moral code that denies humans, and human cultures, the right to defend themselves from extinction or eradication. Joining in such a defense against repression and genocide is a critical aspect of the solidarity that will advance us to a more humane future.

Self-Criticism

But particularly if we are going to use violence in self-defense, a vital factor in finding a lasting solution is self-criticism. If we only identify the problem outside ourselves, we will never come to grips with the totality of the problem. If we only criticize others, we will have no credibility. We have all internalized oppressive aspects of the system and society, and we must all internalize the struggle as well. Otherwise, we will demonize "the racists" without confronting our own racism. We will alienate people who like ourselves must change and participate in the struggle.

Self-criticism is also vital because nobody is exempt from the struggle. The oppressed must not turn around and become the oppressor. This has happened all too often in the past. Perceiving oneself exclusively as a victim leads eventually to becoming a victimizer, to seeking revenge rather than justice. Without self-criticism, for example, anarchists may be no less likely than statists to reproduce the oppression they claim to be overthrowing.

The Jewish people were targeted for genocide by the Third Reich, and abandoned by many others to their fate; but Israeli Jews have turned around to become expropriators and oppressors of the Palestinians. The Serbs of Yugoslavia were victims of Croat collaborators with Hitler during World War II; but today the Serbs are participating in a genocide against Muslim Slavs and a criminal war among Serbs, Croats, and Muslims. The Chinese were oppressed by various imperial powers, particularly England and Japan; but now the Chinese violate the human rights of the Tibetans, and the Chinese government imprisons dissidents.

It is a mistake to regard the oppressed as simply powerless, exclusively as victims. The oppressed in fact have power and are capable of exercising it— otherwise, a revolutionary transformation and an end to oppression would be impossible. And therefore, the oppressed people, like anyone else, are capable of abusing and misusing power, now or later. Self-criticism is essential to preventing this. It is necessary to recognize that the object of bigotry can also be bigoted. Thus, self-criticism on the part of anti-racists and liberation activists is essential to becoming worthy of the trust and participation of the ordinary people who must risk everything to make a significant change in the world. Their common sense of fair-play and justice requires that everyone be held to a common standard.

I once held to the view that, because racism required both prejudice and power, people of color could not be racist. I now see this as a mistaken view. There are various forms and sources of power, ranging from physical force, to political organization, to the application of knowledge, to physical and social phenomena, to wealth. People of color can and do at times exercise these powers, individually and collectively. So, people of color can be prejudiced and can have the power to put their prejudices into practice—to be racist.

Such racism, whether between people of color or against whites, should be opposed, not excused. White supremacy is the particular world historic form of racism tied to colonialism and European world domination. It is the dominant and systematic form of racism today. It is still the ruling idea and practice of the global system, but it is not the only form of racism. As a dominant ideology, it acts as a magnet and model for other forms of racism and discrimination. For this reason, as well as because it is the key prop of a global system of injustice and exploitation, white supremacy must be the principal target of anti-racists.

But principal target does not mean exclusive

target. The Japanese are people of color, yet they have a strong imperial drive in their history, a history of racism and colonialism towards other Asian peoples, including the Chinese and Koreans; and manifestations of racism towards whites and blacks are not uncommon in Japanese society. Most Mexicans are of indigenous origin, yet racism and discrimination against unassimilated indigenous people is quite strong in Mexico. Certainly people of color within the U.S., the strongest and wealthiest country on earth—even though they are colonized and discriminated against within this country—are not exempt from this pattern. So while we need strategically to seek to dismantle the overarching system of white supremacy and colonialism, tactically it is vital to oppose all forms of racism from all sources.

This argument does not mean to equate all forms of racism. Clearly, the hate and fear of the oppressor for members of oppressed groups is based on guilt and a desire to maintain privileges; whereas the hate and fear of the oppressed for members of the oppressing groups is based on a survival instinct and the desire to end oppression. Nonetheless, it remains true that both the oppressor and the oppressed, even if for different reasons, must overcome this hate and fear. Revenge is not the solution to oppression, particularly if that revenge is aimed simply and indiscriminately at all people of the same skin color, nationality, or religion of the oppressing group.

Nor is opposing other forms of racism besides white supremacy the same as claiming that affirmative action is "racism in reverse." Steps to overcome and compensate for racism are not racist; we do not become color-blind by simply declaring ourselves so, in the face of huge social and economic disparities based on color and nationality. Affirmative action, reparations, the redistribution of wealth, can all be necessary and justifiable measures.

What I am arguing, quite simply, is that self-criticism is vital for members of oppressed groups as well as for those born into oppressor groups. Strategic thinking requires that the enemy be defined precisely and according to his actions; it is racist, and therefore illogical and self-defeating, to blame all Blacks or all whites, all Jews or all Christians, all men or all women, for the actions of some.

Socialism

Finally, in addressing solutions, we must look to socialism in some form as a replacement for the current economic system. Racism and colonialism are bound up inseparably with the system of private wealth and private control of land, resources, and labor. Democratic, anti-authoritarian socialism is necessary to remove the profit motive from racism and to protect the earth. Such socialism does not mean simply replacing corporate ownership with state ownership; it certainly doesn't mean imposing the dictatorship of a political party or state apparatus over all economic or social or cultural activity.

But some form of social ownership of the "common-wealth" is essential, as well as some systematic way of ensuring that no form of ownership will violate the rights of people or the sanctity of the land. The pre-existing relations of people to land in the

Americas, Africa, the Pacific Islands should be restored along with the sovereignty of the indigenous peoples, and the rest of the world should learn from their example.

Racism 101

For the past several years, white supremacist groups like the Ku Klux Klan (KKK), and David Duke's National Association for the Advancement of White People (NAAWP) have been claiming that they are not racists. They say they are not motivated by hate, but are simply proponents of "white rights." Duke, Thom Robb and Shawn Slater of the KKK, Tom Metzger of WAR (White Aryan Resistance), and others say they are trying to redress what they claim is current discrimination against white people.

Some people have been seduced by these arguments. But their essential dishonesty should be evident. No white racists, claiming that Black people now enjoy unfair advantages, would be willing to exchange their own conditions of existence and their own supposed "oppression" for the situation of Black people in America, or that of most Africans, Mexicans, Puerto Ricans, Central Americans, Asian/Pacific Islanders, or native people.

Yet, even though the specious nature of these claims is evident, many white people claim that they "don't see what Black people are always complaining about." A lot of white people say that they themselves are not racists and they don't see that racism is such a big problem. They wish that Black people would stop making such a big fuss about "past discrimination." Perhaps this is only a case of, once again, none being so blind as those who will not see. But in the interest of taking at face value these arguments and protestations of ignorance as to what the problem is, and in hopes that, by treating them as sincere, such ignorance may be dispelled, let's look at a summary of the material reality of racism, in particular as it regards Black people in the U.S. Such a summary will demonstrate that racism is rooted in colonial power relations.

Racism and the Criminal Justice System

The racial skew in U.S. courts and prisons is so extreme that it is not an exaggeration to assume that the system is expressly designed to criminalize Black people. A study in the 1980s in Los Angeles, for example, showed that Black people go to state prison about 20% more often than white people arrested for the same crimes, and serve sentences of from one to two years longer, on average. This is so despite another study by the Rand Corporation that showed that higher percentages of Blacks and Latinos than whites were released after being arrested because of insufficient evidence to substantiate the charges.

The U.S. Supreme Court has upheld the constitutionality of the death penalty, ruling that it is legal even though there is a racial disparity in its application. The death penalty is much more likely to be imposed if the victim was white than if the victim was Black. The prison population in the U.S., the largest in the world, is disproportionately Black, Latino, and Native American, and the disproportion is even greater on Death Row. U.S. Blacks are more than three times as likely as South African Blacks to go to prison; eight times more likely than white Americans. Current statistics show that one in three Black male youths are in custody or under some form of parole or probation.

Against these underlying realities, the acquittal of the white police who brutalized Black motorist Rodney King, and the decision of a judge not to impose any prison time on the Korean woman grocer who killed Black teenager Latasha Harlins, served to ignite the 1992 L.A. uprising. These cases underlined the extent to which the "justice" system is designed to victimize Black people, not protect them. Such discrimination is a manifestation, among other things, of the comparative exclusion of Blacks from the legal profession and from the judiciary.

Only in 1992, for example, did the Justice Department begin to apply the provisions of the Voting Rights Act to the drawing of districts for the election of judges; such districting had long been designed to diminish the chances of Blacks to win judgeships. Moving the L.A. police brutality case to suburban Simi Valley, with virtually no Blacks in the jury pool, was only a more blatant manifestation, by a panel of judges and the white cops' defense attorneys, of a common prosecutorial habit of excluding individual Blacks from juries.

George Bush, for example, once tried to appoint to the federal appeals court a man whose job had been to defend death penalty convictions on appeal. He defended as justified cases where the D.A. had divided jurors into four groups: strong, acceptable, weak, and Black. In New York, it was recently disclosed that white jurors from suburban areas of Long Island were brought in to Brooklyn courthouses that were drawing substantially Black and Latin juries; whereas the opposite is never the case, even though juries in Nassau and Suffolk are predominantly white, and Black and Latin jurors from Brooklyn would provide the corresponding "balance."

The drug war is another example. Surveys consistently show that illegal drug use is, if anything, more extensive among whites than Blacks. Yet in both media portrayals and reality, Blacks are a disproportionate percentage of those arrested and convicted for drug crimes. In federal courts, enhanced penalties for sale are overwhelmingly sought against Black and Latino offenders. Sentencing for possession of crack cocaine, generally used by poor Blacks, is much more severe than for powdered cocaine, generally used by rich whites.

A visit to the criminal courts is a lesson in the nature of race-based colonialism. The lawmakers, law enforcers, jurists, and jurors, are predominantly white, the defendants predominantly Black and Latino.

Racism and Economics

It is widely recognized, even in official unemployment figures, that unemployment is always at least twice as high among Black people as among whites. Official figures also undercount the larger percentages of under-employed and "discouraged" Black workers. This gap persists during good times and bad. It tends to get worse when the economy contracts or stagnates, but sometimes it worsens even when the economy improves. In Milwaukee, for example, as total employment rose in the 1980s, it shifted from manufacturing to non-manufacturing. Unemployment among whites dropped from 5.3% to 3.8%. But among Blacks, official unemployment rose from 17% to over 20%. Actually, among inner city Black and Hispanic youth around the country, joblessness is over 50%.

Black men's earnings are lower than those of white men; Black women's lifetime earnings are the lowest, even in comparison with those of white women. These differentials have persisted in the years since civil rights ordinances and affirmative action have outlawed employment discrimination. This is because affirmative action is at best an individual solution to a collective and institutionalized problem, although it is certainly justified. Far from reducing standards or abilities, affirmative action provides access to the talents and abilities of people previously excluded from the system. But it directs Black people seeking economic improvement into competition for a place in the white corporate and government power structure, and is no substitute for community-based economic development.

Nor has affirmative action created a bias in favor of Blacks in hiring. A study by the Urban Institute in Chicago and Washington, DC, in 1991 showed that in roughly 500 audits of pairs of Black and white young men who were closely matched in education, age, size, experience, and other attributes, the Blacks faced discrimination 20% of the time. In comparison, only 7% of the whites were denied equal treatment.

In fact, income and employment differentials

understate the extent of Black–white economic differences. A study of wealth, a more accurate measure of economic well-being, showed that, based on
the 1990 census, whites on average were three
times as wealthy as Blacks. White households'
wealth was four times their income; Blacks' assets
amounted to only 2.5 times income (in addition to
being based on a lower income). White wealth was
more heavily concentrated in financial assets (which
make money). What wealth Blacks possessed, was
mainly in household goods (homes and cars).

What's more, poor Black and Hispanic people
are tightly concentrated; recent census figures show
that over 80% of poor African Americans live in poor
census tracts. Sixty to seventy percent of poor
Latinos live in poor areas. But among whites, only
30% of the poor live in poverty-stricken areas.
Relatively speaking, the white poor are dispersed
among other white people, while poor Blacks and
Latinos are isolated not only from whites and the
larger society, but even from better-off members of
their own nationalities. Again, this is a manifestation of colonialism and neo-colonialism. Poor whites
live with rulers of their own nationality; members of
the colonized groups who collaborate with the colonial regime disassociate themselves physically from
the colonized.

What is less widely recognized is the extent to
which all other discriminatory economic conditions
intensify this colonial situation. People who express
puzzlement about how African American youth could
destroy "their own" community in the L.A. rebellion
fail to understand that the community was not their
own. Black areas had 30% fewer businesses per

capita to start with than other areas of L.A., yet even many of those were not owned by Black residents. What's more, those areas had a disproportionately high concentration of liquor stores compared to other parts of the county (and those liquor stores therefore formed a vastly larger percentage of all the businesses). Black areas are redlined for insurance, loans, and housing, driving out those Blacks with some economic wherewithal to other areas where they will at least face less discrimination from banks and insurance companies.

This discrimination is practiced not only in L.A., and not only for housing; a study of industrial development in the south showed that corporations have avoided areas with large Black populations. During this same period, Blacks lost their farmland at a rate 2-1/2 times higher than small white farmers. More than 95% of all Black farms have been lost since 1920, compared to a 54% decline in white-operated farms in the same period.

Again, these are manifestations of a system that must be described as colonialism. Black people do not control their own economic circumstances, land, or labor. As a result, they are forced to pay more for shoddier goods, and work harder for less pay.

Racism and Health

The health and medical situation of Black people in America is so dismal that it reduces the life expectancy and raises the infant mortality rate overall for the entire U.S. population. Despite an overall decline in infant mortality rates, Black babies are almost twice as likely as white infants to die in the first year of life. In 1950, the Black infant death rate was 61% higher than that for whites; by 1979, it was 91% higher. Even among well-to-do Blacks, infant mortality is high, apparently due to disproportionately low birth weight. Infant mortality in poor inner-city communities in the U.S. such as Detroit is higher than in many "Third World" countries, including much of Central America.

This reflects the absence of medical care and the exclusion of Blacks from medicine. While medical school enrollment increased by 50% in the U.S. between 1972-82, it remained virtually flat among Blacks. The total number of Black physicians increased slightly, but declined as a percentage both of all doctors and of the Black population. Again, such disparities are a manifestation of colonialism. The medical schools, hospitals, and insurance companies are outside of Blacks' control and do not respond to their needs. And since government also reflects this colonial dynamic, government services do not improve matters. One recent federal study, for example, showed that for 30 years, Blacks with serious ailments have been much more likely than whites to be rejected for disability claims under Social Security, especially on appeal.

Disparities show up in every area of medical care. Whites, for example, are 3-1/2 times more likely than Blacks to receive potentially life-saving coronary artery bypass surgery. Life expectancy for Black people has actually been dropping steadily. Until 1984, Black life expectancy, while shorter than that for whites, increased at roughly the same rate and narrowed the gap in actual years. But since 1985, as white life expectancy has continued to inch up, the average life span for both Black men and women has grown shorter. In other words, a bad situation for Blacks is getting worse even while the situation for whites is improving.

Blacks in America do not suffer only in comparison to whites. Because colonialism persists within America, the situation is often worse than in some Third World countries. Black men in Harlem are less likely to live to age 65 than men in Bangladesh—55% of Bengali men, but only 40% of Black men in Harlem live to reach 65 years. Infant mortality rates among Blacks in Detroit are worse than those in Honduras.

A study of U.S. Black death rates compared to U.S. whites in the 1980s showed an annual excess of 59,000 Black deaths over the number that would have died if the white death rate had applied. This excess represented 42% of all deaths of Black people annually. In L.A., for example, Black and Latino gay men have been diagnosed with AIDS at twice the rate of whites. Recent studies have shown that Black and Latino AIDS patients are much less likely than whites to receive life-extending medicines and other therapies. Government cuts in medical care fall disproportionately on communities of color, leading to the revival in these communities of virulent strains of tuberculosis and many childhood ailments that had been thought conquered.

Racism and Immigration

For many generations, immigration to the U.S. was limited on a consciously racist basis. For many Asians, immigration was either outlawed entirely for long periods or restricted to men. Women were not allowed in, so the U.S. could take advantage of

Chinese, Japanese, and Filipino laborers, while preventing them from establishing families or having children in this country.

Immigration throughout most of this century was controlled by laws written while the KKK was at the height of its power as a mass organization, and reflected the Klan's anti-immigrant politics. The explicit bias in what immigration was allowed was towards northern Europeans, by establishing quotas for admission to the U.S. from each country based on the percentages of the U.S. population from those countries in the previous century. The U.S., for example, closed its doors to most Jewish refugees from Hitler's terror (while later happily admitting a host of nazi collaborators who had desired scientific or espionage skills).

More recent reforms modified the open racism of U.S. immigration policy, and allowed increased immigration from Asia and Latin America, to fill jobs this country needs to have done but can't fill from among the ranks of white labor. But this has only sparked a new wave of explicitly racist anti-immigrant organizing. Visa lotteries and new immigration laws have restored a bias in favor of northern Europeans. Studies conducted under the Immigration Reform and Control Act have shown that such measures as employer sanctions have resulted in wholesale discrimination against all Hispanics and Asians; this is because the hostility towards "illegals" is focused on a racially selective basis, ignoring Irish, Eastern Europeans, and others who enter or stay illegally, and targeting "non-whites."

In fact, U.S. immigration policy has always been two-faced. The history of importation of people of color to do the back-breaking work is central to U.S. development, beginning with the slave trade, and proceeding through the use of Asian and Mexican labor on the railroads, mines, and fields of the west. Illegal U.S. immigrants to Mexico, who refused to abide by that country's ban on slavery, fomented first Texas independence and then the U.S. war on Mexico to expand slavery and make the U.S. into a continental power (thereby setting the stage for both the U.S. Civil War and the subsequent Indian Wars). Having incorporated a massive and resource-rich section of Mexico and imposed a new border, the U.S. can hardly be surprised to find that border is porous. To this day, illegal immigration of Third World workers is an economic enterprise akin to the drug trade— it is made illegal not to prevent it, but to keep it more profitable as a black market, and to keep the workers more easily exploitable, less able to defend their rights and organize.

Racism and the Environment

The 1993 global ecology summit in Rio de Janeiro, Brazil, focused attention on the relationship between protection and restoration of the environment and the set of issues referred to as the "North–South" conflict, between the developed and the developing nations. The real issue here is a history of race-based colonialism. Western economic growth and environmental devastation has been based on a history of land theft and genocide of native peoples in all corners of the globe by the European powers and their settler colonists.

Vast areas of the world were and continue to be

dedicated to growing crops desired by the Europeans. The threat to the rain forest presented by the need for land on which to graze enough cattle to produce another billion hamburgers had its origins in the "mono-culture"—one-crop—economies imposed on the Third World by companies like United Fruit and immortalized in such popular phrases as "there's an awful lot of coffee in Brazil." Today, adding insult to injury, the U.S. and other developed nations want to export their waste and their toxic industries to the Third World.

What's more, this pattern is reproduced within the U.S. Toxic waste dumps and polluting industries are located disproportionately in communities of color. In a city like L.A., where it would seem that air pollution would not discriminate, the existence of toxic hot spots that correspond to areas with predominantly Black and Hispanic populations demonstrates that even the air which we breathe can be the vehicle of discrimination. A recent study of Black and Latino youth from south L.A. who had died of non-medical causes (mostly violence) showed that these teenagers were already losing their lung capacity to pollution-caused lesions; had they lived, they would have been candidates for severe lung diseases like emphysema or cancers by their 30s. Such situations are repeated around the country, from uranium mining on Indian reservations to pesticide poisoning of mostly Chicano farm workers and their families.

Of course, in the long run, none of this race-related ecological destruction can be confined to one group. The classic case of the massively devastating effects of colonialism might be Oklahoma. Land-hungry white settlers swept into this beautiful, green, forested Indian territory. They stripped the land of its ancient and "unproductive" forests to create private agricultural holdings. Within a couple of generations, the loss of the forest affected the climate of the region and produced a sustained drought. The precious topsoil, without the trees to anchor it, dried up and blew away, in the famous Dust Bowl of the 1930s, driving the white Oklahomans before it.

The issues that are gripping California and the country—"jobs vs. the environment," crime, immigration—can all be seen to have roots in systematic and institutional racism and colonialism. The disparities we have touched on here are not statistical flukes, or fading remnants of earlier discrimination, but evidence of a worsening crisis of racist oppression and exploitation, of marginalization. Similar and sometimes even worse comparisons can be drawn with the educational, environmental, economic, medical, and judicial discrimination against Chicanos, Puerto Ricans, and other Latinos; Native Americans, Alaskan Inuits, and indigenous Hawaiians; Chinese, Vietnamese, Koreans, Samoans, and other Asians and Pacific Islanders. To ignore this racism and colonialism, or to buy the racist line that whites are now the oppressed minority, is to be incapable of solving any of the problems facing our society.

The Ku Klux Klan in U.S. History

White Racist Terror and the Role of the State

The Ku Klux Klan poses two problems central to a correct understanding of the reality of American history and society, particularly since the twentieth century reemergence of the KKK in 1915, and in its essentially continuous existence since then.

First, what is the role of an openly white-supremacist organization in a country that, at least since the abolition of slavery and the elimination of the color line in the Constitution, and certainly since the post-World War II civil rights reforms, has professed to be a pluralist, multi-racial democracy?

Second, what is the relationship of a secret paramilitary organization to the monopoly on the legal use of violence enjoyed by a supposedly democratically controlled state apparatus?

An examination of history will show that these two factors are directly related. The KKK and its successor and fraternal organizations are deeply rooted in the actual white-supremacist power relations of U.S. society. They exist as a supplement to the armed power of the state, available to be used when the rulers and the state find it necessary. The KKK has been so used at certain critical moments when the direct application of state power was either insufficient or inadvisable. At other times, when paramilitary KKK-type activity is seen as less desirable, or even embarrassing, the state tightens its leash considerably.

At times, the KKK, through terror directed against oppressed and struggling people, and through open white-supremacist, jingoistic, super-patriotic organizing of white people, has served to strengthen the state apparatus. This has helped the state to deal with revolutionary threats. In the period before and after the First World War, the KKK was not a marginal anachronism based on an idealization of the pre–Civil War South, as it is sometimes portrayed in history books and the media. The KKK was an expression of the central political dynamics of the growth of the U.S. as a global economic and military power. It was central to the role of white supremacy in that development, and in the consolidation of a new concept of "America" as a "white nation" within the white population.

To understand this, we need to look at the first, Reconstruction-era KKK, on which the twentieth-century revival consciously modeled itself. Prior to 1865 and the military defeat of the slave aristocracy, the KKK was unnecessary. The African population in the U.S. was directly suppressed by the slave-owners and overseers, and by the local, state, and national government apparatus they controlled. White supremacy was enshrined in the U.S.

Constitution, through such mechanisms as the prohibition on abolishing the slave trade and the
counting of African slaves as three-fifths of a person
for purposes of determining the size of the
Congressional delegation from slave states. White
supremacy (against the indigenous people as well as
the slaves) served as the basis for the organization
of society as well as government, despite challenges
from the slaves and from some white abolitionists.
The Supreme Court ruled repeatedly that slaves had
no rights a white man or the white government was
bound to respect.

The day-to-day repression and exploitation of
the slaves was in the hands of their owners. When
rebellion or unrest broke out, or slaves escaped,
patrols were deputized. The entire power of the
national government guaranteed the right of the
master to reclaim his fugitive property if a slave
broke free. At times when the Africans were able to
link up with Native Americans in large numbers,
surpassing the power of the slave patrols, the army
was used against them. Moreover, even many of the
"democratic" impulses of the white population were
white-supremacist and colonialist in nature, such
as the movement around Andrew Jackson, a notorious Indian killer and conqueror of native lands for
white settlement.

But the balance between North and South,
maintained through a series of constitutional and
congressional "Compromises," was undermined by
the westward expansionism that culminated in the
annexation of Texas and the invasion and seizure of
much of Mexico's territory (where the Mexican government had outlawed slavery since achieving inde-

pendence from Spain). The few politicians, like Lincoln, who claimed to oppose the war with Mexico, were ready to vote to finance it once it was declared. The whole doctrine of "manifest destiny" that justified it was racist in conception; it was a classic use of racial ideology to justify colonial conquest. This potential new territory, which would have provided for the expansion of the slave system to the Pacific, was the prize that set the stage for Civil War.

However, the struggle of Black people at that time for freedom and for control of the land they were working proved irrepressible. They seized on the emerging contradiction between the industrial capitalists of the North and the slave owners of the South to press their struggle. They began to make inroads into the political base of white supremacy through the abolitionist movement and the Underground Railroad. Eventually, once the Civil War broke out, they struck decisive blows against the Confederacy through strikes, guerrilla warfare, and participation in the Union Army. In fact, their uprising contributed to the overthrow of the whole previous form of government and society in the U.S. This transformation was codified in the 13th, 14th and 15th amendments to the Constitution, which tried to reconstitute and democratize the state and federal governments, in order to incorporate and contain the revolutionary potential of the newly free population, who were attracting allies from among the poor whites.

After the war, two strategies emerged within the former ruling groups about how to deal with this potential. Some northern industrialists and reformers proposed a series of radical measures that would co-opt the Black struggle and contain its demands for land redistribution, education, and economic development. They wanted to use its popular force to create a new federal system, in which the central government was clearly predominant over the states. They felt that they would thereby be strengthened to carry out the tasks of integrating the U.S. as a single national industrial economy, subduing the Indians, and integrating the territories stolen from Mexico through the war a generation before.

The former southern ruling sectors, despite their defeat in war, wanted to restore the *status quo ante*, the previously existing arrangements. They wanted to regain their control of Black labor and their resulting domination of white society. At the very least, they wanted to regain the political and economic power, based on slavery, that had allowed them to contend for national authority.

Black people continued to struggle after the war for their own demands, for their political rights and the land that was their due. This forced the contradictions that had led to the Civil War to break out again into war of a different form. The Klan, which had been organized as a fraternal society among former Confederate officers almost immediately after the war, was called upon to play a new role some two years later. After the national government struck down the state regimes that the old rulers had reestablished, the southern rulers, dispossessed of state power to enforce their will, took up the weapon of the KKK, a secret, paramilitary organization, to carry out the repression that the state at that point was incapable of.

The KKK began a campaign of terror against free Blacks and their white supporters. Over the course of a decade, disarmed by the Union Army and abandoned by the white abolitionists, Black people were defeated in this struggle. By 1872, former Confederate Gen. Nathan Bedford Forrest, a founder of the Klan, was able to issue a call to disband the KKK. By 1876, the national government and the Republican Party had struck a deal with the southerners to respect "state's rights." This meant accepting the re-enslavement of Blacks through tenant-farming and share-cropping, and the disenfranchisement of Blacks through discriminatory legislation and economic coercion.

Once again, suppression of Black people's freedom, and control of dissident elements among whites, was carried out directly by the state. There was no need for the full KKK organization, although lynchings, beatings, killings, and other extra-legal attacks continued to take place. As a new generation of Black people born after abolition grew up, the laws to enforce their subordinate status became more onerous, and the terror to thwart their resistance became more naked, in order to maintain the system. Supreme Court decisions like *Plessy v. Ferguson* upheld these new discriminatory laws. The system of share-cropping and "Jim Crow" segregation, similar to the apartheid system later created in South Africa, was the law of the land. Support for white supremacy became such a mass phenomenon among the white population, particularly in the south, that lynchings and burnings of "uppity" Blacks were virtually a recreational activity. During this period, the Klan was unnecessary.

40

The Klan in U.S. History

However, with the dawn of the century, a new America was emerging that would call forth the KKK again. Black resistance began to grow. Ida Wells Barnett campaigned tirelessly against lynchings. To oppose segregation and terror, new organizations like the NAACP sprang up, and Black people undertook militant self-defense. Twenty-five hundred Black people were lynched between 1885 and 1910, in a period when the KKK did not exist. Refugees from this terror, Black people began to make their way north in large numbers at this time. But they were met with hostility there as well. White race riots against Black people occurred in Wilmington, North Carolina; Springfield, Ohio; Atlanta, Georgia, and Springfield, Illinois among other cities. Between 1910 and 1920, the Black population of Chicago doubled, Cleveland's tripled, and Detroit's increased 600%. The Mexican population in the U.S. also doubled at this time.

Simultaneously, the U.S. had a tremendous hunger for cheap labor to fuel its explosive industrialization. It began to act as a safety valve for the restive workers and peasants of the European empires. One million, two hundred thousand legal immigrants entered the U.S. in 1914 alone. Increasingly, they were from Catholic southern and eastern Europe, and they were harder to absorb into the dominant white Protestant society than earlier waves of northern Europeans had been. Industrial labor organizations grew up among such immigrant workers, sometimes favorable to socialism and (less frequently) supportive of Black rights. Also, as war passions grew in Europe, U.S. citizens, who were mostly of European descent, began to choose up sides based on the stances of their former home-lands: Swedes opposed Russia, Germans opposed England, Anglo-Americans opposed Germany.

The war fever came at a critical time for the U.S. Increasingly dependent on international trade for markets for its factories and farms, the U.S was making loans and investments in the European economy, and seeking new customers, especially the Allied powers. Between 1914 and 1916, U.S. exports to England and France tripled to $2.75 billion. At the same time, fear of the war fueled socialism, pacifism, and labor radicalism among the working people who were not benefiting from these gains.

To resolve its growing internal contradictions while carrying out its ambitious plans for a new world role, the U.S. state needed a movement among white people that would mobilize and disci-pline the white population, promote "Americanism," and keep Blacks and other oppressed people in their place. Ultimately, this would strengthen the hand of the state. In response to this need, the KKK was re-organized as a national organization, after a 40-year hiatus, with the blessings of the highest ranks of the federal government.

President Woodrow Wilson, a segregationist Democrat from Virginia and a white Protestant supremacist in his thinking, was confronted by the prospect of war in Europe and a divided and anti-war electorate at home. At the behest of his old col-lege roommate, Thomas Dixon, Jr., (the author of the novel "The Clansman" about the reconstruction-era KKK,) President Wilson arranged for a private screening of D. W. Griffith's new film "Birth of a Nation." The movie, the first full-length, multi-reel feature film from Hollywood, was based on Dixon's book. Its favorable treatment of the Klan was highly controversial, not only among Blacks, because it was deemed by many to support a secessionist view of the Civil War and Reconstruction. The NAACP of the day particularly protested the film's racist depiction of Blacks and "mulattos."

D. W. Griffith, the director, had used the most advanced technology and techniques available to the fledgling film industry, inventing most of the "vocabulary" of cinema for the work. The movie, almost magical in its technologically primitive context, worked persuasively to organize white people to support racist violence, portraying Black people as a threat to white womanhood and civilization. President Wilson gave the film his seal of approval after viewing it.

Dixon then arranged a showing of the movie for the U.S. Supreme Court, through his friend Josephus Daniels, the Secretary of the Navy. Chief Justice of the U.S. Edward White announced his support for the film's theme. He said that he had been a member of the KKK himself as a youth in New Orleans. With this high-level government imprimatur, the movie overcame the initial controversy and opposition it had generated, and became a great national success. It drew huge crowds everywhere it played, and grossed the then phenomenal sum of $18 million.

Sensing the chance to capitalize on the film's popularity and propaganda value, a southern colonel, William J. Simmons, recruited several former members of the original KKK and a number of other supporters. The group, which included the speaker of the Georgia legislature, decided to burn a cross—the symbol of the KKK—on a hillside overlooking Atlanta on the eve of the film's opening in that city. They declared the rebirth of the Ku Klux Klan. D.W. Griffith was later so upset about the outcome of his film that he tried to make amends by filming a denunciation of prejudice through the ages called "Intolerance."

The KKK immediately began to build itself in the South and around the U.S. by policing the nation to achieve victory in World War I, which broke out soon afterward. Founder Simmons joined a group called the Citizen's Bureau of Investigation, similar to the government-sponsored American Protective League. Klansmen broke strikes, hunted draft dodgers, harassed pacifists and other opponents of the war effort, and marched in patriotic parades. The Klan joined the other fraternal organizations like the Lions and the Elks in the ranks of the new urban business middle class. It was to be an instrument of inculcating Americanism among whites, replacing their old national allegiances with an identification with white supremacy.

In the aftermath of the war, the KKK took off nationwide. In 1920, its organizers and salesmen used the newly developed techniques of mass marketing to sell its solutions to white Americans worried about uppity Blacks, communist immigrants, liquor and crime in the streets, emancipated women. What distinguished the Klan from other political groups that supported a similar program, and from other fraternal groups that adopted similar secret handshakes and mumbo-jumbo, was its propensity for vigilante action.

Its program coincided well with the needs of the government in that period. It was the era of the Palmer raids by the Attorney General against suspected "reds," and a huge, war-fed increase in the powers of the central government. KKK chapters sprang up nationally to spy on radicals, put down bootlegging in the Prohibition era, and terrorize returning Black war veterans, who were intent on winning their equal rights after risking their lives and after tasting life in less race-conscious societies in Europe. W.E.B. DuBois, a founder of the NAACP, expressed the attitude of Blacks in this period: "We return. We return from fighting. We return fighting."

The Black struggle at that time was linked to a world-wide upsurge against colonialism and racism in the wake of the war among the old empires of Europe. The first Pan Africanist Congress was held, to demand independence for colonized Africa. A militant movement for Black empowerment and African liberation, the United Negro Improvement Association (UNIA) sprang up, under the leadership of a West Indian, Marcus Garvey. Headquartered in Harlem, New York, it had chapters across the U.S. and in several African-populated countries in the Western hemisphere. The KKK sometimes professed to support Garvey as a Black separatist, but in fact his appeal to the Black masses struggling for freedom was anathema to the Klan.

Malcolm X, the Black freedom leader of the '60s, gives us eloquent testimony about the true attitude of the growing KKK towards the UNIA in the 1920s. Malcolm's father, Rev. Little, was a Garvey organizer in Nebraska. He was the target of harassment and night-riders. When the family moved to

Michigan to get away from these attacks, they were set upon repeatedly by the Black Legionnaires, a KKK-offshoot composed of white industrial workers. Malcolm's father was found dead, his head beaten in, his body thrown across the train tracks.

This story was repeated dozens of times across the country, as the KKK rode the crest of a wave of white-supremacist violence in major northern cities. In 1919, there were 25 anti-black race riots in U.S. cities, from Longview, Texas to Washington, DC, to Chicago, Illinois.

The KKK was effectively promoted at this time by some ostensibly negative publicity and media coverage. Press "exposés" glamorized and served to build the Klan. Hundreds of applications for membership came in to the KKK clipped out of articles in the mainstream press. The final boost to national status and success came from a Congressional investigation. In his testimony to Congress, Colonel Simmons was able to drape the Klan in Americanism; it was a personal and organizational triumph. The chairman of the Congressional committee was defeated in the next election, and politicians across the U.S. began jumping on the KKK bandwagon. Simmons later recalled, "Congress gave us the best advertising we ever got. Congress made us."

Central to the organizing strategy of the Klan was racist violence. Beatings, tar-and-featherings, and murders were the hallmarks of their presence in a community. These Klan actions actually swelled their ranks. The KKK beat and branded Blacks in Texas, and striking Black cotton pickers were terrorized. In Oklahoma, the KKK flogged scores of Blacks in the early '20s. The Klan marched against "loafers and prowlers" in Columbus, Georgia.

In Oregon, a Black bootlegger was nearly lynched and driven from town. The KKK sponsored an Arkansas-Louisiana Law Enforcement League to patrol the state border and prevent "cohabitation between whites and blacks." The list stretches across the country for half a decade. A Black state agricultural expert was kidnapped and beaten in North Carolina; in California, Klansmen kidnapped a Mexican they suspected of bootlegging, and got into a shoot-out with constables. The Colorado KKK operated as the Denver Doers Club and sent threatening letters to Blacks, Mexicans, and their sympathizers; they organized a paramilitary formation called the Klavaliers.

Hooded Klansmen attacked Black migrant farm workers in Missouri. In West Virginia, the KKK killed a white woman while attacking a Black home. Klansmen posted signs reading "Nigger, don't let the sun set on you" in towns in Indiana and Ohio. The KKK led a white mob in Detroit in attacking the home of a Black surgeon, who was then tried for murder for defending himself. In Arizona, the Klan whipped a Black bank janitor. A Catholic priest taking a group of Black youths on an outing was kidnapped by the KKK in Virginia. Two truckloads of hooded men fired at a group of Black Boy Scouts in Pennsylvania; in New Jersey, crosses were burned in Black communities; and so on in almost every state in the union.

Far from isolating the Klan, this campaign of terror initially led it to legitimacy and political power. It was sometimes deputized by local law enforcement; more often, it numbered police and sheriffs in its ranks. Operating within the Democratic Party in the South and in the Republicans in the North and West, the KKK elected mayors, aldermen, congressmen, senators, and governors across the country. Harry Truman, later President, and Hugo Black, later Supreme Court Justice, were only two of hundreds of major and minor political figures who joined the KKK in this period, whether from conviction or opportunism.

The vice-president under Calvin Coolidge expressed his support for the Klan's goals, if not all its tactics. In Illinois, a former federal revenue agent named Glen Young led armed Klan patrols against bootleggers which were officially deputized by U.S. prohibition agents. The KKK reached its height of electoral success in 1924, and the following two summers saw the KKK march thousands strong in hoods and robes down the streets of Washington, DC.

At this point, the state began to pull the plug on the Klan, feeling that the group had fulfilled its purpose and was beginning to overstep its bounds. The KKK had served in particular as half of a two-pronged strategy among white people: its Protestant nativism had been the stick that served, along with the carrot of big-city political machines, to inculcate "Americanism" into Catholic immigrants from Europe. Much of the Klan's anti-immigrant program was enacted into law, and in 1921 and 1924, severe restrictions were placed on further immigration into the U.S., especially against Asians and Latinos, with quotas based on the census of 1890 (when northern Europeans were a larger percentage of the U.S. population). But as the KKK continued its call to expel immigrants, its open use of violence and intimidation against other whites within the electoral process began to be seen by the elite as too crude and unsophisticated.

Once government support was withdrawn, the Klan began to deflate as rapidly as it had swelled up. Anti-mask laws were passed in a dozen states. Indictments were brought against leading Klan figures for financial irregularities and violence. Once it was clear that the Klan's ability to terrorize with impunity was over, KKK candidates for local, state, and national office were defeated. Leaders and politicians abandoned the KKK, and its membership dwindled.

The state had used the KKK as a mass movement and a terrorist organization to suppress revolutionary Black struggle, to integrate millions of first- and second-generation Europeans into a new, national white culture; and to strengthen the state apparatus in dealing with the problems of a vast industrial work force and of global power. Once it fulfilled this assignment, the KKK was tossed aside. Of interest is that a number of Klansmen of German origin made their way back to their homeland in this period of the '20s, bringing the Klan ideology of racism and white supremacy with them, and helping to form some of the cells that later coalesced in the Nazi party.

In the light of arguments often made that the KKK grows in response to hard times, during which white workers are looking for a scapegoat, it's interesting to note that the Klan was at its greatest height during the relative boom years of the 1920s, when the U.S. became a creditor nation for the first time, and advanced to the first rank in industrial and agricultural output. During the subsequent depression of the 1930s, the KKK never regained its earlier strength, though it did persist as a mass organization in reduced size until 1944. At that point, preparing for a post-war world, the federal government decided to liquidate the Klan as a mass, public organization by driving it into bankruptcy through a claim for non-payment of back taxes. The KKK wasn't consistent with the need to project the U.S. a friend of liberty and leader of the "Free World" and a neo-colonial approach to Africa, Asia, and Latin America. (The KKK had also worn out its welcome by trying to make common cause with the nazi-oriented, "fifth column" German-American Bund at the outset of the war, leading to charges of sedition.)

Jimmy Colescott, the leader of the KKK at this post-war juncture, made a noteworthy remark: "We had to sell out our assets, turn the proceeds over to the government, and go out of business. Maybe the government can make something of the Klan—I never could." The government could indeed make something of the KKK. Liquidated nationally, it re-emerged in the Cold War period as an informal association of small, local Klans, with a secretive membership. Many such KKK groupings were infiltrated, or sometimes organized, by FBI agents. The Klan was a flexible instrument for clandestine terrorist and paramilitary bombings and shootings against the Black liberation struggle throughout the '50s, '60s and '70s. The FBI was in the midst of Klan groups that carried out bombings and shootings against civil rights workers and the Black freedom movement in this period. The FBI and police involvement in the Klan in this period is explored in more details in the chapter "Blue by Day, White by Night."

In 1979, a new period emerged, sometimes referred to as the nazification of the KKK, which remains in effect with some modification to this day. Klan organizers themselves sometimes refer to it as the fourth era of the KKK (after Reconstruction, the '20s, and the post-war, civil rights era). This period is marked by the turn of the KKK towards a renewed alliance with consciously nazi, radical elements, this time with a "revolutionary" strategy (rather than fighting to maintain the status quo) and a commitment to developing a clandestine terror apparatus. Again, the government has played a pivotal role in this new alignment.

The period begins on the eve of the Reagan era with the killing of five anti-Klan activists in Greensboro, North Carolina by members of a United Racist Front of KKK and Nazis. The Nazi group involved was infiltrated and armed by an agent of the Bureau of Alcohol, Tobacco and Firearms (ATF), Bernard Butkovich. The KKK group was virtually led by an FBI/Greensboro police informant. The two government plants did nothing to impede and may have advanced the unification of the two groups. Local police were suspiciously absent from the scene when the KKK–Nazi group attacked an anti-Klan march. The killers, although they were caught in the act on videotape, were eventually acquitted in both state and federal trials; though the victims' families later won a civil suit for damages from the police and others. Part of the Klan–Nazis' defense was that they killed the anti-Klan activists because they were communists, not out of racial prejudice, and therefore were not guilty of civil rights violations.

The message that the KKK could again kill with relative impunity was not lost on a new generation of white-supremacist leaders; nor was the example of "success" through a unity of white racist forces regardless of organizational affiliation. In the years following, we saw the emergence of the Order, a white-supremacist paramilitary underground. The government slapped them down hard when they turned to bank robberies and counterfeiting to finance the racist right. Yet in a show trial in Fort Smith, Arkansas similar to the Greensboro acquittals, the generally acknowledged master minds of the Nazi–Klan conspiracy were let off on federal conspiracy charges. Two of the jurors became romantically involved with the white supremacists. In another, more recent North Carolina trial, a former member of the White Patriots, a paramilitary Klan faction that emerged after the Greensboro killings incorporating many former and active-duty marines, was acquitted of the execution-style slaying of three men he thought were gay.

The general outlines of the story of the racist underground paramilitary organization called the Order, *Bruder Schweigen,* or Silent Brotherhood, are widely known and were swiftly sensationalized through Hollywood's hunger for newsworthy hooks for films. The film "Talk Radio" focused on a character loosely based on the group's most famous victim, Alan Berg; "Betrayed" began with that same assassination by white supremacists of an acerbic Jewish talk-show host and went on to explore the just-folks nature of the Aryan warriors and their families; "Dead Bang" with Miami Vice's Don Johnson told the fictional story of a street cop's unwitting discovery and rapid destruction of an underground network of survivalists, fundamentalists, and Nazis while the FBI stumbled around on his heels. A baker's dozen films and TV shows have used the rise and fall of the Order as a backdrop for socially-conscious heroics by their good guys.

The neo-nazi underground was rooted in the network of Christian Identity–oriented survivalist camps that had sprung up in the late '70s. They perpetrated a series of killings and robberies. Order founder Robert Jay Mathews provides a microcosm and metaphor for the genesis and ultimate obliteration of the group as a whole. The rise and fall of the Order was situated in a historical process that included the development of significant power in the Republican Party and the presidency by some of the same hard right forces that formed the early thinking of Mathews. Years of polemicizing by such key racist right figures as Bob Miles, Louis Beam, and Tom Metzger laid the basis for the Order's practice, but the government failed in its attempt to convict Miles, Beam, and Richard Butler of conspiracy in the Order's crimes.

According to the authors of the book "The Silent Brotherhood," who interviewed Mathews's mother, he was a white boy who moved rapidly from playing cowboys and Indians to white power war games in the southwestern desert. A major role was played in that development by the Goldwater campaign, the John Birch Society, and the tax protest movement. Under his apparently charismatic leadership, the

Order carried out killings, counterfeiting, and thefts, recruited insiders at Brinks, and came into possession of plans to power plant systems in the northwest. The plans were meant to be used for sabotage, reflecting the racists' belief that provoking chaos, economic deprivation, and racial unrest would elicit a white backlash in their favor and hasten the exterminationist race war they planned for.

Yet despite the threat the Order posed, the government's effort against them was surprisingly weak and undeservedly lucky. According to the account in "Silent Brotherhood," as the Order jumped off, the feds were only sniffing around the perimeter of the hard core racist and survivalist right. They were able to rather swiftly snuff the Order itself because of the political and security weaknesses of the plotters, a couple of lucky breaks in tracking people through their weapons, and at key moments, the tips of informers (whom the feds had not previously recruited from or placed in the racists' ranks, but who had simply had a failure of nerve when they found themselves in over their heads).

Why was the government not better prepared to fight or infiltrate the Order? What was the state's role in the consolidation of Nazis and Klansmen and the turn towards violence that led to the emergence of the Order—most obviously in the Greensboro massacre? The book documents that Mathews took his fateful decision to initiate the armed activity of the Order when one of his mentors, Aryan Nations head Richard Butler, was arrested in a cross-burning in L.A. But the connections of the Order to this cross-burning are never further explored, despite the fact that five of the participants were among the central members of the racist underground. The cross-burning was essentially a celebration of the unification of the Nazis, the KKK, the Aryan Nations, and the White Aryan Resistance. Was it also secretly an attempt to establish an anchor for the Order in California? Butler, WAR leader Tom Metzger, or Frank Silva, the local Klan leader who brought them together and then signed up as a soldier in Mathews' army, could tell us, but they aren't talking. One of the main participants in the Order gave the FBI a deposition that the group distributed much of the money it stole to Metzger and other public white-supremacist leaders.

The final chapter of the story of the Order is not yet written. Some of the original plotters have already been released. Others will be out of prison shortly. Most are unrepentant. Many of the key players walked away scot free to turn their attention to base building and recruiting a new generation of "Aryan warriors" from among the neo-nazi boneheads and other racist youth. Springing from the same soil as the Order have come at least two similar efforts at clandestine racist terror: the so-called Order II, involving other followers of the Aryan Nations; and a recent effort to bomb gay bars, Korean businesses, and Black, Jewish, and anti-racist targets in the northwest which was infiltrated and broken up by the FBI. In the southeast, people in the same mold as Glenn Miller, who brought significant elements of the KKK paramilitary apparatus into the neo-nazi underground before turning state's evidence, have also reappeared. Recent federal indictments, including that of a Green Beret sergeant, have exposed a massive racist operation stealing vast quantities of military weaponry.

The path that Robert Jay Mathews trod is being followed again today, with greater rapidity and virulence, by a cadre of racist and violence-prone young people. Some are nazi boneheads, some not—but all are being guided by racist veterans who have learned lessons from the immaturity and amateurishness of the Order, who have hardened their commitment to race war, their hatred of Blacks and Jews, and their disdain for most white people and for the government. Tom Metzger, who constantly preaches support for those he terms the Aryan prisoners of war of the Order, is wooing white youth to the same brand of racist "revolutionism" that birthed the Order. The next time around, the combatants that carry this ideology out may prove harder to bring down.

Currently, the government is moving actively against the spreading menace of nazi skinheads who are being organized by older KKK elements. This may be because the grass roots nazi-skin upsurge is not as easily infiltrated or controlled, and its violence is therefore less susceptible to direction by the state. In the 1993 case of the Fourth Reich skins in L.A., who were infiltrated and in part financed by government agents, the feds testified that they moved to make arrests only when they felt the skins were getting out of their control. One can perhaps conceive of this crack-down as a kind of obedience training of the new reserves of the Nazi–Klan movement; the thugs are to be kept on a short leash until the government is clearer about what may be acceptable targets.

Meanwhile, the phenomenon of organized white-supremacist activity inside police departments and the military continues to grow at an alarming rate. [See "Blue by Day, White by Night," which documents dozens of such cases, and their increasing incidence over the last decade.] This is apparently one key new area of KKK organizing, along with several mass movements such as the anti-immigrant, anti-gay, and anti-abortion movements. Several white-supremacist and anti-Semitic groups have been trying to attach themselves to the Ross Perot movement or otherwise to duplicate the electoral breakthroughs of David Duke into the mainstream. These efforts are also looked at in greater depth and detail in succeeding chapters.

In any case, the evidence of more than a century is clear; we cannot rely on the law enforcement or legislative apparatus to eradicate the KKK and its off-spring, because when it serves the interests of the ruling powers they will be unleashed again. Instead, we have to win people who might be drawn to the Klan or Nazis away from those formations, or prevent others from acting independently on their racist inclinations, through the strength of the anti-racist movement.

Blue by Day, White by Night

Organized White-Supremacist Groups in Law Enforcement Agencies and the Military

The investigation of police brutality in Los Angeles after the beating of Rodney King exposed the problem of organized white-supremacist groups inside police forces. In the wake of the brutal beating, Black officers came forward to report harassment within the department by the use against them of Klan insignia and calling cards. The L.A. sheriff's deputy who was involved in the shooting death of Arturo Jimenez in East L.A. had been exposed as a member of a white-supremacist gang, the Vikings, while serving at the Lynwood station, and forced to change assignments. Another sheriff's deputy, Brian Kazmierski, dismissed from the force for burning a cross inside the county jail, was reinstated by the elected sheriff in time to kill a Mexican national after making racist remarks.

A civilian investigator for the L.A. Police Commission was investigated by the LAPD's Anti-Terrorist Division in 1992 after being seen at racist gatherings with Tom Metzger in Orange County, and was found to have used police computers to run background checks on Metzger, Jewish activists, and possibly as many as 200 others.

But this problem is not isolated to one or two cases, nor is it only a local problem in Los Angeles. In Houston, Texas in 1991, the Klan conducted an intensive and reportedly successful recruiting drive among police officers. In Indianapolis, a cop whose membership in the National Socialist White People's (Nazi) Party was exposed 10 years ago when he was suspended from the force for killing a Black man, killed another Black man under suspicious circumstances in July, 1991. In the southeast, a number of white cops organized a national organization of white male cops opposed to affirmative action. In New Jersey in 1993, a cop busted for dealing in illegal weapons was found to have white-supremacist and neo-nazi propaganda in his home. In 1994, Black agents of the federal Bureau of Alcohol, Tobacco and Firearms, brought a discrimination lawsuit against the agency that disclosed unpunished acts of racist harassment and Ku Klux Klan affiliation and activity among white ATF agents. What is the background for these developments?

White-supremacist groups like the Ku Klux Klan have always had a contradictory relationship to the federal governmental system of the U.S. Although these groups are extra-legal by nature, and often carry out illegal acts, they have played a big role in maintaining the political, social, and economic order. As a result, they have often been protected by the state apparatus—especially the most racist elements within that apparatus.

Also, because the KKK and other neo-nazi groups seek power, and have been inclined to use violence to gain their ends, they have looked for recruits and allies in the ranks of the police and the military. Collusion and joint membership between the KKK and law enforcement agencies was common around the country during the Klan's heyday in the 1920s, when whole klaverns were deputized for Prohibition raids, as well as throughout the South during the civil rights era. But this is not only a matter of history, it's a current-day reality. Common perceived interests of the white racists and the police have created a symbiosis and overlap even as the demands of multi-racial, multi-ethnic democracy should create law enforcement opposition to violent white supremacy. This raises troubling questions for any objective person about the true nature of the "criminal justice" system.

After briefly sketching the historical background of the links between the KKK and other white-supremacist groups with law enforcement through the 1960s, we will concentrate on developments since the Greensboro killings of five anti-Klan activists by a North Carolina Nazi–KKK alliance in 1979, which marked the beginning of a new period, in which many white supremacists adopted revolutionary and anti-state rhetoric. Despite this stance, cop–Klan collusion is still very much a current problem. This is not a comprehensive analysis of the broader issue of racism in police forces in general, nor of the widespread problem of racist brutality and deadly force by cops. It focuses on the relationship between the cops and the Klan.

Organized police forces and organized, extra-legal white-supremacist groupings like the Klan had their origin in roughly the same period of U.S. history, after the Civil War. Prior to that, the government was still a relatively weak element of society compared to the massive force it wields today. Slave codes were enforced by slave-owners and their overseers, who would deputize slave patrols from among the white population. Urban populations were relatively small. Militias were called up from the armed white male population to put down rebellions among the lower classes, the African slaves, or the Native American nations.

However, with the conquest of northern Mexico, the abolition of chattel slavery, the defeat of the Native American nations in the center of the continent, and the growth of industrialization, new ways of controlling both society and individuals were required. The KKK sprang up to terrorize and disenfranchise the freed slaves and to restore the old slavocracy to power in the South. Throughout the country, a permanent army and professional law enforcement bodies began to develop.

The federal nature of the U.S. government meant there would not be a single national police, but rather a large number of small local and state forces. In sparsely populated areas, as settlers began to take Native American land in the west, U.S. marshals were appointed (again with the power to deputize white men) to lay down the law until the local white population could grow large enough to establish its own civic authorities. In the territories conquered from Mexico, "agencies" such as the

Texas Rangers and the Arizona and California Rangers were established—initially hardly more than vigilantes—to lay down the law and suppress the resistance of the indigenous population to colonial control.

In the larger eastern cities and west coast ports like San Francisco and Seattle, with large laboring classes, police departments were set up on the British model of constables on patrol (c.o.p.s) to keep a lid on and enforce property relations. From the outset, many of the people (mostly men) attracted to these agencies have been individuals imbued with authoritarian and racist values, intent on protecting the powers-that-be and the status quo.

To this day, law enforcement in the U.S. is a patchwork of more than 15,000 different city, state, county, and federal agencies. In the largest cities, like New York and Los Angeles, the schools, the housing authority, and the rapid transit system may all have their own police departments in addition to the city cops who patrol the streets. Also, there are more and more private security forces, whose tradition goes back to the union-busting efforts of the Pinkertons. These private cops were hired by the mine-owners and industrialists to control their workforce in the early days of industrialization, when government police agencies had not yet developed sufficiently to meet the demand for enforcement. With the highest incarceration rates in the world, the U.S. also has a massive and growing cadre of prison guards and jailers.

The relationship between groups like the Klan and these official armed bodies has often been intimate. Particularly before the civil rights reforms of the '60s, the KKK and the police tended to share many common values and enforce the same social order. Thus, during the '20s, when the Klan was a mass movement throughout the U.S., operating within both the Republican and Democratic parties and holding judgeships, governorships, and other elected offices, the KKK would on occasion be deputized to fight rum-runners.

However, the state is very jealous of its official monopoly on the use of force through the police and military, and at times has cracked down on the vigilance committees and lynch mobs. For example, the law against "lynching" in fact makes it a crime to take someone from police custody (and has therefore been used in modern times against demonstrators who help people evade arrest). Clearly, the state was more concerned with its own right to use force and violence without opposition, than with the rights of the Blacks and others who were victims of lynch mobs.

After World War II, when the U.S. became the pre-eminent global power, the so-called national security state developed on the framework of a permanent war mobilization. The state apparatus became even stronger, and the national government began to impose its will more on local and state authorities. Police departments began to be reorganized on a military model, a trend in which L.A. played a vanguard role. Confronted by the Soviet Union and facing an upsurge against colonialism in Africa, Asia, and Latin America, the U.S. became concerned with cleaning up its image, if not its act.

The KKK, which had been driven into bankruptcy by the government after getting involved with the Nazi-oriented German American Bund prior to the Second World War, was resurrected as a useful tool to fight the reds and to suppress the civil rights movement without dirtying the government's hands openly. However, the new political climate made the relationship between the state and Klan more problematic than before.

Officially, the government was, under pressure, doing away with the official trappings of apartheid. Jim Crow legislation was being abolished, and the law would no longer maintain segregation and political disenfranchisement. The KKK fought a rearguard action, along with groups like the White Citizens Council, to maintain the old order. And the leaders of this fight were often office-holders and law enforcement officials. The killing of Medgar Evers, a Black civil rights leader, is one instructive example of this. The killer, Klansman Byron de la Beckwith, was not convicted until his recent retrial. A state government agency designed to combat federal civil rights reforms interviewed prospective jurors and provided the information on them to de la Beckwith. On the other hand, an FBI informant in the Klan heard Beckwith practically boast of the killing, but this information was never provided to the prosecution.

Similar incidents abound in the history of the civil rights movement. The killings of Schwerner, Chaney, and Goodman, fictionalized in the film "Mississippi Burning" into a story of the heroism of the FBI, was actually an example of the clear involvement of local law enforcement with the KKK. The killers were never charged with murder locally and only prosecuted for federal civil rights violations.

The true role of the FBI in this period is particularly ugly, in fact. Under the guise of infiltration, the FBI actually rebuilt the Klan in the south, setting up dozens of klaverns, sometimes being leaders and public spokesmen. Gary Rowe, an FBI informant, was involved in the Klan killing of Viola Liuzzo, a white civil rights worker. He claimed that he had to fire shots at her rather than "blow his cover." One FBI agent, speaking at a rally organized by the klavern he led, proclaimed to his followers, "We will restore white rights if we have to kill every negro to do it."

Eventually, however, a number of key reforms finally changed the old legal order once and for all, without necessarily touching the social and economic base of racism. The Voting Rights and Civil Rights Acts passed in the wake of the Kennedy assassination and Johnson's landslide opened the door to Black elected officials. Civil rights lawsuits ended legal segregation of the schools—and of police departments. These measures did not end racism in the U.S., or even materially improve the conditions of the majority of Black and other oppressed people in this country, but they did change the political terrain for both advocates of liberation and justice, and for the proponents of white supremacy. White supremacy had been replaced as the official ruling ideology by multi-cultural pluralism. Even most Klan groups now couch their demands in terms of "white rights," depicting themselves as members of an oppressed group that's only seeking what it's entitled to.

Of course, this is only lip service, masking the true virulent racism that preaches white superiority and depicts Blacks, Jews, and others as sub-human or satanic. And some of the most hard core racists remain within the police departments and other armed bodies of the government.

In the '70s, the KKK and other racists were trying to regroup. A major political realignment was taking place in the South, and elsewhere in the country. Whites from areas that had been solidly Democratic since Lincoln were finding a home in the Republican Party just as newly enfranchised Blacks had begun to vote Democratic. Possibly the vanguard of this racist defection from the Democrats occurred in New York City in the '60s, where the police union, the Patrolmen's Benevolent Association, united openly with the John Birch Society and the American Nazi Party of George Lincoln Rockwell to overturn a civilian "police complaint review board", through a referendum that won overwhelming support in white ethnic neighborhoods. This was a precursor of Nixon's "silent majority" and "southern strategy" to incorporate George Wallace's supporters into the Republican electorate. But the Republicans were an odd amalgam of established pro-big business economic conservatives, racists, and hard core old and new right ideologues. A stratum of racists with anti-establishment or "populist" leanings were uncomfortable with this mix and wanted to rebuild the Klan on more modern, but still openly racialist lines, as a voice of white grievance and reaction rather than of white satisfaction with the new status quo.

This group included a number with backgrounds in the military, particularly military intelligence or other state counter-insurgency programs such as Bill Wilkinson (in Naval Intelligence) and David Duke (with USAID in Laos), and their local lieutenants like Louis Beam of Texas, Tom Metzger of California, and Virgil Griffin and Glenn Miller of North Carolina (all former soldiers or Marines).

These new-age Klansmen shared an ideology that abandoned the old red-neck hooded image for a combination of three-piece suits and paramilitary camouflage. They continued to draw on police and military forces for their recruits. A Klan klavern loyal to David Duke was organized by Metzger supporters at a Marine base in California in the late '70s, resulting in violent confrontations with Black servicemen. The military dealt with this by scattering its members to other bases around the country, thus simply planting the seeds for Klan organizing in Texas, North Carolina, and elsewhere, laying the basis for the infamous Greensboro killing by the United Racist Front of Klansmen and Nazis.

Although a split has developed in the racist ranks—David Duke and others opted for the appearance of legitimacy in the political mainstream of electoral activity, while Tom Metzger, Beam, and others adopted a stance as racist revolutionists opposed to the establishment—they have all carried out their activities with a surprising degree of impunity. As in the case of the Klan–Nazi killings in Greensboro, even where federal authorities have chosen to prosecute, the racists have often won acquittal, due to poor handling of their cases by the prosecutors and sympathy for their racism among jurors. Most of the major court setbacks for the Klan and Nazis in the last 10 years have come from civil suits, not criminal prosecutions (except for the break-up of the

Order, a neo-nazi underground, and the local trials of numerous nazi skinhead gangs for their racist, anti-Semitic violence).

But throughout the past decade and a half, there have been a series of exposures of KKK-type groups operating inside police and correctional agencies, the military, and even fire departments. The armed might of the state was used to protect the Klan's "right" to organize its campaigns of racial hatred under the guise of "free speech." In the same period, the KKK returned the favor by organizing to "support the local police" in cases of racist brutality and killings by police. And several neo-nazi leaders, notably Tom Metzger, have continued to carry out their activities with impunity from or even protection by the state. We'll look at each of these issues in turn.

Klan-Nazi Operations Inside the Police and Other Uniformed Services

KKK operations inside police agencies are by their nature clandestine in the current period. Unlike the '50s, when sheriffs were open proponents of white supremacy, law enforcement today is supposed to be color-blind, and departments are no longer uniformly white. Yet a troubling number of cases of neo-nazi infiltration of or organizing in such agencies have come to light. It is hard to believe that these cases, numerous as they are, represent every single manifestation of the problem. If what has become public knowledge is instead only the tip of the iceberg, the problem of organized racism in police ranks is massive indeed.

A listing of some military units, prisons, and

police departments affected, and of some incidents since the late '70s, will begin to show the magnitude of the problem:

1976, *Camp Pendleton, CA:* A den of David Duke's Knights of the KKK (led in the state by Tom Metzger) is exposed at the Marine base. The Corps disperses the members to other locations after racial fighting erupts.

1976, *Ventura, CA:* A KKK gathering in a local bar is exposed and photographed. Several local police officers are identified among the participants.

1977–78, *Napanoch, NY:* A KKK klavern is exposed among prison guards and inmates at a New York state prison. Earl Schoonmaker, a civilian instructor at the prison, and guard Glen Wilkinson, incorporated the Independent Northern Klans in the state. Guard brutality leads to a rebellion by the prisoners.

1979, *Sacramento, CA:* Pistol targets depicting a fleeing Black man are placed on the State Police firing range and on several police lockers. The targets award points for hitting various parts of the Black man's anatomy.

1979, *Childersburg, AL:* Police Officer William Rayfield, a Klan member, is indicted for, but acquitted of, civil rights violations for shots fired into Black leaders' homes.

1979, *Euless, TX:* Klan members from Ft. Hood Army base, dressed in combat fatigues, stand guard with weapons over a nearby Klan rally.

Blue by Day, White by Night

1979, U.S.S. Concord, Independence, and America:
Klan groups of Bill Wilkinson's Invisible Empire
form on several Navy vessels, holding a cross-
burning on the *America,* wearing robes on the
Independence, and provoking racial incidents on
the *Concord,* based in Norfolk, Virginia.
Wilkinson, a former member of Naval
Intelligence, is later exposed as a long time FBI
informant.

1980, San Diego, CA: The police department, through a
reserve officer assigned undercover to the KKK,
provides funds, radio equipment, and help in
gathering ballot signatures to qualify Klan leader
Tom Metzger for a run for Congress. (Metzger
won the Democratic nomination but lost the
general election.) Later, the agency destroys all
their files and gives the FBI a chronology actually prepared by Metzger himself. The undercover
reservist, abandoned by the department after he
is exposed, later wins a civil lawsuit against the
police.

1980, New Britain, CT: Auxiliary cop Gary Picotanno is
exposed as the local Grand Dragon of the
Invisible Empire of the KKK. He obtains a gun
permit because of his police auxiliary status.

1980, Houston, TX: White prison inmates, fighting a
court integration order detailing the racist and
brutal operations of the Texas prisons, form a
group called "Advocates of the Ku Klux Klan,"
with the support of the local Klan and sympathetic white prison guards and officials. Klan
robes are found in a guard's locker.

1981, Frankfurt, Germany: The U.S. Army hires Gene
Neill, a convicted drug smuggler and gun run-

71

ner, after his early release from prison. Neill, who has become an open member of the Invisible Empire KKK, writes a regular column for its newspaper, *The Klansman*. Styling himself an "evangelist," he is assigned by the chaplain's office of the Army's V Corps to preach to the troops.

1981, Fort Monroe, VA: Five members of the 560th Military Police Company are reassigned when their membership in the KKK becomes public.

1982, Signal Hill, CA: Four cops from the local agency near Long Beach, which is under fire for beatings and killings of Black people, are suspended for wearing t-shirts showing a gallows, a hangman's noose, and the words, "Signal Hill, Stairway to Heaven." The officers bought the shirts at a camp-out of cops sponsored by the Southern California Memorial Peace Officers Association. The shirts were sold by an ex-cop from another department to more than two dozen officers from various agencies. The Signal Hill chief protects the identity of the other officers and departments involved.

1982, Pritchard, AL: Off-duty police Sgt. Bob Morris is seen putting up KKK placards on a city street. (He's fired from the force for "conduct unbecoming an officer").

1982, Meriden, CT: Joseph Hard, the public leader of the KKK in Connecticut, is identified as a state prison guard, just before a "National White Christian Solidarity Day" rally he organized, featuring Bill Wilkinson. Pressure from the anti-Klan movement forces the state to fire him for organizing white guards and prisoners into the Klan.

Blue by Day, White by Night

1983, North Carolina: White supremacists organize among white inmates and prison guards. Glenn Miller's Confederate Knights of the KKK burn a cross outside the home of Bobby Person, a Black prison guard who was trying to win a promotion and became the target of harassment.

1983, Richmond, CA: The Cowboys, an organized white-supremacist group inside the Richmond police force, is exposed after two of its members are involved in the killing of at least two Black men. At one point, the Cowboys even wore cowboy hats and boots while on patrol. The group circulates a flyer showing a white hunter grinning over a dead deer with the caption, "choke hold, good for killing big bucks," after a Black man is strangled to death by four guards inside the Richmond jail.

1983, Chicago, IL: In an effort to defeat Black mayoral candidate Harold Washington, the cops form "Police for Epton" (the white Republican). They wear plain white buttons or buttons with a circled watermelon with a slash through it. The white cops circulate racist flyers, and concoct a plan for massive arrests in Black neighborhoods on the eve of the election, which is derailed at the last minute after being exposed by the Black press.

1983, Los Angeles, CA: An uproar develops over spying by the Public Disorder Intelligence Division, (the L.A.P.D.'s "red squad," which maintained surveillance and dossiers on many of the leading civic and political figures in the city, including opponents of police brutality). With the approval of superior officers, a lieutenant in the unit takes files home that were supposed to be destroyed under court order. He funnels materials to the domestic espionage apparatus of the Western Goals Foundation, an extremist right-wing outfit run by the head of the John Birch Society, with ties to the racist, anti-Semitic World Anti-Communist League.

1984, Battle Creek, MI: Larry Guy, Black leader of the Coalition to End Police Brutality and Racism, is the target of a series of Gestapo raids by the police, and grand jury indictments. Guy, who had earlier exposed links between the local cops and the Klan, including a 1980 cross-burning at a Coalition member's home, is arrested along with his son. Then another cross is burned on the lawn of another Coalition member.

1985, Louisville, KY: Alex Young, a 13-year veteran with the Jefferson County police, long active with the Klan, is fired after admitting that he had "probably" accessed the National Criminal Information Computer on behalf of the KKK on non-police business. Young, who had widely distributed Klan propaganda to people who knew he was a cop, is exposed when a Black family that had been victimized by racist arson brings suit. Young is forced to reveal the identities of police members of a Klan chapter he had formed in the department, called COPS (Confederate Officers Patriot Squad), but a court order keeps their names secret from the public.

1986, St. Pauls, NC: Active duty Marines from Camp Lejeune and soldiers from Fort Bragg engage in para-military training with the KKK and the White Patriot Party, an armed racist group.

1986, Chicago, IL: Black FBI Agent Donald Rochon sues

the Bureau. He is the target of harassment and death threats from white agents in the field office. His wife receives KKK-type material and threats. (Rochon ultimately wins $1 million in a settlement of the suit he brings against the agency. Ironically, when with the L.A.P.D., Rochon had infiltrated, spied on, and disrupted Black community groups opposing racist police brutality such as the killing of Eula Love.)

1987, Canton, OH: Jewish police officer Steve Silver finds a poster of Adolph Hitler stuck on the wall of the locker room in the police department.

1987, Los Angeles, CA: Assistant Chief Robert Vernon, a fundamentalist minister, is disclosed to be recruiting hundreds of "born again" Christians from the department to his church. Vernon earns a substantial second income selling right-wing Christian books and tapes, and all his staff people at the department are "born again." Vernon is later caught accessing the department's computer to provide information about Michael Zinzun, a former Black Panther running for office in Pasadena, to a right-wing candidate supported by his wife.

1988, Youngstown, PA: Former Police Chief David Gardner is indicted for providing armed security to white supremacist James Wickstrom, head of the Posse Comitatus, as part of a scheme to produce counterfeit U.S. currency to finance the racist movement.

1988, Des Moines, IA: Racist and sexist incidents of harassment within the P.D. provoke a series of lawsuits. In one case, two white cops tried to terrorize a Black officer by donning white robes over their uniforms.

1988, Ogden, UT: The Ogden police hire Richard Masker, a spokesman for the racist League of Pace Amendment Advocates and the Aryan Nations, to lecture them about the far-right movement. In 1983, Masker was fired from a job with the city of Corvallis, Oregon for sending Hitler birthday cards to local Jews.

1989, San Bernardino, CA: Black officers seeking promotion become the target of harassment. They find threatening racist letters, signed by the Brotherhood of the Aryan Police Officers Association, in their lockers inside a secured area of their police station.

1989, Exeter, NH: A part-time officer with the local cops is fired for alleged involvement with the KKK. Thomas Herman was exposed when he ran for a seat on the local Board of Selectmen. (He was defeated.)

1989, Los Angeles, CA: Two white sheriff's deputies are suspended after burning a cross inside the county jail with a home-made blowtorch to intimidate Black inmates. Reinstated by Sheriff Sherman Block, one of them, Deputy Brian Kazmierski, later shoots and kills a Mexican national. In 1989–90, allegations surface of organized white - supremacist groupings in the Sheriff's Department, at the Lynwood station (the Vikings), the Peter Pitchess Jail facility (the Wayside Whities), and possibly East L.A. (the Cavemen). Based on evidence related to the Vikings, a federal judge issues an injunction against the department, requiring them to obey their own written guidelines on the use of force.

Blue by Day, White by Night

1990, Boise, ID: Two Army Rangers from Ft. Lewis are called to testify at the trial of their associate Bob Winslow, an ex-Ranger discharged in February from Ft. Lewis, who then joined the Aryan Nations. Winslow and two others are convicted of plotting to bomb a gay bar, a Jewish temple, and Korean businesses in Seattle, Washington.

1990, Oak Harbor, WA: Three Navy men are arrested for burning a cross in the wake of the civil trial of racist Tom Metzger for the death of an Ethiopian refugee. The three are attached to the Whidbey Island Naval Air Station. (Whidbey Island is where racist leader Bob Mathews was killed in a shootout, and has been a site of a pilgrimage by neo-nazis who support Mathews's strategy for exterminationist race war.)

1990, Fort Worth, TX: Sgt. Tim Hall is dismissed from the Tarrant County sheriff's department after it is revealed that he is secretly "J. D. Calhoun," the kleagle, or chief recruiter, of the local Klan. Hall's exposure leads to the firing of two other sheriff's department employees and six of his fellow military police at Carswell Air Force base. Hall later tries to get a job with a department in Century, Florida, but is forced out after Dallas papers report on his background. Hall had previously been with the police in Santa Rosa, California.

1990, Cambridge, MA: Tech Sgt. Hank Stram of the Air National Guard is arrested with a cache of more than 500 weapons, 50,000 rounds of ammunition, a mortar, an anti-tank gun, a rocket launcher, a swastika poster, and Nazi and survivalist propaganda.

1991: In Los Angeles and San Francisco, California and in Blakely, Georgia, Klan activity is uncovered inside the fire department. In San Francisco., there is harassment of Black firefighters; in L.A., a fire captain dons a Klan-type hood to intimidate a Black woman employee, and most of the Black firefighters quit the union when it supports the captain; in Georgia, local Black residents win a settlement in a law suit brought after the fire chief's affiliation to the Klan is disclosed by anti-Klan organizers.

1991, Los Angeles, CA: In the wake of the beating of Rodney King by police from the L.A.P.D.'s Foothill Division, it is disclosed that an organized Klan faction was operating at the Foothill station. At least two Black officers, a man and a woman, had been harassed and had received Klan calling cards in locked areas of the station. Following disclosures that a paramilitary Klan faction with close ties to Tom Metzger has been attempting to recruit L.A. cops, Chief Daryl Gates assigns the Anti-Terrorist Division to investigate, but as of this writing, no results have been made public. The Commission investigating the police in the wake of the King beating turns up police computer transmissions referring to klavern meetings, and numerous racist, sexist, and anti-gay comments between officers and dispatchers.

1991, Ft. Bragg, NC: Sgt. Mike Tubbs, Warrant Officer Jeff Jennett, and two civilians are arrested for stealing and stockpiling military weapons. Tubbs was brought back from Saudi Arabia to face charges. The four were part of a group called Knights of the New Order with plans to attack Blacks and Jews.

Blue by Day, White by Night

1991, Indianapolis, IN: Officer Wayne Sharp, a member of the Nazi party who had attended Nazi meetings in Illinois and Virginia, and founded a party cell in his home town, shot and killed a Black shoplifting suspect. In 1981, Sharp had killed a Black burglary suspect and been briefly suspended. He has been involved in other shooting incidents as well during his 18-year career on the force. It was disclosed that as local leader of the Nazis, he had sent letters to Jewish organizations.

1991, Beverly Hills, CA: Scott Dafoe, an off-duty white cop, and three body-building buddies from New York are charged with the brutal gay-bashing of a Latino man outside a West Hollywood restaurant.

1991, Alameda, CA: Four white police officers are suspended after a check of mobile data transmissions turns up "jokes" about killing a nigger and wearing Klan robes. They are eventually let off with a slap on the wrist. It is later disclosed that the city destroyed the tapes rather than turn them over in a lawsuit by two bars charging the cops with bias.

1991, San Francisco, CA: The chaplain of the S.F.P.D. is exposed as an activist in the anti-abortion movement who has led prayer revivals for Operation Rescue.

1991, Northridge, CA: Then L.A. Police Chief Daryl Gates agrees to attend a rally sponsored by Students for America, the youth group of Pat Robertson's Christian crusade. The chapter had also been involved in local Populist Party organizing. (The Populists are a Nazi front group which ran David Duke for president.)

1992, Los Angeles, CA: Garland Hardeman, a Black cop who had been ostracized and verbally abused by fellow officers since testifying about racism in the L.A.P.D. to the Christopher Commission, finds a chalk outline in front of his locker like those at homicide scenes, with the indication of two bullets to the head. A police spokesman says it "is too early to characterize it as a threat."

1992, Merriville, IN: The chief of police and a deputy are suspended after making racist slurs.

1992, Savannah, GA: Three soldiers from Ft. Stewart are arrested for the racially motivated killing of a Black man. Residents believe that a white-supremacist ring may be operating on the base.

1992, Chicago, IL: A fire-fighter and his brother are arrested for shooting at their Puerto Rican neighbor. Nazi paraphernalia and massive quantities of weapons, ammunition, and explosives are found in their home.

1992, Lanett, AL: A review board upholds the city's dismissal of two officers who taunted a prisoner with racial slurs and made him wear a Klan hood.

1992, Denver, CO: Two sheriff's deputies, one white and one Latino, dress up in Klan robes in an attempt to intimidate Black inmates at the jail. In another incident, a cop flashes a KKK hand sign at Chicanas on their way to protest a Klan rally. Meanwhile, the Army issues a ban to prevent active duty personnel from attending the rally.

1992, Grovetown, GA: Scott Lowe, the former fire chief who had been exposed as the grand titan of the Christian Knights Klan, is arrested for having burned a cross in 1987 outside a Black family's home.

1992, Boynton Beach, FL: Officer Dave Demarest, fired from the force for flaunting a swastika tattoo at a Jewish woman officer and several other cops, seeks reinstatement by claiming that racism and Nazism were widespread and accepted in the department. He presents a photo of two officers dressed as Nazis which had been posted in the deputy chief's office.

1992, Ft. Benning, GA: Police arrest Klan leader Bill Riccio and several Confederate Hammer Skins and Aryan National Front members for posses-sion of military weapons and explosives at an Aryan Fest racist rock concert. Further arrests of military personnel are expected at the base.

1993, Dallas, TX: The Christian fundamentalist sheriff opens a special, plush section of the jail reserved for "born again" Christian inmates, and off-limits to the press and lawyers for other inmates. Even after the sheriff is removed for other illegalities, his successor, also a funda-mentalist Christian, continues the practice.

1993, Washington, DC: In separate incidents, gangs of sailors are involved in a gay bashing and the murder of a gay sailor, apparently in response to efforts to lift the ban on openly gay or lesbian service-members.

1993, Paterson, NJ: A cop is busted for dealing in illegal weapons with a undercover officer in a sting operation. An extensive weapons cache, Nazi paraphernalia, and white-supremacist material is found in his home.

1993, Somalia: The existence of a network of neo-nazis inside the Canadian military and Special Forces, linked to Canadian associates of Metzger's WAR organization, is exposed by the execution-style slaying of a Somali by a member of Canadian forces included in Clinton's "humanitarian" invasion of Somalia. A series of trials of the white supremacists involved in the murder and in racist paramilitary training ensue, embarrassing the Canadian government.

1994, Los Angeles, CA: A Jewish officer for a suburban police department wins an out-of-court settlement for a lawsuit he brought charging anti-Semitic harassment within the department, carried out with the apparent approval of superior officers.

1994, Los Angeles, CA: Bobby Marshall, a Black cop who talked to the Christopher Commission about Klan and racist activity in the L.A.P.D., and author of a forth coming book, "Inside the Blue Klux Klan," is convicted in a third trial on what he alleges are frame-up charges of involvement in a robbery ring. The only evidence is the testimony of a convict offered a deal by police and prosecutors to finger Marshall.

This string of incidents makes it clear that organized, violence-prone white supremacists, who make up a small element of society at large, are much better represented in the ranks of law enforcement and the military. This is no accident. The ideology of law enforcement, the "us against them" mentality which guides their daily lives and contacts with the public, makes the police suscepti- ble to white racist preachings. The police—even if polite, respectful, and individually not personal racists—carry out a commitment to suppress threats to the hierarchy of the state and society which leaves Black people and other people of color on the bottom. Organized white supremacists within the police forces find fertile soil for the argument that democratic and egalitarian values, and concern for human and civil rights, hem them in needlessly. The Klan portrays such procedural safeguards as only so much hypocrisy that interferes with cops' ability to protect themselves and to get tough on crime.

Cops Protect the Klan; Klan Returns the Favor

One aspect of the relationship between the police and organized white supremacists is massive police protection for white supremacists' organizing drives under the guise of maintaining freedom of speech. Time after time, particularly in the early '80s when the KKK was on an upswing, using public hooded rallies to promote their cause and to lay the basis for further night-riding, police forces around the country have come out in force to enable the Ku-Kluxers to carry out their strategy, and to suppress or intimi- date opposition to the Klan in the community.

In city after city, police and National Guards- men, sometimes numbering in the thousands, were

83

mobilized as phalanxes around handfuls or several dozen neo-nazis or Klansmen. Police attempted to intimidate and sometimes brutalized anti-Klan demonstrators. On many occasions, in Washington, DC, Atlanta, Georgia, Austin, Texas, and elsewhere, pitched battles broke out between community residents outraged by the Klan and police enforcing the white supremacists' line of march. Some anti-Klan groups that work closely with the police put the blame for these incidents on hot-heads in the anti-Klan movement. This echoes the line of the police, and the KKK itself. In fact, the violence that erupts at Klan rallies is in the first instance the fault and responsibility of the Klansmen and neo-nazis themselves, who violate the rights and humanity of their victims with their hateful slogans, and who use the public rallies to build the base for their clandestine terror. Everywhere the Klan has organized publicly, racist violence and terror, such as cross-burnings, shootings, and assaults have quickly followed.

In the particular rallies that have erupted in violence, police over-zealous in "protecting" the Klan by trying to intimidate and suppress anti-Klan protests have often played an important role. Police who have pushed and bullied anti-Klan protesters, declared counter-protesters to be unlawfully assembling, or cordoned off whole sectors of downtowns to separate neo-nazis from anti-racist demonstrators have brought the ire of the counter-demonstrators on themselves. Police have often been brutal in the arrests they make in these situations, making it seem that their sympathies and affinities lie with the Klansmen they are protecting. This pattern was repeated twice in 1992 in Simi Valley, California by local police and Ventura sheriff's deputies. White supremacists had been attempting to capitalize on the notoriety generated by the acquittal there of the cops who beat Rodney King by rallying to "support the police." Despite a call by anti-racist groups, the Simi Valley police chief and the Ventura County sheriff never publicly repudiated this racist "support." Meanwhile, a Black former deputy has filed suit for damages against the Ventura department for failing to stop racist harassment of him, and for allowing Klan activity among deputies, including the sale of knives inscribed "K.K.K."

For their part, Klansmen and other organized white supremacists have often made one of their top priorities defense and support of the police, particularly in cases where the cops are under attack for racist killings or shootings. In Miami, Florida for example, after racist police violence resulted in a Black rebellion in the '80s, Bill Wilkinson rushed in to hold a Klan rally to support the police. (It should be noted that Clinton's Attorney General, Janet Reno, failed to get a conviction in this case as local county prosecutor, and subsequently refused to prosecute most Miami cops in racist brutality cases.)

In Los Angeles in 1983, the local Klan Wizard, Frank Silva, launched a "support the police" campaign after a cop was killed in a shooting incident with a Black man married to a white woman. Silva's campaign culminated in the burning of three crosses by the Klan and the Nazis that he billed as a religious memorial to Lt. Verna and other fallen cops. Silva and his supporters struck a deal with cops from the Foothill Division to disperse counter-demonstrators from the Jewish Defense League, and allow the cross-burning to go forward, with an L.A.P.D. helicopter flying overhead, and then for the racists to be arrested. But this cross-burning gives the lie to the Klan's alleged support of the police. Among the participants were Tom Metzger, head of the White Aryan Resistance (WAR), Stan Witek, head of the L.A. Nazi Party, and David Tate and Richard Butler of the Idaho-based Aryan Nations.

According to testimony in a successful civil suit, Metzger was involved in the Russian-roulette interrogation of a police infiltrator of WAR. Witek was convicted of assault on an Amtrak cop when he smashed him with a standing ashtray after a demonstration while Witek was on trial for the cross-burning. Tate, who became a fugitive from federal charges while facing trial for the cross-burning, eventually was captured and convicted of killing a Missouri state trooper. The cross-burning, which supposedly memorialized fallen police officers, turned out to be the cementing of a KKK-Nazi-Aryan Nation alliance that gave birth to the Order, a clandestine neo-nazi armed group that killed a talk show host, robbed a Brink's truck and banks, and plotted the assassination of judges and other public and political figures. "Police supporter" Silva himself became a federal fugitive and is now doing time for his criminal involvement in the Order conspiracy, as are several of his cross-burning co-defendants.

Nazi–Klan Impunity from Prosecution

The 1983 L.A. cross-burning is instructive in regards to another aspect of the relationship between law enforcement and the white supremacists: the ability of the Nazis and KKK to get away with murder. Although more than 15 racists were arrested at the time of the cross-burning, only four did any time for the cross-burning itself.

The then district attorney, a Republican appointee, refused to prosecute after the original arrests were made, saying that the police arrest reports were faulty. The city attorney then filed misdemeanor charges against the participants. The case dragged slowly through the courts, until a Municipal judge suddenly dismissed the charges, buying the neonazis' argument that the cross-burning was a protected act under their constitutional rights to free speech and free exercise of religion. The city attorney's office appealed the dismissal. Eventually, an appellate court overturned the lower judge, and the city attorney was allowed to refile. By this time, however, several of the defendants had vanished. Four had become federal fugitives, exposed as members of the Order and wanted for crimes ranging from bank robbery to counterfeiting to murder. Had they been prosecuted effectively and convicted and jailed for the cross-burning, several lives might have been spared.

The story does not end there, however. The second time they were brought to court, the city attorney in the case needed surveillance and bodyguards because of racist threats related to the Order. The defendants demanded to be tried on felonies (most of the counts could be treated as either misdemeanors or felonies), thus bumping the case back up to the District Attorney and starting things from scratch again.

This strategy of the racists proved successful

when, after another long series of hearings, a judge again threw the charges out of court before an actual trial could begin. Prosecutors again appealed, and again the charges were eventually reinstated by a higher court. This time, in the interim, cross-burner Tom Metzger, one of the few remaining defendants after the Order fugitives were severed from the case, was found liable in a civil trial in Portland, Oregon for the Nazi skinhead killing of an Ethiopian refugee, along with his son John. (John Metzger had in fact participated in and been taken into custody at the L.A. cross-burning in 1983, but as a minor at the time had been released to his mother without even juvenile charges being filed.) Again, one can only speculate who might still be alive today if the Metzgers, father and son, had been held to account for the cross-burning when it first happened.

More than eight and a half years after their act of racist terror Metzger and a few co-defendants, including Witek, were finally convicted. A prosecution that failed to expose the race-war strategy espoused by Metzger allowed him to distance himself from the others, and he received the lightest sentence after getting a hung jury on several counts. The D.A. decided not to refile on the undecided charges, and Metzger was sentenced to only six months. He was released by a judge after less than half the sentence because of the illness of his wife (which proved terminal). Within days after his release and the burial of his wife, Metzger was involved in organizing for a neo-nazi, anti-immigrant mobilization on the border with Mexico. Subsequently, Metzger violated the terms of his probation by illegally entering Canada and consorting with white racists there. He was expelled by the Canadians, yet the L.A. county D.A. and judge never violated his parole or returned him to jail to serve the rest of his sentence. In 1994, Metzger was appealing his conviction, and stands a chance of overturning it.

As noted earlier, Metzger also enjoyed a charmed life with the San Diego police. Despite the intelligence reports submitted by Doug Seymour, a police reservist assigned to infiltrate Metzger's Klan and White American Political Association operations, which documented criminal activities by members of Metzger's group that included allegations of the beheading of Mexican migrant workers, the S.D.P.D. never brought any charges against Metzger. Instead, they let agent Seymour twist in the wind until his cover was blown, and he had a breakdown after being interrogated at gun point in Metzger's house. Seymour eventually won a civil lawsuit against the San Diego police in the case.

Another Nazi with a charmed life in the L.A. cross-burning case was Richard Butler, head of the Aryan Nations, based in a paramilitary compound in Idaho, which has been the breeding ground for a series of neo-nazi combatants who were eventually captured and convicted of killings and bombings. Yet Butler himself always walks away, just as he has thus far from the L.A. cross-burning. A bench warrant was issued because Butler refused to return to L.A. for trial, yet even after the conviction of his cohorts, he has not been extradited because the L.A. charges are only misdemeanors. Butler also was indicted on federal charges while the L.A. case was pending. He was one of 13 leading white supremacists tried for seditious conspiracy for plotting attacks on federal judges, counterfeiting, and other crimes to advance the white-supremacist movement. But the prosecution, held in Ft. Smith, Arkansas, was mishandled, just like the Greensboro killing case. The white supremacists were acquitted of all charges. At least two of the jurors became romantically involved with the defendants after the trial.

Summing Up

In regard to several key parameters, the relationship between the cops and the Klan is problematic for a democratic society. The organizing of white supremacists within police and military forces, the involvement of the FBI and of (former) intelligence operatives at the highest levels of Klan organizations, the apparent impunity enjoyed by many key white supremacists, all point toward troubling conclusions. At a minimum, these realities make the case that we cannot rely on the cops and the courts to deal with the Nazis and the KKK.

We cannot ban the Klan, and laws designed to do so are more likely to be used by the state against liberatory forces than against white supremacists. Even imprisonment, while well deserved for many of the white supremacists' crimes, is not a solution, given the existence of racist groups like the Aryan Brotherhood that function among white prisoners, and the fact of Klan organizing among prison guards.

The solution to the problem of racist organizing and terror must lie in anti-racist organizing, in building support for the victims of bigoted violence, and building alliances among such communities that support self-determination and social justice.

Blue by Day, White by Night

Anti-Klan organizers in particular must maintain a healthy skepticism of, and distance from, the law enforcement apparatus to maintain credibility with the communities that are at least as victimized by police brutality and repression, and by economic discrimination and exploitation, as they are by the neo-nazis. We must oppose racism and brutality in the police, militarism in U.S. foreign and domestic policies, and economic domination by the multinational corporations and banks, along with our opposition to the stone racists of the Nazis and the Klan.

Warren Christopher and His Commission

Foreshadowing a Clinton Administration

An update and revision of "L.A.'s Christopher Commission: Elite Blueprint for 'Enlightened' Repression," a research report originally prepared for People Against Racist Terror (PART), an anti-racist group in Los Angeles

The grey eminence of the Clinton administration is Secretary of State Warren Christopher. Christopher has been the architect of Clinton's chief foreign policy success, the neo-colonial "peace" agreements between Israel and the Palestinians and Jordanians. Christopher was also the chief talent scout for Clinton in selecting cabinet officials during the transition from the Bush administration. One of Christopher's choices, Zoe Baird, a protege at his high-powered corporate law firm who went on to serve as private counsel to such union-busting firms as General Electric, was the first embarrassing flame-out of Clinton's new administration. Her indiscretion in having hired two undocumented immigrants as domestic servants, failing to pay their social security taxes while she and her law professor husband earned over a half a million dollars a year, caused such an outpouring of resentment from around the country that official Washington was unable to blink it off.

With Christopher her only patron, Baird was forced to step down as nominee. Clinton subsequently gave her the consolation prize of an appointment to his Foreign Intelligence Advisory Board, a post that requires no confirmation, after she became yesterday's news, overshadowed by subsequent media tempests. Christopher himself emerged unscathed from the brouhaha over Baird, though some questioned his judgment in recommending a right winger with ethical problems to head the Justice Department.

Neither Christopher's critics nor his adherents have delineated his politics clearly. Most criticism of Christopher has simply called him a manager with no clear policy views. On the other hand, a well-orchestrated burst of publicity appeared a couple of months into Clinton's term, including a fawning puff-piece by Bob Scheer in the *Los Angeles Times* magazine which lauded his humanitarian instincts. Other articles painted him as the most effective member of Clinton's cabinet. But Christopher has a clear politics, a neo-colonial strategy of the iron fist in the velvet glove, which has eluded clear analysis by either his critics or his fans.

In 1991, while the controversy over the L.A.P.D. and its then chief, Daryl Gates, was raging in Los Angeles in the wake of the police beating of Rodney King, People Against Racist Terror (PART) issued a paper demonstrating that the so-called Christopher Commission report on the L.A. police—while it provided valuable evidence about the degree of racism and sexism inside the department—was ultimately a whitewash of the problem. The "Independent Commission," jointly appointed by Mayor Bradley and Chief Gates, was led by Warren Christopher, then known primarily as a leading L.A. power broker and a former federal official. The PART report, which predicted—in hindsight, correctly—that Christopher's proposals were not merely too little, too late, but would in fact make matters worse in L.A., takes on renewed relevance today. It has accordingly been rewritten here, with an eye towards its larger, national relevance to activists wondering how to deal with the Clinton administration.

PART strongly but unsuccessfully urged progressives in L.A. at the time not to divert our efforts against police brutality and racism into support for the Christopher Commission report. The report was issued by Christopher and his fellows at a critical moment. The L.A.P.D. had been exposed locally and internationally by the video-taped beating of Rodney King; the city government was paralyzed by the refusal of Chief Gates to step down in the face of massive opposition; a grass-roots movement around police brutality and injustice, more widespread and generalized than that over any single previous case, was growing locally and inspiring similar activity nationally. At that juncture, Warren Christopher stepped in; this proved to be a temporarily successful effort to clean up what was, from an elite perspective, an embarrassing and potentially explosive mess.

Yet the very effectiveness of the report, short term, in derailing the grass-roots movement, and the inability to step up truly independent efforts to expose the real problems, were key factors leading to the eruption in L.A. the following year, after the police who beat Rodney King were acquitted. Now, that history, as well as the exposé of the true nature and interests of Warren Christopher and the other commissioners, hold important national and international lessons, not only around the issues of police brutality and reform, but general issues of neo-colonial strategy for managing the American empire in the "post–Cold War" period.

Warren Christopher and Mickey Kantor, the two principal architects of Bill Clinton's transition and his top administration staffing, who now both hold cabinet-level appointments with international policy responsibilities, served together on the L.A. commission. A third Clinton cabinet-level appointee, James Woolsey, the Director of Central Intelligence, is a right-wing, cold-war Democrat who served at Christopher's law firm, O'Melveny and Meyers. In addition to the unsuccessful attempt to name Zoe Baird Attorney General, several top sub-cabinet officials, particularly at the State Department, are Christopher proteges from his law firm or previous federal offices. Activists dealing with war and peace, the economy, and other areas now falling under the authority of Christopher and his cohorts, as well as those dealing with police racism and brutality, would be well advised to examine this record closely. Christopher intends to carry out globally the same counter-insurgency strategy he attempted in L.A. Activists must not be deluded or disarmed by it.

Warren Christopher

The Christopher commissioners in 1991 were, unsurprisingly, representatives of the business and professional elite that has long guided the destiny of L.A. Warren Christopher, who chaired the commission came with an impressive national resume as a former Deputy U.S. Attorney General under Lyndon Johnson and Deputy U.S. Secretary of State under Jimmy Carter. He had served as vice-chair of the McCone Commission, headed by the CIA chief, which made some similar recommendations in the wake of the 1965 Watts Rebellion. It was fear of a reenactment of that rebellion, under conditions where 50,000 or more Black and Latino youth are armed with automatic weapons, which motivated the Christopher Commission to issue its report, PART said at the time; so perhaps it is fitting that the report in fact ultimately led to just such an uprising.

As PART pointed out at the time, Christopher made his political career trying to put out the fires of the Black liberation struggle. The McCone Commission set the standard in 1965 for expressions of establishment concern about lamentable economic and social inequities and for reform recommendations, which somehow never bore fruit. It was a model followed in dozens of cities shortly thereafter.

The supposed expertise on handling "civil unrest" that Christopher gained by serving on the McCone Commission was called on repeatedly during his government career. Lyndon B. Johnson sent him in to Detroit, during the 1967 Black rebellion there, as his personal troubleshooter. When Blacks in Chicago erupted in April 1968, following the assassination of Dr. Martin Luther King Jr., LBJ again sent in Christopher, by that time a sub-cabinet official in the Justice Department. Christopher coordinated, along with then Deputy Secretary of Defense Cyrus Vance, the use of the U.S. Army to suppress a rebellion that had exceeded the capabilities of even the vicious Chicago Police Department to put down. As PART reported in 1991, during confirmation hearings when Christopher became Vance's deputy at the Jimmy Carter State Department, allegations were raised that Christopher had approved the use of U.S. military surveillance of domestic dissidents during his stint at the Johnson Justice Department, particularly against peace activists organizing around the summer 1968 Democratic convention.

At the time of the 1977 confirmation, Warren Christopher denied having been aware of or approving this domestic spying by the Army. He claimed that military intelligence had only collated raw material obtained from the field agents of local police forces. However, during the new hearings in 1993 to confirm Christopher as Clinton's Secretary of State, evidence emerged of a written memo detailing the assignment of Army Intelligence operatives to carry out surveillance of movement activists. The memo is clearly initialed and approved at the relevant point by "WC"—Warren Christopher. Yet despite this new evidence, indicating that Christopher apparently not only approved the initial spying, but later lied about it under oath to obtain his earlier confirmation, the story sank back below the surface like a stone. Christopher is obviously too valuable a manager and policy-maker to have to worry about minor matters like perjury or the unconstitutional domestic use of the military to repress dissent. Other recent reportage has exposed the close tabs Army Intelligence kept on Martin Luther King right up to his assassination in Memphis. No legislator has asked Christopher or Vance what they knew about that.

It was his experience in handling "civil unrest," and in particular containing and suppressing the Black rebellions of the '60s that qualified Christopher for his assignment at the head of the "Independent Commission" in L.A., along with his undeniable standing in the top ranks of L.A.'s business elite as head of the leading corporate law firm of O'Melveny and Meyers. O'Melveny and Meyers is not the "LA Law" of TV fame; they are a giant corporate law firm and are sophisticated union busters who have long helped their multinational clients keep their work forces unorganized. Even the L.A. City School Board, in its attempts to break the United Teachers Los Angeles, had retained O'Melveny and Meyers as outside counsel. After the L.A. teachers were recently browbeaten, with fearmongering about another L.A. rebellion, into accepting a contract calling for a 10% pay cut, attorneys at O'Melveny and Meyers went to work behind the scenes to sabotage the deal because they thought it gave away too much to the union!

Warren Christopher himself was the managing partner of the firm. He is also a member of the elite Trilateral Commission, whose theorists have maintained since the late '70s that the U.S. and other Western nations are suffering from an "excess of democracy." This theory holds that marginalized, disenfranchised, and economically oppressed groups are destablizing the system with their demands for an effective voice, and that steps must be taken to limit democracy and harden the state apparatus. These are the views that he was carrying out at the L.A. Commission and which he brings to his new federal service.

It was at the Independent Commission that Christopher first worked very closely with Mickey Kantor, a partner in another high-powered law firm, Manatt, Phelps and Phillips. Kantor was a long-term Democratic Party king-maker and fund-raiser. His firm, too, mainly represents multinational clients and is closely associated with effective lobbying inside the Washington beltway. He and Christopher went on from the Commission to the Clinton camp; they had keys roles in screening and suggesting staffers to the president-elect for his incoming administration. Kantor is now Clinton's U.S. Trade Representative, a crucial position that straddles domestic and international policies. He's one of the architects of Clinton's victorious adoption of the North American Free Trade Agreement (NAFTA) and manager of the crucial U.S. economic relationship with Japan. Kantor's post is central in Clinton's depiction of U.S. foreign interests as being defined in the first place around U.S. economic productivity growth. "Productivity growth" simply means that companies are able to exploit greater profits from the work of fewer employees; as we have already seen under Bush and Reagan, it does not translate into economic well-being or secure employment for most people.

In addition to getting themselves placed in cabinet-level positions, Christopher and Kantor also had Clinton's ear on policy and personnel matters.

Warren Christopher

Throughout the campaign, echoing the Christopher Commission recommendations, Clinton promised to oversee a national increase in the number of cops on the beat. As in L.A., this growth in police forces is designed to implement "community oriented policing," in which the cops take on an organizing role, trying to mobilize residents into auxiliary forces of law enforcement. It is planned as a continuation of Bush's "Weed and Seed" program. This came to fruition in Clinton's crime bill, which massively extended the death penalty, made membership in a street gang a federal crime, and sweetened the pill with a few "weed and seed" type counterinsurgency social programs.

PART said at the time that the Christopher Commission issued its report that the Commission had two primary concerns. First, Christopher wanted to enable the police department and the city to put the crisis caused by the beating of Rodney King behind it, hoping that once off the front pages and TV screens, the issue would lose some of its heat before it erupted into uncontrollable turmoil. Second, he and the others sought to end the embarrassing political paralysis in Los Angeles city government and at the L.A.P.D. that had resulted from the stalemate over the issue of police accountability between Mayor Bradley and Chief Gates's backers on the City Council.

That's why the Commission finally, but very politely, concurred in the chant raised by thousands of demonstrators that "Gates Must Go!" To the Commissioners, Gates remained a loyal servant, commended in the report and urged only to retire, not resign, and to stay on until a successor could be

101

chosen. Reading between the lines, Gates was sent the message that staying on indefinitely would endanger the elite he served and the social and economic order he was paid to protect. But in fact, the report ultimately allowed Gates to stay on long enough to make matters even worse during the rebellion that followed the police-beating acquittals.

For many organizations and activists at the time, stymied by the City Council's support for the chief and his backing by many white homeowners, the report by the Independent Commission seemed a godsend. It did amass incontrovertible evidence of the reality of a police department permeated by racism, sexism, homophobia, and a culture of violence. It demonstrated that neither the department's management from Chief Daryl Gates on down, nor civilian authority in the Police Commission, the City Council, or the D.A.'s or Mayor's office, did anything to check or correct this abuse. The commissioners were apparently shocked—shocked!—by the overwhelming evidence of racist police brutality having gone unpunished, indeed often having been rewarded with promotions. They knew they had to act when they discovered blatantly racist, sexist, and anti-gay messages throughout a random sampling of interdepartmental computer transmissions.

The Commission did document the extent of conscious racism and sexism in the department by releasing more than 80 pages of computer printouts from police patrol communications filled with vile racist slurs, boastful accounts of chases by car and on foot, intentional beatings and shootings, and harassment of women and minority police officers. Samples of these transmissions appear in the appendix, though these particular exposures are less significant with the passage of time, and the general parameters of the whitewash more striking. The message did go out at the time, however, to other departments around the country to tighten up their management and avoid similar embarrassment by carefully auditing their paper trail. The commissioners understood that the King beating and its aftermath had national political consequences, and they sought to defuse the issue before widespread concern and outrage could be mobilized into an effective political movement.

But many local progressive activists apparently felt that Christopher, demonstrating the openness of the city's power elite to reforms in the police and to a transfer of power from Gates to a new, more accountable chief, was the horse to back. They failed to recognize that such concessions came only out of fear that a grass-roots movement might extract much larger victories if it continued to grow. Joe Hicks, then director of public relations for the ACLU, and now head of the local Southern Christian Leadership Conference, considered the Christopher report to be a substantial victory for civil libertarians. "Shortly before the report was released," he said, "we were worried that we might have lost the momentum and impact that was built for significant reforms as a result of the videotaping of the King beating."

He claimed that the report adopted 85% of the ACLU's proposals. Hicks detailed how the ACLU had reacted to the success of Gates's efforts, before the report was released, to capitalize on the fears of white liberals and homeowners, and to portray the issue as Blacks versus the cops and Gates. Rather than taking on this racist strategy head on, the ACLU tried to counter it by appealing to such pocketbook concerns as the cost of judgments and out-of-court settlements against the city and the L.A.P.D. in brutality cases. In the wake of the Christopher report, the ACLU, NAACP, and others focused their campaign almost exclusively on its adoption.

Warren Christopher was allowed to be seen by most as simply a leading corporate lawyer with a lauded history of far-sighted "public service." He and the other commissioners were authentically troubled by the racial polarization in the city over the issue, with even the most moderate African American and Latino leaders expressing fear and resentment of the L.A.P.D. at a series of hearings, while the commission was flooded with letters in support of Gates and the force from the white West San Fernando Valley (in a campaign organized by Gates). They knew that such an extreme polarization was bad for business in the new multi-ethnic international marketplace.

But perhaps even more than the polarization, they feared the radicalization of the African American community. They sought to forestall the possibility of grass-roots links between Black and Latino victims of police repression, and the discrediting of moderate leaders unable to "do something" about Gates and the cops in favor of more militant leadership. Like the judges who ruled at the time to change the venue of the trial of the officers who beat Rodney King out of L.A. (and who set the stage for the Simi Valley acquittal), their deliberations and decision were shaped by a fear of "social unrest" and rebellion, though the commissioners were not as frank in acknowledging this as were the judges.

In fact, as damning as the report was, it was still a whitewash! It is ironic and fitting that the commissioners' strategy and the judges' decision led to the most massive "social unrest" in the history of the U.S. by people frustrated with their inability to get rid of Gates or to get justice from the system. Sadly, the local progressive movement at the time seemed incapable of understanding or exposing the true agenda of Christopher and his ilk; of providing leadership that might have substantially weakened the cops' repressive power and the elite's control of the city; or of channeling the people's anger into effective political action.

In the wake of the subsequent rebellion, there have been no more Christopher or McCone Commissions or reports calling for social reform; instead, former FBI and CIA head William Webster was charged with figuring out how to improve police command and control functions and riot control operations. Governor Wilson assigned someone to help the National Guard strengthen its rapid response capabilities to deal with "civil unrest." The Christopher "reform" recommendations have been absorbed into Clinton's repressive crime bill.

Even the new "reform" police chief, Willie Williams, appointed under the Christopher-reformed city charter to replace Daryl Gates, pulled out all the stops to disrupt a 1993 rally against police brutality on the corner of Florence and Normandie where the 1992 rebellion started. The L.A.P.D. is now committed to using rubber bullets and pepper gas to break up opposition. This strategy was put into practice at a cost of over a million dollars a day when the verdict came down in the federal civil rights trial of the cops who beat Rodney King. The massive police presence, and the mobilization of the National Guard and the Marines, was justified through media-induced paranoia about another uprising, and was repeated during the trial of those accused in the Reginald Denny beating, as well as for the sentencing of Koon and Powell and, in a lower key, for King's civil lawsuit against the city.

When they issued their report, Christopher and his fellow commissioners wanted to regain control of the agenda and to reestablish the legitimacy of the police. Thereby, the L.A.P.D. could actually increase the effectiveness of its repressive capacities by incorporating elements of the community as snitches for and adjuncts to the police. At the time, confessing some of the sins of the L.A.P.D. was necessary to the Commission's credibility. Yet a report which was principally designed to provide political cover to Gates' allies in the politically risky task of easing him out, became the big tent under which many opponents of police brutality crawled as well.

With no major progressive group offering a truly independent critique of the police and the system they serve, and without systematic grass-roots pressure and exposure, education, and action, there was no real change in the use of brutality and violence by the police to enforce a racist status quo, no transformation of the criminal "justice" system from its role in oppressing rather than protecting people of color.

The ruling elite saw to it, as PART predicted, that the Christopher Commission proposals were adopted;

former Police Chiefs Reddin and Davis helped push the proposals through the City Council. Despite PART's analysis, grass-roots anti-racists failed to take a different tack. As a result, Christopher at the time succeeded in taking the steam out of the movement. Yet his "success" led to the rebellion a year later, as neither elected officials nor the old-line civil rights movement and religious leadership had any credibility on a street level, nor any ability to disguise or protect injustice from people's anger.

Christopher was not only the chair but the pre-eminent member of the L.A. Commission, whose other members attributed its "success" to his tenacity and facilitative skills. The other members of Christopher's Commission came from the same corporate mold that he does, including Roy Anderson, the chairman emeritus of Lockheed, the aeronautics defense contractor. Anderson was then head of "LA 2000," an elite planning group for the 21st century. Anderson shared membership with Christopher himself on the Board of Trustees of Stanford University and on the Board of Directors of both Southern California Edison and First Interstate Bank. Anderson, in addition, was a director of ARCO, whose downtown offices were where Gates got the final word from the Atlantic-Richfield chairman that he had to go. Anderson rose to the top at Lockheed in the wake of its defense contract bribery scandal, in which he was judged to have been only a minor participant, the cleanest of a dirty lot involved in paying off officials in Japan and other countries.

Other members of Christopher's Commission besides Kantor and Anderson included Andrea S. Ordin, a former U.S. Attorney, deputy California

Attorney General, and head of the County Bar, who subsequently resisted Bradley's efforts to appoint her to the police commission; Richard Mosk, a former member of the Iran–U.S. Claims Court (a previous area of Christopher responsibility under Vance at State) who learned how to handle high-level Commission cover-ups as a staff member of the Warren Commission appointed by LBJ to keep the lid on the Kennedy assassination; and Commission Vice-Chair, Gates appointee John Arguelles, who had been appointed to the California Supreme Court by Governor Deukmejian after the right-wing ouster of Rose Bird and several other justices. Even the "minority community" members of the Commission, like John Brook Slaughter, a Black man connected to the Urban League, come from the same corporate mold. Slaughter was a member of the corporate boards of IBM, Monsanto Chemical, and Union Bank.

The report adopted by these representatives of the ruling corporate elite was not meant to serve the interests of the working poor and oppressed communities of L.A. Essentially, these members of the city's establishment only came around to the view espoused by then Mayor Bradley and the *Los Angeles Times,* that Gates ought to go for the good of the L.A.P.D. and "the city"—meaning for the good of the privileged and powerful. After the 1992 rebellion, these same forces congregated in the Rebuild L.A. (later RLA—"Our" L.A.) effort to place private enterprise at the helm of reconstruction and revitalization. The passage of time has shown the pretense and futility of these efforts, and now even ARCO, of which Anderson was a director, has slashed the

Warren Christopher

funding and spending of its ARCO Foundation on non-profit community service programs.

The Commission report did lay the problems of the L.A.P.D. directly at the doorstep of its top management. Refusing to accept Gates's declaration that the beating of Rodney King was simply an "aberration," it identified a hard-core group of problem officers who continued to use excessive force with an impunity that actually made them role models who were emulated by new recruits, rather than negative examples. (A follow-up study by the *Los Angeles Times* showed that two years after, many of these problem officers had yet to be effectively disciplined.) But ultimately the Christopher Commissioners had no interest in exposing the extent of the real, systematic problems that lead to police brutality. As a result, the report sloughed over serious problems. These omissions helped disclose its real agenda.

What the Commission Didn't Deal With

For one thing, although its addendum reported several police transmissions that refer to the Ku Klux Klan, as well as one about a watch commander with "white hoods," and another police transmission that used the slogan "white power," the report does not deal with organized white supremacist activity inside the police force. Testimony given to the Commission by African American officers about harassment which they attributed to KKKers in police ranks is not reported in the summary, and the Commission neither commented on the publicized efforts of the Klan to recruit in the L.A.P.D. after the King beating, nor looked into Chief Gates's assignment of the Anti-Terrorist Division to investigate Klan infiltration of the Department. No results of that investigation have been made public. The resemblance of the emblem of the L.A. SWAT team (Special Weapons and Tactics) to the logo of the American White Separatists, whose slogan "Racial Purity is America's Security" was on the Ku Klux Klan calling cards left for Black officers inside the Foothill Division, as reported in the Black press, is not dealt with. Since the report, new revelations of such organized white-supremacist penetration of the force have been similarly hushed up. Thus the problem has been allowed to fester and grow since the report was released.

The latest disclosures regarding Robert Bauman, a civilian employee of the L.A.P.D. for 23 years, underscore the continuing seriousness of the problem. Assigned to investigate applicants for police permits, with access to criminal records, tax filings, and other data, Bauman was discovered by undercover L.A. and Huntington Beach cops participating in activities organized by Tom Metzger and other white supremacists in Orange County. Huntington Beach police reported that he apparently engaged in counter-surveillance activity against them, disrupting their attempt to cover the meeting and apparently identifying them as cops to other participants. A subsequent investigation by the L.A.P.D.'s Anti-Terrorist Task Force and by Internal Affairs uncovered other connections to white-supremacist activity, and after a warrant was obtained, a search of Bauman's home disclosed a vast collection of material on the nazis and white-supremacist literature. Bauman, however, claims he is only an independent historical researcher, not affiliated with Metzger.

Whatever his affiliations, Bauman used his access to L.A.P.D. computers to run background checks on Metzger, Stan Witek of the local Nazi Party, Arnold Schwarzenegger, Irv Rubin of the Jewish Defense League, Jan Tucker, a private investigator and Peace and Freedom Party candidate, and as many as 200 others. His defense is that he was obtaining the information for his personal historical research and interest in right-wing and left-wing groups. He says he was angry at Rubin for disrupting a historical society meeting in Pasadena, apparently a reference to the holocaust-revisionist outfit, the Institute for Historical Review. Bauman was given a 10-day suspension, and new Police Chief Willie Williams promised to tighten up access to police computers.

But Bauman appealed his suspension, saying even 10 days is too much, and citing the cases of at least 45 other cops and civilian employees who have been disciplined in the last three years for using the computers for "unofficial business." Most received only reprimands or one-or two-day suspensions. Similarly, the L.A.P.D. has refused to cooperate with an FBI/San Francisco District Attorney investigation of access to confidential police reports to a private eye working for the Anti-Defamation League The private eye later repackaged information he had collected for the ADL on anti-apartheid activists and sold it to the South African secret police.

In its failure to deal with such problems, the Christopher report was used as a model for a similar whitewash of the Sheriff's Department by retired Judge Kolts, appointed by the elected sheriff after a series of racist killings by deputies in the following months. But the Kolts report's most glaring omission illuminates the reality of organized racist activity in the Sheriff's department. In criticizing D.A. Ira Reiner's refusal to prosecute deputies for brutality or murder, the Kolts report cited the case of one deputy who went out "looking for trouble" on New Year's Eve a couple of years ago. The deputy was overheard making racist comments and ended up shooting and killing a Mexican national. Yet Kolts failed to mention that the deputy involved, Brian Kazmierski, had previously been investigated by the FBI and kicked off the force for burning crosses inside the county jail to intimidate Black prisoners. Kazmierski had been reinstated to the department on the express orders of Sheriff Sherman Block. The media went along with this cover-up.

Of course, though focused on the L.A.P.D., the Christopher report had nothing to say about the L.A. Sheriff's Department, whose deputies are involved at least as often as the cops in racist brutality, shootings, and killings, and who exercise direct police powers inside the city of L.A. (in the jails, for example); let alone other local police departments in the county (or the country). To do so would begin to acknowledge that the problem of police abuse is systematic, not merely due to a few "bad apples" or aberrations at the L.A.P.D., or a breakdown in supervision. The killing of a Latino youth by sheriff's deputies on L.A.P.D. turf shortly after the report was issued underlined the interrelationship which jurisdictional niceties do not affect. The problem was and is in fact national in scope, and it is cold comfort that Christopher and Kantor now have a national and international arena in which to operate.

Nor did the Christopher report deal adequately with sexist and homophobic violence against civilians by white male officers in the L.A.P.D. and the mistreatment of women and gay men and lesbians within the ranks of the department. While noting the prior history of discrimination against gay men and lesbians, and of condescencion and negativity towards female officers, the report did little but endorse existing programs (won through lawsuits) to recruit women, Blacks, and Latinos to the force, and the department's newly adopted prohibition on discrimination in hiring or promotion based on sexual orientation. No mention was made of the lawsuit against the department by former officer Mitch Grobeson and other anonymous gay officers, which probably prompted the rescinding of the department's previous explicitly anti-gay policy, nor of any of the testimony provided the Commission about the prevalence of gay bashings by L.A.P.D. officers. Nor, despite a court finding that the L.A.P.D. is liable for a rape carried out by one of its officers while on duty, and despite an epidemic of sexual abuse and assault by law enforcement personnel around southern California, did the report make substantive recommendations for dealing with the cops' sexism.

In general the report was silent about complaints that the L.A.P.D., in its dealings with immigrants, turned not only criminal suspects but also even victims of crime and complainants over to the INS for deportation. The brutal beating by the L.A. cops of mostly Latino "Justice for Janitors" protesters (who were trying to unionize Century City office towers), resulted in permanent disablities and the death of a prematurely born baby. But this notorious incident was not even mentioned, nor was the general hostility of the cops to labor organizing by immigrants and other workers. Thus, the police were given a free hand for their massive turn-over to the INS of undocumented workers arrested for curfew violations and other "crimes" during the 1992 uprising, as well as for the vicious brutality and union-busting tactics employed against striking Mexicano drywall installers by the L.A.P.D. and other forces. Some of the arrested strikers again were held for documentation checks by the INS.

Police violence against anti-war protesters also wasn't mentioned in Christopher's report. Despite noting the lack of effective prosecution of police criminality by the District Attorney, whose prosecutors depend on the police to make their other cases, the commission had no systematic recommendations to make to ensure that such police–prosecutorial collusion does not continue to leave law enforcers "above the law." The report didn't deal with the demands for an overhaul of the K-9 corps, whose vicious dogs aim for the face and the groin, and seem to have been trained and inculcated in the same racism many of the L.A.P.D.'s human officers suffer from. As later noted by Amnesty International in accusing the L.A.P.D. and L.A. Sheriff's Department of human rights violations, the victims of monstrous maimings by police dogs are almost invariably Black and Latino.

Since the Commission was designed to limit the focus of the examination of the problem, the report's proposals for dealing with the problems it identified were sharply circumscribed. The key changes the Commission proposed were to strengthen the Police

Commission and to limit the tenure of the chief. The report called for stricter discipline and enforcement of department policy against excessive force, and racial, ethnic, and gender slurs. It proposed tightening up promotion policies and cutting back on the use of stress disability pensions to allow cops to retire with pay rather than face discipline for excessive force and other misconduct. It called for a wider variety of possible punishments and greater administrative power to discipline officers, including taking into account previous complaints against them, and for Police Commission review of reversals of such discipline by the chief. Those recommendations were good as far as they went—which wasn't very far. But they served to help throttle a campaign for a much more sweeping initiative to establish an elected civilian board to deal with citizen complaints which in fact failed to gather enough signatures to qualify for the ballot after the Christopher report was codified by the City Council (over Gates's continued opposition) and put up for a vote by the electorate.

The worst aspect of the Commission report was not that it was limited, however, but that it moved the L.A.P.D. in the wrong direction in the guise of reform. To replace the department's aggressive paramilitary crime-fighting strategy, the report recommended an alternative model called "community oriented policing." The report proposed that "community based policing's emphasis on officers interacting positively with the public should have the effect of 'humanizing' their perceptions of those whom they police.... [It] would increase the effectiveness of the police and diminish the tension between the public and the L.A.P.D. by eliminating the view of the 'community as the enemy.'"

This laudable-sounding vision that the L.A.P.D.'s relationship with impoverished and exploited Black, Latino, and Asian communities, with Native Americans, with the homeless, could be similar to that enjoyed by the white suburban homeowners who also fall within its jurisdiction, was at best wishful thinking, a fantasy. In fact, the community policing slogan masks an even more ominous reality, given the racial dynamics of U.S. society.

The Commission reported, as an example of current community-based programs within the L.A.P.D., the experiment in "community policing" begun in 1989 known as "Operation Cul-de-Sac," in which the police erect barricades and street barriers, posted "Narcotics Enforcement Area—Open to Residents Only." Officers on foot, horseback, and bicycle saturate the area and require identification of people entering. The program is actually another Gates innovation, like the SWAT team and the DARE program, an example of "community oriented policing" that puts uniformed, armed cops in the classroom as "teachers." Operation Cul-de-Sac had its antecedents during the "anti-terrorist" hysteria at the time of the 1984 Olympics in L.A., when the Black community surrounding the University of Southern California, one of the main Olympic venues, was cordoned off.

Operation Cul-de-Sac is aptly named: it's a dead end. Even the Commission's report acknowledged criticisms of the program for operating only in minority neighborhoods and for resulting in harsh treatment of suspected gang members, while having only an illusory effect on crime by simply displacing it to other nearby streets. The report failed to mention the coordination of some of these operations with the INS to identify undocumented immigrants. Having created the conditions of poverty, degradation, and hopelessness that breed crime, the ruling elite's proposed solution—"community policing"—amounts to a prescription of a police state as the solution to these woes.

Although the new chief, Willie Williams, came in with a commitment to this strategy, the only funding for such policing came, in the wake of the April–May 1992 uprising, from the federal "weed and seed" program, designed to beef up law enforcement. "Weed and seed" puts what little community development money is available from Washington under the control of law enforcement officials at the Justice Department and requires that any local programs so funded be supervised by local law enforcement. This is essentially the strategy also followed by Clinton's crime bill.

Some in the affected communities, tired of drive-by shootings and other forms of criminal victimization, may be ready to accept the Commission's proposals. We can expect, under a Clinton administration in which Christopher and Kantor play a large role, that the counter-insurgency "weed and seed" programs will continue. These plans are aimed at weeding out not criminals, but any independent, radical leadership in oppressed communities, while beefing up the police presence. Just as the Law Enforcement Assistance Administration (LEAA) under Nixon provided massive armament and new centralization to police departments in the wake of the '60s rebellions, "community policing" as proposed by Christopher will be the rubric that allows a similar intensification of police control of the community in the 1990s. In L.A. itself, community opposition initially forestalled acceptance of the "weed and seed" millions; but the program was rechristened CPR and adopted. But no amount of "CPR" will restore a moribund system that cannot meet people's legitimate needs.

It is true that then Chief Gates himself, along with a substantial portion of both the police brass and the rank and file, perceived the few changes as personally and institutionally threatening. The Police Protective League, the L.A.P.D. union, emerged as an opponent of the reforms, in particular those which would require psychological testing of cops or make it easier for police management to discipline officers for excessive force and for ethnic slurs and intimidation. (Interestingly, several opponents of the reforms were appointed to high positions by the incoming mayor.)

In the same way, police unions and vigilantes have acted as a racist vanguard against police review boards, even though the evidence shows that civilian boards are at least as lenient on cops, if not more so, than internal department reviews. However, this institutional opposition by the most retrograde forces should not mean that we allow our movement to be guided by the establishment elite, or our strategies to be written by the Warren Christophers.

When PART wrote its initial report on Christopher and his Commission, we said, hopefully, that it remained to be seen whether progressive forces could regain the initiative in shaping the debate over and response to the Commission's report. It must be stated now that we failed to do so, with the consequences the whole world has seen. Here in L.A., a few Black youths were scape-goated for the entire uprising; as the KKK and other white-supremacist groups attempt to organize "to support the police," it is urgent to recover from that failure. Christopher and Kantor, architects of that strategy, are attempting to repeat their "success" in L.A. on a national and global scale, to deal with insurgency in Mexico, the Palestinian intifada, human rights issues in China. It is equally urgent to arm grass-roots movements with the knowledge and perspective that will enable us to shape our own movements and our destinies, and not fall prey to Christopher's counter-insurgency efforts.

Appendix: Racist and Sexist Transmissions by L.A. Cops

The one undeniable contribution by the "Independent Commission on the Los Angeles Police Department" (Christopher's Commission) is that it issued 84 pages of normally unavailable transcripts from L.A.P.D. mobile digital terminal (MDT) communications between police cars and dispatchers, and those routed by central communications between two police vehicles. These MDTs are computer terminals. The messages are not oral; they are typed in usually in a kind of e-mail shorthand, and codes allow them to be directed to particular patrol cars. The commission randomly selected 182 days out of a year-and-a-half between November 1, 1989 and March 4, 1991 (until immediately after the beating of Rodney King), for which they checked the printouts of all the computer communications.

On practically every one of the days they check-ed, the commission staff found outrageous examples of open racism, sexism, and homophobia towards other officers as well as civilians, bragging about violence, and a virtual blood lust about engaging in pursuits, beatings, and shootings. The commission found it particularly shocking, and proof that the department's top management was unconcerned about racism and the unjustified use of force, that so many officers felt so free over such a protracted period to engage in such remarks, knowing they were being recorded.

Excerpts follow (corrected for grammar and spelling with date and time noted. Indentations indicate a response to the previous transmission, dialogue style. Comments in brackets are editorial comments by the author.

11/7/89 1:30 AM:

> Where you be?
> In the projects.
> Roger...good hunting.

11/7/89 7:48 AM:

I'm off this Friday. Let's do lunch. Do you still have that KKK meeting?

11/9/89 12:40 AM:

A day without violence is like a day without sunshine. The sun shone last. Raaa Grrr.

11/12/89 3:41 PM:

If you hear a help call from me, call in an air-strike with napalm.

Warren Christopher

Better than an M-16 is a Heckler-Koch-94.

I'd love to drive down Slauson [in Watts] with a flame thrower. We could have a barbecue.

11/13/89 12:19 AM:

You can see the color of the interior of the vehicle, dig? You stop cars with a Black interior.

Bees they naugahyde?

Negrohide.

Self-tanning, no doubt.

11/17/89 8:28 PM:

I left a 14-year-old girl I met yesterday handcuffed naked to my chinning bar wearing nothing but a blindfold and salad oil. I'd like to check on her.

11/20/89 7:51 PM:

This hole is picking up. I almost got me a Mexican but he dropped the damn gun too quick, lots of witnesses.

11/22/89 12 noon:

It sure is nice to be labeled emotionally unstable.

Stress pension. Just go in twirling your gun on one finger and say "Who's next?"

11/23/89 12:51 AM:

I have an NHI [No Human Involved—a term used repeatedly, apparently in reference to gang members fighting with each and also in reference to altercations between gay men.] Two guys in mutual combat with bottles. Do I have to make an arrest?

11/24/89 5:27 PM:

Is that call safe for me?

It should be. It's north of the jungle.

121

1/13/90 11:49 PM:

Monkeys in the trees, monkeys in the trees, hi-ho the dario, monkeys in the trees. [There are repeated references to Black people as monkeys or gorillas, to monkey slapping time, etc.]

1/14/90 1:04 AM:

[Referring to a female officer] The troops have already nicknamed her Skycunt. The pilot is her niece.

1/16/90 11:40 PM:

Roger, how's it going as a ghetto gunfighter?

Lots of fun, lots of 181 [personnel complaints] but well worth it.

I bought a town house up in Canyon Country. How's your place? Hey, I've been down here for only three deployment periods, and I don't have any 181's, only two "use of force"; not bad for me.

Good hunting.

6/11/90 9:22 PM:

Did you copy?

I sure did.

Must be nice.

It is.... White power.

6/13/90 10:25 PM:

They're Indians, the towel head kind, not the feather kind.

6/21/90 5:12 PM:

Did you arrest the 85-year-old lady or just beat her up?

We slapped her around a bit. She's getting medical treatment now.

6/28/90 10:10 PM:

Mexican means a wetback with no papers and likes to give bullshit to the police, and doesn't speak no English, until he pulls his i.d. out of his ass, then and only then does he become a Hispanic with papers.

6/30/90 1:36 PM:

We're just some studly big city gun-slinging crime fighters doing our job. Enough about us. What's up?

7/1/90 5:43 AM:

I enjoyed that. Torture and sadism can be sssu-uuch a rrruush...hahahahaha.

But it must be done tastefully, of course. I was informing [omitted] of the standard procedure for dealing with such subhuman maggots in Central. Ahh, the good old days.

7/19/90 6:12 PM:

Oh, nooo....We get to thump the janitors again. Should be interesting. We got such good news coverage last time. [A reference to the brutal beating of the Justice for Janitors civil disobedience strike action in Century City, when police permanently disabled several protestors and caused a pregnant woman to lose her baby.]

7/19/90 10:12 PM:

Flat head and Bone head cruising down the street, Flat head says to Bone head, suck the toe jam between my feet; if they get much dirtier, I'll look like Buckwheat.

123

Okay, Spanky.

10/22/90 6:48 PM:

My shooting policy is based on nationality and looks.

10/27/90 9:40 PM:

I saw a lot of white hoods in the watch commander's office.

I know, all sizes.

They said it was for trick-or-treat, but I don't think so.

I think you're right.

10/29/90 1:35 PM:

I don't believe her. I have to be nice to her so I can get a good rating. What a bitch.

You don't have to tell me. She's just like a wife; bitch, bitch, nag, nag.

10/31/90 3:27 AM:

That sucks. Stick it in his ass for being such a pain.

It's his way of getting a free AIDS test.

10/31/90 noon:

Did you educate him? Take one handcuff off and slap him around.

He's crying too hard and there's four detectives here.

Well, don't seat-belt him in, and slam on the brakes a few times on the way to the station.

12/21/90 5:00 PM:

They had another shooting here.... I love it

when good things happen. It clears the air and gives me more space to breathe when one more asshole dies.

12/23/90 9:44 AM:

Too bad UCLA is not in session. We could look at all the good-looking bitches.

Show 'em what a USC grad can do, like give 'em the chorizo [sausage].

12/23/90 3:47 PM:

Ah, so! Did he tell you he was sooo solly to bother you?

Orientals are the most obnoxious when they're drunk.

12/24/90 4:34 PM:

I would just beat and release that fat slob in the suit named Homey Claus...hohoho, mofo.

12/29/90 10:45 AM:

Advise the desk that a blubberous female mammalian resembling a black-skinned human made utterances that she was going to talk with officers at Southwest Station about who-knows-what. She's a psycho.

12/31/90 8:03 PM:

A full moon and a full gun makes for a night of fun.

Everyone you kill in the line of duty becomes a slave in the afterlife.

Then you will have a lot of slaves.

1/19/91 6:01 AM:

Shut up or I'll cut your pigtails off, Hop Sing.

1/19/91 6:34 AM:

What do you get when you cross a Mexican with an octopus?

A maxipuss.

2/24/91 10:40 AM:

What's happening. We're hunting wabbits.

Actually Muslim wabbits.

Be careful one of those wabbits don't bite you.

Yeah, I know. Huntin' wabbits is dangerous.

2/28/91 1:30 AM:

What are you doing at Sixth and Westlake?

Alley sweeps [rousting homeless]. I'm sure you want no part of it.

Why not? I love alley sweeps, especially if they don't want to move...hammer time.

All told, the Commission included in their supplement nearly 700 separate transmissions which they found objectionable on the 180 days they checked over the year and a half prior to the King beating, with repeated references to cholos, wetbacks, mojados, queers, dykes, bitches, negroes, monkeys, Jews, and Muslims, and boasts about beatings and shootings.

Women's Rights: Target for Racist Terror

Neo-Nazi Involvement in the Anti-Abortion Movement

The cold-blooded murder of Dr. David Gunn by an anti-abortionist in Pensacola, Florida, catapulted the issue of terrorism against women's rights onto the front pages around the country. The subsequent shooting of Dr. George Tiller in Wichita, Kansas, drove home the fact that Gunn's killing was not an isolated event by a "lone nut." As this material was being prepared for publication, Paul Hill, a leading ideologue of anti-abortion terrorism, was arrested for the shooting and killing of Dr. John Britton and his escort James Barrett, and the wounding of escort June Barrett, in yet another attack. This forced the government belatedly to offer protection to some clinics and their staffers, and to initiate an investigation of anti-abortionists for involvement in a terrorist conspiracy.

The groundwork for these murderous attacks was laid over the previous decade, however, while the media and the government looked the other way. Since the early 1980s, the so-called Right to Life movement has used harassment of clinic staff and patients, death threats, intimidation, arson, and even bombings, to deny women the right to choose abortion. After the open violence and destruction diminished briefly from their first peak levels in 1985–87, the issue disappeared from the mass media. But the fire-bombings, death threats, and other attacks on clinics and their personnel never ceased. In fact, 1992, even during the course of an election year with an anti-abortion president in office and seeking re-election, registered the highest number ever of acts of violence against women's clinics and abortion providers.

As the pro-choice movement regains the political initiative in defense of women's rights, we can expect renewed violence, not merely out of frustration on the part of the anti-abortionists, but as a key part of their overall strategy. The attempt to use murder, arson, and other forms of intimidation to deny women the right to control their own bodies has in fact continued and heightened. Anti-abortion leaders have explicitly voiced a strategy to make abortion "unavailable" even if it is legal; and thereby to make it possible to later win the legal and political battle to re-criminalize abortion. In the context of aggressive direct action by Operation Rescue and other groups to shut down clinics in particular cities, bombings and other violent attacks have occurred, ranging from the discovery of a hand grenade after a clinic confrontation in New York, to the repeated arson of a women's clinic in Redding, California over the past two years.

Women's Rights: Target for Racist Terror

In 1992, a clinic in Reno, Nevada was fire-bombed, as were two California clinics, including the Pregnancy Control Center in Sacramento in November, which had been the target of Operation Rescue blockades and "minuteman" hits. In February 1993, a clinic in Corpus Christi Texas was firebombed and burned to the ground, causing over a million dollars in damage. Dozens of clinics were the targets of butyric acid attacks (euphemistically called "stink bombs"). The day before the killing of Dr. Gunn in Florida, eight clinics in San Diego and Riverside counties in California were the targets of a coordinated series of such acid attacks, resulting in the hospitalization of four health care workers.

On September 10, 1993, a Family Planning Associates clinic in Newport Beach, California was bombed, shattering the windows. The clinic had been the target of demonstrations by anti-abortionists, and was hit by an unsolved arson the previous summer as well. On September 22, 1993, a second Family Planning Associates clinic in Bakersfield was totally destroyed in a $1.4 million arson attack that also demolished several nearby businesses. The Bakersfield clinic had also been the target of numerous demonstrations. In both cases, demonstration leaders denied any responsibility; each cynically suggested that the clinic might have been the target of a "disgruntled boyfriend."

Anti-abortion rhetoric has fueled other forms of violence and intimidation, as well as the bombings and killings. In July 1993, a security guard hired to escort patients past anti-abortion demonstrators at a clinic in Van Nuys had a heart attack during a clinic protest. The same clinic has been the target of

129

disruptions in 1994. In late June 1993, a San Diego obstetrician who performs abortions as part of his practice filed suit and won a restraining order against Operation Rescue and other anti-abortion activists for trespassing at his home and seeking to intimidate him. Among the people named in the lawsuit was Cheryl Sullenger, who served three years for conspiring to bomb a women's clinic in the area in 1988. Earlier in the summer of 1993, nazi bone-heads were seen participating in an OR clinic blockade in Orange County, being closely controlled by the local head of Operation Rescue. Nazi skins also participated in clinic shut-downs in Portland, OR. A clinic in Ventura County was the target of an acid attack in 1994.

Although southern California is definitely one hot-spot for such tactics, they are becoming predominant all around the country. In Denver, Colorado, during the Pope's visit last year, a doctor charged Randall Terry of OR with threatening his life on a nationally syndicated Christian radio show. Dr. Warren Hern of Boulder had written an op-ed piece for the *New York Times*, describing how he was forced to wear a bullet-proof vest. Terry read from Hern's piece, then called him a "vulgar baby killer," and said, "I hope he is tried for crimes against humanity and I hope he is executed." Terry's comments were aired on a local Christian radio station. Yet another anti-abortionist in Denver, Clifton Powell, was acquitted in July 1994 of charges of making death threats against a clinic worker, despite having yelled at her, "Just one more day, Patty! This is your last day on earth!"

In Boise, Idaho, and Missoula, Montana, in May

1993, the only facilities providing abortion services in a wide area of the northwest were destroyed in arsons. During that same period, a clinic in Kansas City, Kansas was vandalized and Dr. Robert Crist, who works for Planned Parenthood in that city, had shots fired into his home in the middle of the night while he and his wife and son were sleeping. A clinic in Madison, Wisconsin was vandalized for the third time in August 1993. An abortion protester in Sacramento was jailed in September 1993 for threatening staff members at a clinic he was trying to shut down. On September 30, 1993, a Planned Parenthood family planning clinic in Lancaster, Pennsylvania, where no abortions were performed, was firebombed and forced to close. The firebombing, which caused $130,000 damage, was the second such attack; a molotov cocktail had been thrown at the clinic in July.

Such tactics, along with the continued refusal of the government to authorize Medicare coverage for abortions for all needy women, are having their desired effect, in denying women practical access to what is their legal right on the books. Catholic hospitals are merging with non-sectarian ones, and denying abortion and contraception services, or refusing to teach medical residents how to perform abortions. Travelers Insurance and other major carriers are beginning to deny fire and other forms of insurance to buildings that house women's clinics. Although they claim it is a "business decision," not political, the effect has been to drive many of the remaining clinics out of business.

As a result, women are already being forced into back-alley abortions, with predictable results.

In New York in August 1993, a grand jury indicted a
doctor for murder, for performing a botched, illegal
abortion on a Latina woman, Guadalupe Negron,
and allowing her to bleed to death, in "depraved
indifference to (her) life." Another doctor has lost his
license to practice medicine in a similar series of
cases, and is facing possible prosecution. Here in
southern California, a woman in Santa Ana was
also charged with murder in August 1993 for killing
another Latina woman, Angela Sanchez, a mother of
four, on whom she allegedly performed an illegal
abortion. Sanchez had been found dead in January
lying next to her car outside the clandestine "clinic."
But the lives of such Latinas, like the lives of the
doctors, don't matter to the racist, sexist, anti-abortion extremists.

In an example of the simultaneous massifica-
tion and nazification of anti-abortion politics, a
Charles Manson T-shirt is being produced in southern California by the Lemmons brothers of "Zooport
Riot Gear" in Newport Beach; they pay ten cents for
each shirt into an escrow fund for convicted mass
murderer and neo-nazi Charles Manson. But they
are also giving a "a good chunk of the proceeds"
from the Manson shirt—they won't say exactly how
much—to Operation Rescue, Randall Terry's fascis-
tic anti-abortion group. The t-shirt was publicized
and marketed when it was worn by Axl Rose during
a national tour by Guns N' Roses, and Rose put a
song by Manson on the group's latest album.

In defending the shirt, which shows Manson
and the slogan "Charlie Don't Surf," Dan Lemmons
of Zooport said, to the *San Francisco Examiner,*
"People get all worked up over some murders that

happened almost 25 years ago. Why not be concerned with the ... babies who are murdered in the U.S. every year," referring to his anti-abortion beliefs. Lemmons told the press, "There's a good side to Charlie that hasn't gotten out.... Kids today don't look at Charlie Manson as a mass murderer. He's like a rebellious figure."

Look at the hypocrisy of abortion opponents promoting a man whose followers stabbed to death Sharon Tate, a nine-months-pregnant woman, killing her after she pleaded for the life of her unborn child, stabbing her in the abdomen with a fork. Manson and his family originally sought to blame the killings on Blacks in the hope it would foment a race war. (Even after Manson was sent to prison, he continued to associate with such open nazis as Perry "Red" Warthan, head of the Nazi party in Northern California. Warthan used his association with Manson to recruit young followers in the '80s, and then killed one of them for talking to the police about Warthan's distribution of nazi propaganda in the high schools.)

We need to analyze who is responsible for the campaign of anti-abortion terror, where it's leading, and what can be done about it. By draping itself in the mantle of overwhelming moral commitment on a single issue—opposition to abortion—hard-core rightist forces have disguised their true agenda and often won open support from the government and favorable treatment in the media, despite their use of violence and intimidation to achieve their political ends. The "anti-abortion" movement is serving as a radical right united front, in which open racists are winning legitimacy and the use of reactionary political violence is winning adherents.

The Klan and the Killings

The killings, the shootings, the death threats against women, the arsons and bombings, must be seen for what they are, naked acts of terrorism, directed at all women and at all health care practitioners who would defend women's rights and meet their needs. The killing of Dr. Gunn, the shooting of Dr. Tiller, and the murder of Dr. Britton and his escort, and the role in these atrocities of "former" Ku Kluxer John Burt, illustrate this well.

In a paper on the anti-abortion movement I wrote in 1984 for the John Brown Anti-Klan Committee, Pensacola anti-abortion leader John Burt was identified as having been a Florida Ku Klux Klansman. Burt has repeatedly since admitted his Klan involvement, but claimed it was a thing of the past. He has consistently been at the forefront of public fomenters of, and apologists for, violence and terror against women. Yet despite his exposure, he was never repudiated by his fellow "pro-lifers."

In the 1980s, three Florida clinics were bombed by two young white couples who were followers of Burt, in some of the earliest acts of such violence, helping to initiate a national trend of terrorism. Burt had shortly before changed his title from Klansman to "lay preacher," claiming that he was "born again" and no longer a racist. Yet fundamentalist televangelist Jerry Falwell stood up for the "good Christian young people" and their families.

Falwell, then leader of the so-called "Moral Majority," offered to defend and provide financial aid to the four clinic bombers in Pensacola, who came out of families involved in Burt's public picketing. This pattern of terror bombers well connected to the public movement was similar to most of those who have been caught for such bombings and other violent acts such as kidnapping and shooting. Although he didn't condone violence, Falwell said, the four were "probably sincere people," and the blasts had focused national attention on abortions. He compared the clinic bombings with the civil rights movement, and noted that there had been "lootings, burnings all over America" after Martin Luther King was killed. In attempting to equate the clinic bombers with the Black liberation struggle, Falwell chose to ignore the "irony" that the Pensacola bombers were brought into the anti-abortion movement by a former leader of the local KKK. Perhaps this is because Falwell, too, was forced to acknowledge having been an active segregationist earlier in his career.

In the public anti-abortion campaign in 1986 that continued after those bombings failed to shut the clinics down, Burt knocked down the manager of the Pensacola Ladies' Center and a volunteer, when he led six protestors in invading the medical facility, which had already been bombed twice before. Burt and his followers injured two women, one seriously, and damaged equipment in the invasion. Yet despite this history of racism and violence, in which Burt carried over his Klan tactics to his new "calling" as an anti-abortionist, the mainstream movement at the time did not isolate or repudiate him. Its embrace of him then eased the path to new and more fatal violence.

Undaunted by the arrests and unopposed by "mainstream" anti-choice groups, Burt continued his organizing, becoming the leader of forces allied with Rescue America, a national anti-choice group that grew out of the "direct action" wing of the anti-abortion movement, and has been even more supportive of violence than Operation Rescue. Although Michael Griffin, Dr. Gunn's assassin, had asked Burt's congregation to pray for Gunn to come to Jesus, and had publicly stated that he would "bring Gunn to Jesus," Burt and his fellows did not report Griffin's threatening remarks or do anything to stop him from carrying out his murder.

Griffin was no fringe fanatic, but a conscious adherent of the strategy expressed by Randall Terry that "the doctor is the weak link." Doctor Gunn had appeared on a "wanted poster" at an Operation Rescue rally (in Montgomery, Alabama) which gave Gunn's home phone number. After the murder, leaders of Rescue America and other anti-choice groups quickly issued a moral justification for the execution of Dr. Gunn by labeling him a "mass murderer." John Burt drove the point home on national TV, that the "godless" doctors who perform abortions should fear for their lives. Burt referred to the killer, Griffin, and the doctor, Gunn, as equally "victims of the abortion system." John Baumgarder, once Imperial Wizard of the KKK, wrote to the Pensacola papers from Gainesville, Florida, to support Griffin's shooting of Gunn as "biblically justified."

A few early press reports of the killing acknowledged Burt's documented history of Klan activity and of anti-woman violence. But they accepted him at his word as a "lay preacher," and allowed him to claim moral high ground for his cause. A few reports also noted that Griffin's wife had sought an injunction against him to prevent him from further battering her. As earlier versions of this report predicted, these failures to expose the terrorists led to further killings, just as the Pensacola bombings led to further arsons and attacks.

In August 1993, Rachelle Renae Shannon fired four or five times from a semi-automatic weapon and shot Dr. George Tiller twice, after participating in an anti-abortion protest outside his Wichita, Kansas clinic. Shannon, wanted as a fugitive after failing to appear in court following her arrest at an earlier clinic blockade in Milwaukee, had been corresponding with Griffin and also writing to Burt, regarding the need for "pro-life Christians" to support Griffin.

Shannon, who had been a participant in Operation Rescue clinic shutdown attempts around the country for several years, has hinted at her culpability, along with others in her movement, in a string of arsons and other attacks. She had been editing a newsletter for convicted and imprisoned clinic bomber John Brockhoeft. Brockhoeft is serving seven years for having bombed a Planned Parenthood office in Ohio in 1985. In 1988, Brockhoeft was arrested with explosives in his car near the same Ladies' Center in Pensacola, Florida, which had been bombed by followers of Burt, and invaded by Burt himself. Burt, who brought Brockhoeft to the site, was charged with violating the terms of his own probation, for coming too close to the clinic after his own previous attack on it. But Burt was not charged on any explosives counts. Brockhoeft was sentenced to 26 months in prison for that bombing attempt.

Witnesses at the Kansas shooting saw Shannon jump into a get-away car driven by another person, but no one else was charged in the Tiller shooting. Shannon was arrested 160 miles away from the shooting, across a state line, returning the rented car that had been spotted by eyewitnesses. (In a separate incident that same week, an abortion doctor from Atlanta was shot and killed outside a restaurant after he accosted someone trying to break into his car. Authorities denied that there was a political motive in that shooting, although they did so on the basis of no public evidence or identified suspects.)

Brockhoeft's report, which Shannon edited, is one of a number of anti-abortion extremist publications which have been laying the ideological groundwork for the use of deadly force to stop abortions. Just a day or two before the Wichita shooting, Rev. David Trosch, a Catholic priest in Alabama, attempted to run a mainstream newspaper ad advocating the killing of doctors who perform abortions as a form of "justifiable homicide." In the wake of Griffin's killing of Gunn and Shannon's shooting of Tiller, many public anti-abortion figures came forward to support and defend their actions. Andrew Burnett, head of Advocates for Life ministries, said, "I'm supportive of what [Shannon] did. It was a courageous act." Don Treshman, the national head of Rescue America (Burt's current group), said, "This shooting ... will result in babies' lives being saved."

Life Advocate, another anti-abortion publication which promotes the strategies and thinking of the most violent wing of the movement, ran several articles defending Griffin's killing of Dr. Gunn. Said one Protestant theologian in *Life Advocate:* "If the Bible allows the use of force, even killing someone, to defend property (Exodus 22:2), how much more must this apply to innocent little boys and girls.... It's a little troublesome that in this doctrinal 'gray area,' [some] would rather give the benefit of the doubt to the murderous aggressor [the doctor] and let the children die." A Catholic priest is more blunt: "You see how stupid it is for...the U.S. Bishops to call an act of self defense in favor of unborn infants [like the killing of Dr. Gunn], murder? What I am telling you is God's law.... The Bishops should have condemned the abortions that the doctor performed and praised the heroic act... by the pro-life man."

It is probably no coincidence that the latest killings following this line of reasoning also took place in Pensacola, where "former" Klansman Burt is based, and where anti-abortionists conduct a "boot camp" for their shock troops in clinic shutdowns. Paul Hill, who shot and killed two more clinic workers there, was only as good as his published word. A fundamentalist minister who led anti-abortion activities in the southeast, he had put out a broadside advocating the use of force to "defend" born and "unborn" children and had been one of the most outspoken supporters of Griffin. He declared such violence against clinics and medical practitioners to be "Defensive Action," which is what he called his new group.

After the murder of Dr. Gunn, according to a report by the Bay Area Coalition for Our Reproductive Rights, the anti-abortion leaders in Pensacola had made it their highest priority to identify the doctor who replaced him. In a chilling account quoted from their own publications, the anti-abortionists described trailing and spying on clinic workers until they spotted the doctor's license plate. They relayed this information to Burt, who ran a check on the plates, identified the doctor, and publicized his identity—the doctor shortly thereafter shot and killed, allegedly by Hill.

Pat Robertson's American Center for Law and Justice was defending Hill on other charges at the time of the killings. Like Shannon, who was facing other anti-abortion criminal charges at the time she shot Tiller, Hill had been arrested in June 1994 for violating noise ordinances during a public anti-abortion protest. Hill's lawyer on a number of his other cases is Michael Hirsch, who wrote an article for the Law Review of Robertson's Regents University Law School advocating that the killing of abortion providers is justifiable homicide, comparable to the actions of those who plotted to kill Hitler. Hirsch, back when he was the militant head of Operation Rescue in Atlanta, appeared as a featured speaker at a conference sponsored by neo-fascist Lyndon LaRouche.

After the killing of Britton and Barrett, John Baumgardner, the Klan leader who had written to support Griffin's shooting of Gunn, announced that the KKK would hold an anti-abortion protest at the Ladies' Center, to denounce the assignment of federal marshals to guard some of the clinics. Eight hooded Klansmen also joined an anti-abortion picket line outside a clinic in nearby Melbourne, Florida. Even though no abortions were scheduled at the site, women seeking clinic help had to walk a gauntlet of the hooded racists.

Anti-Abortion Violence:
Part of a Racist Right Strategy

Despite this documented record of racism and violence, the right has mobilized and radicalized a mass base of thousands on the basis of the abortion issue, for door-to-door canvassing, direct action against clinics, and electoral activity directed against women's right to control their own bodies. It's out of this mass movement that the bombers, stalkers, and killers have come, the Army of God and other groupings whose extra-legal and para-military actions have been legitimized and justified by the rest of the anti-choice movement. The government, unprepared to use open repression itself to completely outlaw abortion, de facto accepted over a long period of time, the use of illegal political violence to reach the same goal.

One reason anti-abortion violence reached a new crescendo in 1992 was a series of favorable court rulings for Operation Rescue and its cohorts, opening the door to more militant intimidation, and stripping the clinics of the protection they had enjoyed under the Reconstruction-era anti-Ku Klux Klan civil rights act. Recent laws reinstating such protection are only as good as their enforcement. Hill was free and on the streets at the time of the killings because federal authorities refused to prosecute him under the new clinic protection act designed to remedy these court rulings, despite complaints by clinic staff of harassment by Hill which they felt violated the law.

As we look at these past few years of struggle over reproductive rights, three things become clear. First, violence is an inextricable part of the right wing's strategy in the struggle to revoke abortion rights; the violence has been supported by the public movement and winked at by the government. Second, the "pro-life" movement is a racist movement, opening avenues to legitimacy for avowed white supremacists. Third, the right has targeted women as part of a strategy that moves this country towards fascism. We will not be able to combat and defeat the campaign of terror against abortion rights, unless we fully understand the nature and breadth of the movement that confronts us. The rest of this paper examines these three main points in turn.

Anti-Abortion Activists: Apologists for Terrorism

The anti-abortion campaign is making it possible for the right wing to broaden its base and develop a paramilitary capacity through attacks on women. In much the same way, in the 1970s, the mass anti-busing movement tapped widespread opposition to school integration among white people, and made it possible for the KKK to organize openly, for racist terrorists to blow up school buses and attack Black children, and for anti-busing activists to win elections with thinly-veiled appeals to racism. The difference is that in the '70s, the coalition that had supported prior civil rights struggles abandoned black people to these attacks, and did not contest effectively for mass support among white people. Today, the movement for reproductive rights and women's liberation is reasserting itself in the face of the rightist onslaught. But that movement must be strengthened. Becoming aware of the true nature of our enemy is a crucial part of that effort.

142

Women's Rights: Target for Racist Terror

Examples of the relationship between the public anti-abortion movement and the bombers abound. We can look at developments in San Diego, California for instance, as one case study. In that city, the Birth Control Institute was bombed on September 13, 1984 after months of picketing and hostile confrontations by Christian fundamentalists led by Rev. Dorman Owens. After the bombing, public harassment and secret attacks continued. The offices of the clinic's lawyer were burglarized, and files stolen. Owens, who has demanded the death penalty for lesbians and gay men despite his professed reverence for "life," extended his picketing to the local gay-oriented Metropolitan Community Church, which also began to receive bomb threats.

Finally, a clinic bomber linked to Owens, with a history of prior arrests for anti-choice and anti-gay harassment, was caught in the act by San Diego police in the summer of 1988. Eric Everett Svelmoe, a member of Owens' fundamentalist Bible Missionary Fellowship, was arrested by the Criminal Intelligence Unit of the San Diego P.D. on a stakeout at the Alvarado Family Planning Clinic. Disguised in a woman's wig and black-face, Svelmoe drove a pickup with its lights out onto the grounds of the clinic, and planted a pipe-bomb attached to a two-gallon gasoline drum under the clinic stairs. He was followed to his home, where he was arrested; a .357 magnum and ammunition were seized from the truck.

Svelmoe, a 29-year-old aviation mechanic, was arraigned on federal charges of possession of an explosive device and interstate transportation of explosives. Police and investigators from the Bureau of Alcohol, Tobacco and Firearms (ATF) refused to say how they learned of the planned bombing. Federal agents obtained warrants to search the home of Cheryl and Randall Sullenger, who, like Svelmoe, were associated with the Rev. Dorman Owens' fundamentalist church and were two of the most outspoken public anti-abortion figures in the city. Owens, Svelmoe, and Sullenger had all been arrested previously for violating a court order that limited their picketing of birth control facilities in the area.

According to Debra Flemming of Womancare (a feminist health facility which had received a bomb threat the same night that Svelmoe was arrested), Mrs. Sullenger had been suing the clinic for false arrest. Sullenger claimed she was not a member of Owens' church, and not subject to an injunction obtained by the clinic to prevent Owens and his followers from obstructing the clinic. "We know there is a political conspiracy to shut down abortion clinics that goes right up to Reagan," Flemming said at the time. She demanded that the ATF determine and uncover the extent of the criminal conspiracy. Sullenger was the head of an Operation Rescue–like outfit called Operation Jericho (as in "when the walls come tumbling down"), which had been picketing the Alvarado clinic prior to the bomb attempt. Despite her association with the bombing conspiracy, Sullenger remains an active leader of the public anti-choice movement, listed in 1993 as a contact person in San Diego for Operation Rescue's "No place to hide" campaign directed against abortion providers in their homes.

Rev. Owens claimed in 1988 that he was "shocked" by the arrest of Svelmoe, but he called

Women's Rights: Target for Racist Terror

Svelmoe "committed to the Christian cause." Svelmoe's willingness to carry his Christian commitment into illegal action in Owens' causes was a matter of public record. In 1985, Svelmoe's pilot's license had been suspended by the F.A.A. when he buzzed the San Diego Gay Pride parade with an anti-gay banner during an Owens-led counter-demonstration. He didn't have a permit for the banner. At the subsequent year's Gay Pride parade, someone again flew an anti-gay banner in circles over the marchers.

Detective Barone of the San Diego P.D. said that Svelmoe's fused pipe bomb and gasoline could have leveled the clinic had it not been defused. Jim Stathes, head of the local office of ATF, said the investigation was looking into links to two previous unsolved firebombings (of the Birth Control Institute in nearby El Cajon in 1984 and 1985). Flemming of Womancare pointed out that the San Diego events followed the pattern of clinic bombings around the country: "The public picketing either increases (dramatically) or stops suddenly right before the bombing. The Saturday before we got the bomb threat, the usual pickets weren't here." Sullenger's group did picket the Alvarado center the weekend before the attempted bombing.

In the aftermath of the foiled bombing attempt, Owens, his associate pastor, and five followers were arrested by federal authorities and charged with conspiring to bomb the Family Planning Associates Medical group. Owens was also charged with and eventually convicted of witness tampering because of his attempts to get the captured bomber to withhold his testimony about the other conspirators. Svelmoe agreed to cooperate with authorities. Based on his testimony, the U.S. Attorney filed a complaint detailing the purchase of chemicals and gunpowder to build the bomb, and a series of meetings to plan the bombing, one held at Bible Missionary Fellowship Church and another at Owens' home. Authorities alleged that Owens and the others, including Randall and Cheryl Sullenger, also conspired to bomb the feminist Womancare Clinic and the offices of Planned Parenthood. The defendants eventually either pleaded guilty or were convicted of various of the charges.

The San Diego case is instructive in its exposure of direct organizational links between the top, visible public leaders and the terrorist bombers of the anti-abortion movement. Joseph Scheidler, the director of the Pro-Life Action League and political godfather to Randall Terry and to John Burt's Rescue America, came to San Diego in the midst of Owens' picketing campaign, to step up "direct action." He also appeared during the same period in Maryland to picket a clinic there, shortly before it was firebombed by the Army of God. From a base in Chicago, Scheidler criss-crossed the country in the mid-'80s, teaching the tactics to shut clinics down "by any means necessary." Once shunned by "respectable" pro-life groups, Scheidler now is a leader of the mainstream of that movement.

In San Diego, he explained to the press that his group had shut down six clinics in Chicago through its tactics. "Simply by [our] being there, they're upset inside ... and the doctor's nervous.... Women going in are thinking, 'This must be a bad thing to do, to murder my baby'.... The complication rate will go up during the operation. That's not my fault." It is this true callousness about life which allows the

146

public "pro-life" leaders to blink at the bombings, justify them, or as in Owens' case, to conspire to carry the bombings out. It is this same callousness which allows public anti-choice leaders to defend or justify the execution-style slaying of Dr. Gunn, and the wounding and attempted murder of Dr. Tiller.

Other national leaders also made it clear throughout the '80s that the bombings did not faze them. Cal Thomas, then vice president of the Moral Majority under Jerry Falwell, wrote a nationally syndicated column which appeared in the *Los Angeles Times* headed "Bombing Abortion Clinics: It's Violent, But Why Not?" In it, he issued a defense of the bombings after two clinics near Washington, D.C. were blasted in 1984. "The line I like best," he wrote, "came from Jayne Bray of the Pro-Life Action Committee: I am personally opposed to the destruction of property, but I respect the rights of those who do it where babies are slaughtered." In a similar vein, the U.S. Catholic Bishops, who finally condemned the bombings only after more than a year of silence in the face of mounting pressure to speak out, attributed the cause of the bombings to "the violence unleashed on society by abortion."

Sometimes, public anti-abortion forces directly protect the secret terrorists. In Houston, Texas, after four women's clinics were attacked in the 1980s by arsonists (three in a single weekend), a Presbyterian pastor, George Grant, told the *New York Times* that "local people and some people that were called in from outside were responsible." But he refused to give his information to the authorities, because he said he "did not want to incriminate the credible part" of the pro-life movement. "I'm a pastor, and there are times when you don't want to reveal your sources to the big guns."

Given this protection by the public movement, the bombers stepped up their efforts, increasing the number of attacks and the level of violence. In 1984, 30 clinics were bombed or burned. In the following two years, there were over 300 bombings, arsons, threats, and attempted bombings. The bombers shifted to daytime hours, heavier explosives, and letter bombs that can kill people, rather than simply trying to damage the facility. One bomber caught in this period, Dennis Malavesi, had been trained in demolitions in the Marines. His recent release from prison, after a very short sentence, was greeted with welcoming cheers by the wing of the public anti-abortion movement that most emphatically and openly justifies the violence. Yet in that same period, media attention drifted away, allowing the national scope and intensity of the issue to be obscured. Feeling that the bombings and their apologists had served their purpose in establishing the abortion issue on their terms, the anti-abortionists turned their efforts to mass direct action. But at no time have the bombings and death threats come to a complete halt. For example, firebombs caused $75,000 in damage to a clinic owned by Planned Parenthood of Ohio in 1991. The Columbus, Ohio clinic is five blocks from the state legislature, where a bill to restrict abortion rights was under consideration. In 1992, nearly 200 acts of violence against clinics and providers took place.

Support for the open violence continues to come from spokespeople of the public movement. When, just before New Year's 1987, two clinics in

Cincinnati were firebombed during the daytime after a campaign by Americans Against Abortion, the president of the National Right to Life Committee told the *Cincinnati Enquirer* that clinic attacks won't stop until abortions do. "I don't think retaliatory violence will stop as long as the stimulus for it remains." In the spring of 1990, after Operation Rescue was turned back in an attempt to shut down women's clinics in L.A., a local building housing a number of women's clinics and counseling offices was firebombed. In the '80s, right-wing preacher Robert L. Hymers led a so-called "Fundamentalist Army" in L.A. which publicly prayed for the deaths of Supreme Court justices. This appears to have led to at least one death threat which required intensified security efforts by the Secret Service. In February 1991, a "pro-lifer" fired a shot at a California judge who had ordered the Norplant contraceptive implanted in a woman defendant in a trial for child abuse, to stop her from having more children.

Anti-Abortion Violence: Approved by the Justice Department

The shooting of Dr. Tiller was also the culmination of a long process carried out by public anti-abortion forces in apparent tandem with the clandestine violent elements. In June 1986, Women's Health Care Services in Wichita, Kansas, owned by Tiller, was bombed. The explosion, audible two miles away, blew a hole in the wall and broke windows at a V.A. hospital across the street. Tiller had received bomb threats against the clinic, himself, and his family, over many years, before being shot.

At the time of the bombing, Tiller said, "People with this type of mentality encourage this type of thing, and it goes right to the White House, which aids and abets this sort of anarchy."

The attack on abortion rights, as serious as it is in itself, also served as the spearhead for a broader right-wing offensive to gain and maintain state power. Using anti-abortion fervor and the hysteria over AIDS, the right sought to reverse the legislative gains achieved in decades of struggle for women's liberation through attacks on women, lesbians, and gay men. It's more than coincidental that both David Duke and Randall Terry, on almost the same day, declared their opposition to the admission of open gay men and lesbians into the military, signalling that anti-gay organizing would become an important new focus for both of them. Duke's followers, in alliance with fundamentalist Christian rightists, took over virtual control of the Louisiana State Republican party in November 1992. A study currently being conducted by the Center for Democratic Renewal is showing substantial involvement and support nationally for Duke from the ranks of the clinic blockaders. Randall Terry's effort to follow Duke into the political arena with a run for Congress may be derailed by his prosecution for assault growing out of a two-man "minuteman" hit he carried out last year against a clinic in Los Angeles.

In Burbank, California, as in a number of cities nationally, the Citizens for Effective Education, a front group associated with Pat Robertson's Christian Coalition and its "stealth candidate" strategy for winning elective office, is trying to use the issues of abortion, contraception, and gay rights to take over the schools. At a 1993 candidates' night for school board nominees, the CEE questioned candidates closely about their positions on abortion and on "Christian morality." In the subsequent election, the candidate who most affirmatively embraced their stance was elected outright, while the incumbent school board president, who challenged the relevance of the abortion issue to the schools, was forced into a run-off.

In areas of San Diego, the same churches which have provided shock troops for clinic blockades have turned their members out to bloc vote in "pro-family" candidates to several school boards. The San Diego Pro-Life Council, led by clinic blockader Connie Youngkin, originated the stealth campaign tactic, quietly backing 88 school board candidates in 1990, and seeing 50 of them elected, including Rev. Wayne Wilson, head of OR in San Diego, his daughter Cheryl Jones, an OR activist who expressed her disagreement with teaching evolution, and Rebecca Clark, whose mother and employer was an associate of neo-nazi Tom Metzger in his anti-immigrant campaigning.

Ronald Reagan characterized the attempt by the right to reshape U.S. society for the rest of this century as a "Second American Revolution." The "pro-family" coalition through which the right is broadening its base and sharpening its militance is a crucial factor in this retrenchment. Raising the banner of God, mother, and country, the right is attacking women's liberation in a step towards mobilizing people to defend the American empire at home and around the world. With the end of the Cold War as a defining issue for the establishment right, more nakedly racist, anti-woman, and anti-gay politics are coming to the fore.

The Republican Convention that renominated George Bush gave stark evidence of the extent of the power which has fallen into the hands of these forces, under the slogans of "family values" and "cultural war." Although the rejection by most people of these fascist rallying cries forced Bush and Quayle to back away from them, much of the Republican Party apparatus on the national, state, and local level remains in the hands of these Christian rightists.

What was true under Reagan remained true under Bush, who made his first public address as president to an anti-abortion rally, and whose 1992 re-election platform called for a Constitutional amendment to outlaw all abortion under any circumstances. It remains to be seen how vigorously the Justice Department under Clinton appointee Janet Reno will prosecute the anti-abortion terrorists and whether Clinton will fight to keep abortion and contraception services in his health care reform.

When Reagan himself finally spoke out against the bombings (once, briefly), he refused to call them terrorist, carefully classifying the bombings as "anarchy and unlawful." These views continue to be the official policy and practice in federal law enforcement until they are explicitly repudiated. William Webster, when he was FBI Director (before going on to the CIA), held a special press conference to explain that investigating the clinic bombings was not a priority of the Bureau, because the bombings were not terrorism. "I'm trying to hold the line and not call everything terrorism," explained the FBI director, who previously had stoked the hysteria about terrorism in attacking the Black liberation movement, Arab-American supporters of Palestinian rights, and other dissidents. Webster elaborated that clinic bombings did not fit the FBI definition, because the bombers weren't "trying to shift the government," and added "[their] objective is social." The bombers weren't trying to shift the government—because the government was on their side.

If Clinton is to do anything to reverse this, it will only be under unrelenting mass pressure for women's rights. Apparently, the confessions and hints offered by Shelley Shannon, the attempted assassin of Dr. Tiller, and the support petition for killing of abortion providers as justifiable homicide circulated by Paul Hill, have opened a window for federal agents into this underworld of anti-abortion violence.

But the opportunity existed for nearly a decade of federal inaction. Dan Hartnett, the head, under Reagan, of the division of the Bureau of Alcohol, Tobacco and Firearms charged with investigating the bombings in place of the FBI, claimed there was no conspiracy involved in the bombings. He maintained, for instance, that the Army of God did not exist, even after the group claimed credit for several of the bombings, kidnapped in two different states doctors who had provided abortion services, and sent death threats to the Supreme Court Justice who wrote the *Roe v. Wade* decision which upheld women's privacy rights and legalized many abortions. Perhaps given Shannon's involvement in anti-clinic attacks in numerous states, along with several confederates, and Hill's circulation of a petition calling the killing of abortion providers justifiable homicide, which was signed by dozens of the top anti-abortion leaders, some federal investigation and prosecution may finally be forthcoming.

The death threats and bomb threats against Supreme Court justices and doctors alike were made credible by the bombings, and the government's policies only served to justify or minimize them. With Dr. Gunn's execution, the threats became reality. It is a series of short steps from the Republican platform accepting opposition to abortion rights as a litmus test for federal judges, to Pat Robertson's announcing in his fundamentalist campaign for president in 1988 that he does not recognize court decisions as law, to Rev. Hymers of the Fundamentalist Army in Los Angeles flying a banner with his prayers for death over the public appearance by a Supreme Court justice, to the carrying out of such threats.

Racism and the Right: Whose Right to Life?

The anti-abortion movement provides an opening to the radical right not only by legitimizing terrorism, but also by providing an avenue to respectability for open racist forces.

The violence committed by Operation Rescue and similar groups in their attempts to close down women's clinics, and the violations of women's right to choose, are part of a larger strategy by the right wing to turn back the gains of the women's movement and other progressive forces. Within the so-called Right to Life movement, racists and other fascist right forces are seeking to build a mass base and to sharpen the tools of repression and intimidation with which to crush all dissent. For example, in Dallas, Texas in 1991, five Klansmen marched with Operation Rescue to shut down a clinic. They proclaimed that the Ku Klux Klan opposes abortion. This practice was repeated by nazi skinheads in California and Oregon in 1993.

These are not isolated instances. Tom Metzger, a national racist organizer based in southern California, has long proclaimed that "abortion is white genocide" in his newspaper *WAR* (White Aryan Resistance). A former Grand Dragon of the California KKK associated with David Duke, Metzger declared on his telephone hate-lines in six California cities, "Almost all abortion doctors are Jews.... Almost all abortion nurses are lesbians.... Jews must be punished for this holocaust and murder of white children along with their perverted lesbian nurses."

This rhetoric, which has gone unchallenged by the mainstream anti-abortion leaders, has directly precipitated violence. In the summer of 1983, for example, in one of the first instances of physical violence against individual clinic staffers, a California Klansman who had been a member of the prison-based Aryan Brotherhood killed one man and then took two women hostage at a Los Angeles west side women's clinic. He injured one of the women severely before being killed in a shootout with police.

Yet another example of this is the shooting attack on a Grand Rapids, Michigan Planned Parenthood facility on September 30, 1992. Agents of the Bureau of Alcohol, Tobacco and Firearms (ATF) identified Leland Smart, an associate of local white supremacist Terence Paul, as a suspect. Suspicion fell on Smart after a raid of Paul's home netted five fully automatic assault rifles, two Uzis, live grenades, and 57,000 rounds of ammunition, along with Aryan Nations, Klan, and neo-nazi propaganda.

WAR Youth, led by Tom Metzger's son John, and the Aryan Women's League, which moved its headquarters down to Metzger's home base of Fallbrook, California and is run by his daughter, have propagandized nazi skinheads and white racists to join the anti-abortion movement. In the San Francisco Bay Area, the Aryan Women's League, whose logo is a women's symbol above a swastika, has called on white women to have more babies to "propagate the race." After the Hill killings in Pensacola, Tom Metzger declared on his hate line that if the killings saved "Aryan lives," he would "condone them."

David Duke has also attached himself to the anti-abortion cause. Louisiana's harsh anti-abortion law, which he supported, was passed as an amendment to a bill originally designed to legalize physical attacks on flag-burners.

Joe Fields, a one-time associate of Duke and Metzger, and a long-time open nazi from L.A.'s Harbor area, led a group of his Populist Party supporters in picketing a pro-choice electoral rally in L.A. in October, 1992. Fields, who was running for the state assembly, carried "Abortion Kills Children" and "Abortion Is Murder" placards. The Populists harassed a pro-choice, anti-racist activist, but left after failing to disrupt the rally or confront the Democratic women Senate candidates who were present, Barbara Boxer and Diane Feinstein. At this writing, Fields, who is now running for Congress, is still a strong abortion opponent; simultaneously, he is pushing a measure that would deny prenatal care and hospital delivery to undocumented immigrant women, even though the babies, when born, would be U.S. citizens. [For more on Fields and the Populists, see the chapters "Front Man for Fascism" and "Sin Fronteras."]

Lyndon LaRouche, the imprisoned neo-nazi presidential candidate, is another fascist oriented "politician" who has embraced the anti-abortion movement. Joe Scheidler and other public anti-choice leaders (such as OR leader Michael Hirsch, later attorney for accused anti-abortion assassin Paul Hill) were guests of honor and featured speakers at a LaRouche-sponsored conference in 1991. LaRouche's group featured their remarks and photos in its newspaper.

But the linkage of racism to the anti-abortion movement is not restricted to hard-core neo-nazis. Father Paul Marx was a one-time director of the Human Life Center, which was an anti-abortion think tank in Minnesota, and more recently head of HLI (Human Life International). He made it clear that even the establishment right-to-life groups are mainly concerned with white life, or the "American way of life." In an interview with the *Minneapolis Star* centering on his fear that "the white Western world is committing suicide," he explained his opposition not only to abortion but also to contraception—for whites. "I guess we have 250,000 Vietnamese here already, and they are going to have large families; the Orientals always do," he stated. "God knows how many Mexicans cross the border every night.... And if we ever have to fight the Russians, I wonder if these people will be willing to stake their lives."

Pat Buchanan, former presidential adviser to Nixon and Reagan and syndicated columnist and TV talk show host, who challenged Bush for the presidency and then was allowed to speak in prime time at the 1992 convention, spewing anti-woman and anti-gay hatred, has a long history of favoring such racist rationales for opposing abortion rights. In August 1989 he proclaimed that Islam would destroy Western civilization, because white Europeans and Americans, under the domination of Planned Parenthood, were not having enough babies. Echoing Metzger's racist rhetoric, he related an account from Rev. Marx, claiming that Turkish doctors, to support their own growing families, were aborting German women at a feverish pace. This preposterous story flew in the face of the fact that abortion at the time (prior to German reunification) was illegal and harshly repressed in West Germany, as it had been under Hitler. The West Germans even arrested women returning to Germany who were suspected of having had abortions in other countries. In Germany, the chief political party championing the hard-core anti-abortion stance, which masquerades as a "green" group, has ties to neonazis and holocaust revisionists.

Rev. Marx's racist rhetoric leads not only to continued attacks against women and women's clinics, but also to violence against gay men and lesbians, Jews, Moslems, Blacks, Hispanics, Native Americans, and Asians. In La Verne, California in 1990, for example, a group of nazi skinheads were convicted of attacking an Iranian couple and their infant because they were outraged that they had brought "another Jewish nigger baby into the world."

In general, the political forces leading the so-called Right to Life movement do not truly care about life. They are unconcerned about the death of women who were or would be butchered in back-alley abortions. In particular, they don't care about the lives of Third World people in the U.S., about an infant mortality rate for Black children double that for whites, about genocidal rates of sterilization among Puerto Rican, Native American, or Black women ranging up to 40% of those of child-bearing age.

Although the anti-abortion movement likes to justify itself by comparing abortion to nazi genocide in World War II, the movement is in fact a breeding ground for fascism and white supremacy. Pat Robertson, for example, explaining why the family had to be strengthened, stated, "The home is the basic unit of the church,... of society. When this goes, you have problems, the flotsam and jetsam of the ghetto, where people don't know who their parents are."

The racism of Robertson's views is echoed by those of the National States Rights Party (NSRP), which proclaimed its opposition to the Equal Rights Amendment in its newspaper *The Thunderbolt:* "The time is now to act to protect the family and motherhood itself.... A negro judge in Chattanooga has already used these equality laws to lock a White woman in the same cell with a black man. She was then raped." The Republicans who tried to distance themselves from David Duke in Louisiana because he was a "former" nazi and KKK leader instead supported his primary opponent, an ex-governor's brother, who had himself formerly been a member of the racist NSRP. In the aftermath of Duke's election to the legislature, these same Louisiana politicians supported his proposals to restrict births among welfare recipients.

Tom Metzger is more honest than the rest of the anti-abortion movement about the connection between abortion and nazi genocide. "In Germany under Adolph Hitler," he wrote, "abortion was a serious crime." In fact, the right wing's program today is very similar to the slogan of "Kinde, kuche, kirche" (children, kitchen, church) which the nazis used to express their vision of women's role in the Third Reich.

Steps towards Fascism

Just as its defeat of the Equal Rights Amendment only whet the appetite of the racist, anti-woman right, the ugly successes in the attack on abortion will not satisfy it. Within the anti-abortion movement we can see the nucleus of an incipient fascism: the coordinated use of state power, mass mobilizations, and paramilitary terror to achieve the liquidation of women's rights and the struggle for women's liberation. The anti-abortion movement is now a key avenue through which the right is seeking to popularize new ideological underpinnings for the U.S. empire—not as the "free-est country in the world," but as a divinely ordained bastion of white Christian civilization. The status and rights of women are a key battleground in this effort.

The right's intent to re-criminalize abortion,

160

and its willingness to use terror to accomplish that goal, gives the lie to its libertarian rhetoric. The racist right is marshalling its forces in attacks on women and gays, and on immigrants, for a whole-sale increase in the repressive powers of the state. Despite the differences that they have with each other, their unified opposition to abortion allows them to aggregate their forces.

When Pat Robertson was girding up for his run at the White House in 1988, he announced that the Constitution was written for a Christian nation, "but turn it into the hands of non-Christians and athe-ists, and it will destroy society." In Arizona in 1990, the Robertson wing of the Republicans united with toppled governor Evan Meacham to take control of the party, seeking the support of Supreme Court Justice Sandra Day O'Connor for the notion that America is a Christian Republic. This is a premise very close to the Christian Identity doctrine of America as the promised land for the Aryans, the so-called British Israelites. In November 1992, a similar alliance of Christian fundmentalists and David Duke supporters took virtual control of the Louisiana Republicans.

Phyllis Schlafly of the anti-abortion, anti-ERA Eagle Forum has proclaimed the "right" of children "to be taught from textbooks that honor the tradi-tional family as the basic unit of society, women's role as wife and man's role as protector and provider." The rights of the "unborn" are the same kind of "right"—a pretext for the state to exercise control over the lives of women and children. Schlafly may have best summed up the right wing's chilling vision of the role of women in defending the empire, as homemakers, and if necessary as fighters. She has written in her 1981 book *The Power of Christian Woman*, of her support for the role of women in instigating the military coups that overthrew the democratically elected governments of Goulart in Brazil in 1964 and Allende in Chile in 1973, ushering in decades of brutal fascist dictatorships and "death squad" governments.

"Christian Woman," Schlafly wrote, "starts with the knowledge that America is the greatest country in the world.... [She] must be a patriot and defender of our Judeo-Christian civilization....[Chile under Pinochet] offers an outstanding example of how women can save a nation from Communist takeover.... It is primarily the women who deserve the credit for the overthrow of Allende.... Anything that Brazilian and Chilean women can do, Christian American women can do." But first, apparently, American women must be Christianized, forcibly if necessary. Schlafly had been propagandizing in favor of the coup which overthrew Goulart as early as 1967, calling the elected president a "militant pro-Communist and possible secret Communist," and comparing him thereby to liberal Democrats in this country. Only after years of beating the drums for militarism and interventionism did Schlafly turn her propaganda skills to the battle to defeat the Equal Rights Amendment with the claim that it would mandate unisex toilets.

The right is intent on not only eliminating abortion and other reproductive rights but on strengthening the "family" because it wants it to serve as an instrument of social control over women and children. It is seeking a new generation of "Christian soldiers" to march to war. It is using its still growing power to coerce opposition and dissent, to put women "in their place" while mobilizing them as shock troops for reaction, just as middle-class women were used to hold the pots and pans marches that helped destabilize the popularly elected Allende socialist government in Chile, so that a CIA-backed coup could topple it. The mass graves that resulted from this "defense" of Christian civilization are still being uncovered in Chile two decades later. Through the anti-abortion movement, anti-woman and anti-gay groups in the U.S. have been linked up with a larger right-wing network that includes opponents of busing, segregationist white Christian academies, and supporters of U.S. interventionism.

The pattern established around abortion, where Reagan minimized the violence of the Right to Life bombers, while attacking abortion rights and identifying himself with the "pro-life" movement, has been repeated in other areas. The power of the state is used to confer legitimacy on right-wing initiatives. For example:

- The repeated ballot qualification of Lyndon LaRouche's AIDS quarantine measure in California was preceeded by the Justice Department's ruling that employers could fire employees with AIDS for health reasons, and by Reagan's personal recommendation that people self-donate blood rather than give to or rely on blood banks.

- The campaign by former KKK Grand Dragon Tom Metzger to seal and militarize the border with Mexico is legitimized by liberal Democratic Senator Barbara Boxer's plan to mobilize the National Guard along the border. It was mirrored by the proposal of L.A. Supervisor Mike

Antonovich in running for the U.S. Senate to abolish the 14th Amendment, which recognizes the citizenship of everyone born in the U.S. Abolishing the 14th Amendment is a key platform of the racist right, which wants to expel all "non-Aryans" from the U.S. Yet Antonovich's position has now been adopted even by liberals like Representative Tony Beilinson (Dem.-L.A.).

• The bombings of Arab American groups in Washington, Boston, and Orange County, California, was implicitly sanctioned by Reagan's rhetoric and military assault against Libya. The Justice Department continued under Bush to be unable to bring Zionist terrorists to justice in the U.S., reflecting U.S. support for Zionist terror in occupied Palestine. The FBI interrogation of Arab Americans about opposition to the Gulf War helped legitimize an outburst of anti-Arab violence in this country in the wake of Desert Storm.

There is a deadly symbiosis between groups focusing on race and gender issues and those seeking continued U.S. domination in the world. Fundamentalist groups like the Christian Broadcasting Network raised millions to support the murderous contras in Nicaragua. Jerry Falwell was both a principal spokesman of anti-gay reaction and a chief defender of U.S. and Zionist aggression in the Middle East. Fundamentalists in this country were supportive of Guatemala's General Efrain Rios-Montt, who waged a genocidal war against his own country's indigenous population, and who was just returned to the halls of power in his country's recent elections.

Connecting the demand for a stronger family and an attack on women's liberation with racism and support for a stronger empire is no accident. Whatever their differences, the Ku Klux Klan, the fundamentalists, and the Republicans share a view that it is essential to drive women back into a subordinate position within the family in order to strengthen a chauvinist social base that will fight to "make America great again." The denial of access to abortion is an attempt to imprison women within their reproductive capacities, and propagate the mechanisms of male supremacy which are essential to this society.

The actual destruction of families, the increase in child abuse and pornography, the violence against women which the right wing cynically exploits, are the product of the very system of empire we're being called on to defend. In fact, violence against women, in the streets and in the family, is a hate crime. This applies as much to wife battering as it does to the killing of woman science students by a crazed male chauvinist in Canada; it applies as much to the doctors and corporations who profited from dangerous breast implants as to the sicko who carried out the hostage taking and sexual torture of coeds in Berkeley in the summer of 1992. Hatred of women is so common in our culture that we have a word for it: misogyny.

Though the right is winning converts, it has no solutions. Neither Pat Buchanan, Randall Terry, nor Tom Metzger has the desire or the capacity to end the abuse of women and children within the male-dominated capitalist family. Criminalizing porn, as the right and some feminists propose, would only give the state additional weapons to attempt to define women's and men's sexuality, without eliminating porn; driving it underground would only make it more profitable. Pornography and the degradation of women cannot be suppressed by the censorship efforts of the capitalist state, because they are always the flip side of the attempt by class society to define and control women's sexuality and identity.

Thus, it was no surprise when New Right U.S. Senator Roger Jepsen, paragon of Christian morality, was caught patronizing a sex club, or when conservative Congressman Dan Crane was disclosed to have seduced a teenaged girl who worked as a page in his office, or when the Archbishop of Arizona confessed to having had sex with a number of women barely or not yet out of their teens, or when televangelists like Bakker and Swaggart were caught in notorious sexual pecadilloes. The string of such embarrassments for Congressional conservatives and Christian leaders continued into the '90s with Republican Rep. "Buz" Lukens, who was convicted of sex with a minor but still sought to retain his Congressional seat.

To defend women's right to choose, and other rights of reproduction and sexuality, it is necessary to wage a counter-offensive on many fronts. We must expose the links of the public anti-abortion groups to the violence, target the government's tacit acceptance of this campaign, and oppose the right's broader program of racism and militarism. The right has a strategy for the '90s. Do we?

"Sin Fronteras"

Anti-Immigrant Hysteria and the Rise of the Racist Right

The wave of ugly anti-immigrant violence which has swept Germany in the last years (and caused an outpouring of anti-nazi activism in that country) has been paralleled over the past several years by similar developments in the U.S. Yet organized opposition to such racist and anti-immigrant violence, outside of the immigrant communities themselves, has been much less massive or noticeable in this country. It's vital to mobilize people of conscience to a pro-active stance that can help forestall further anti-immigrant hostilities. We must deny support for repressive government agencies like the Border Patrol, and prevent U.S. neo-nazis from successfully mobilizing even broader strata of the population through their anti-immigrant scapegoating.

This is one of the most crucial issues facing the social change movement today. It touches on a central aspect of the elite strategy for dealing with the enduring U.S. economic crisis. It confronts a pivot of neo-nazi strategy for gaining real power. Even more so than in Germany, it deals with defining elements of U.S. history and consciousness—the expansionist

167

frontier, the border, the "nation of immigrants."
Concern about immigration is demonstrably a mass
issue today, not only in California and not only
among white people. It's an issue the left must
address meaningfully if we have any hope of shaping
mass consciousness and building an effective
counter-force against racist forces in the state, the
right, and in society at large.

What we are seeing today is similar to the 1920s,
when the KKK became a mass organization,
entrenched in both the Democratic and Republican
parties. The Klan reached the height of its power in
that period, combining racist terror with political
action to shape U.S. immigration law on an explicitly
racist basis for three generations. The Klan not only
shaped the debate over immigration in that period,
but its policies of excluding Asians and establishing
racial and ethnic quotas based on the make-up of the
U.S in the previous century, were enacted into law by
Congress.

Many of the leading figures in the KKK and the
racist right today came to prominence through anti-
immigrant organizing early in their careers. Tom
Metzger and David Duke led a so-called Klan Border
Watch in the 1970s; Texas Klan and Aryan Nations
leader Louis Beam led attacks on Vietnamese fishing
people in the same period. Even Klan groupings in
the southeast have jumped on the bandwagon,
attempting to organize all-white trade unions to
scapegoat Mexican immigrant workers for problems
in the lumber and other local industries in Georgia,
Mississippi, and elsewhere. Openly racist and fascist
groups are making continuing efforts to seek legitimacy and acceptance by targeting immigrants.

Such organizing has become a key element unifying various neo-nazi and other hard-core racist right elements with more establishment political figures across the spectrum. "Bo" Gritz made anti-immigrant posturing one of the key points in his Populist Party campaign for the presidency, as did Pat Buchanan in the Republican primaries. When L.A. County supervisor Mike Antonovich ran for the U.S. Senate some years ago, his campaign manager was videotaped mimicking the firing of an automatic weapon at undocumented workers crossing the border when Antonovich tried to use them as the backdrop for a TV commercial. James Jones, local organizer in L.A. for Richard Barrett's Mississippi-based Nationalist Movement, led an anti-immigrant protest in November 1992 in the Harbor area against President Lines. (Jones was subsequently voted out of his position as a United Auto Workers shop steward for his racist actions. But labor remains a target of organized white-supremacist campaigns on the immigration issue.)

Barrett himself, Tom Metzger, and others put anti-immigrant organizing at the center of their politics. Metzger justified the killing of Ethiopian refugee Mulugeta Seraw by his nazi bonehead followers by saying Seraw had no business in this country. Barrett received favorable comment and coverage from newscasters for depicting his 1992 white-supremacist rally in Simi Valley as defending white workers against illegal alien criminals. The racists seek adherents in the unions, in the environmental movement, and elsewhere by offering immigrants as handy scapegoats for an assortment of problems.

Just as in the '20s, many established politicians

of both parties have jumped on the immigrant scape-goating bandwagon, seeing it as a political wedge issue. Immigration became a hot-button issue in the 1993 L.A. mayoral race. Several candidates proposed massive deportations; Latino moderate Julian Nava became a target of hostility for proposing that legal residents who are not yet citizens be allowed to vote in municipal elections. Republican and Democratic legislators have offered a host of bills designed to deny education and medical care to undocumented residents; to toughen or militarize the border; even to repeal the 14th Amendment guarantee of citizen-ship to those born in the U.S.

In L.A., immigrants were scapegoated for the April–May 1992 uprising. The use of the National Guard in L.A. in 1992, along with massive sweeps by Border Patrol agents and the turnover by the L.A. Police and Sheriffs of people arrested without docu-ments to the INS for deportation, went virtually unchallenged outside the Latino community. We hear calls for the use of the Army or National Guard to "seal the border." Perhaps, if Mexico had enforced its immigration laws more strictly when the slavers and gold-hunters encroached on its territory and fomented a war to expand the U.S. in the last centu-ry, none of the current problems would be facing us.

The ten-foot-high wall put up by the U.S. mili-tary along the border is being steadily augmented. But at the same time, walls are being built internally as well. Police and federal agents in L.A., for example, imposed a virtual state of siege in parts of the city in their so-called war on drugs. In suburban Sepulveda and in the central-city Pico Union area, known as "la Centroamericana," a year prior to the L.A. rebellion

170

police erected barricades on street corners and imposed a residents-only policy, stopping cars and pedestrians and checking i.d.s. In spite of the claim that the barricades were an anti-drug measure, few drug arrests were made in either area. Instead, there were charges that in the inner city, police worked with the INS to intimidate undocumented immigrant residents. Similar barricades and chain link fence installations were installed in South Central and downtown L.A. in anticipation of a reaction to the verdict in the federal trial of the cops who beat Rodney King.

Immigrant-baiting is no longer restricted to right-wing politicians like Mike Antonovich and Bruce Herschensohn. Even a "liberal" politician like Rep. Tony Beilinson signed on to a racist effort to scrap the 14th Amendment and amend the U.S. Constitution to deny citizenship to the U.S.-born children of the undocumented. Liberal U.S. Senators Boxer and Feinstein in California went out of their way in their election campaigns to emphasize their support for strict enforcement of immigration laws, and since their election have put forward a number of measures to strengthen enforcement. At this writing, Feinstein is portraying herself as "tough on illegal immigrants" in her re-election campaign. Meanwhile the left has done little to build a countervailing force for solidarity.

"American Spring at the Mexican Border," held at the U.S.–Mexico border at San Ysidro in June 1992, and again in 1993, was a recent example in a series of racist mobilizations aimed at stirring up anti-immigrant hysteria and blaming immigrant workers for all the growing problems of our society. It can serve to illuminate several key aspects of the issue.

In front of the ten-foot border wall, the American Spring nazis raised the confederate battle flag and flashed the Hitler salute. The rally united an assortment of right wingers, open nazis, skinheads, and "White Nationalist" Richard Barrett. It resulted in physical attacks on Chicano-Mexican protesters and the stoning of migrant workers by the nazi boneheads. It was the outcome of a continuing unity of purpose between repressive agencies of the government, reactionary and demagogic politicians, and hard-core racist elements which pose as being anti-establishment, but actually work hand in glove with the state to maintain exploitation and oppression.

In 1994, American Spring attempted to attach itself to a border rally planned by Ross Perot's United We Stand America organization (UWSA). UWSA had provided most of the petition circulators for the so-called Save Our State ("S.O.S.") initiative, placed on the November 1994 state ballot. Proposition 187 aimed to deny all education, health, and social service benefits to the undocumented, and require teachers, health care practitioners, and social workers to report "suspicious persons" to the INS, including even the parents of U.S. citizen school-children.

UWSA put together a united front of S.O.S., represented by former Western INS coordinator Harold Ezell, FAIR (the Federation for American Immigration Reform), represented by former INS Commissioner Alan Nelson, Americans Against Illegal Immigration (AAII), led by Bill King, the former head of the Border Patrol in the San Diego region, and a number of more right-wing fringe anti-immigrant groups. Joe Fields, the neo-nazi spokesman for American Spring, tried to

172

attach his operation to this. Fields himself showed up for a UWSA planning meeting in Orange County; groups that work closely with him, promoting a racist reaction against all immigrants, legal or not, such as Stop Immigration Now, were part of the UWSA coalition.

Fearful that a small turnout would hamper their electoral organizing, and possibly embarrassed by the connection with open white supremacists, the Perot forces canceled the August 20 rally at the last minute; American Spring apparently also fell through for 1994 as a result. But three weeks before the scheduled rally, a group of men in military camouflage uniforms attacked a migrant worker camp in San Diego County, beating a number of workers without regard to their status as legal residents or undocumented workers. The week after, Fields appeared at the Jubilee Jubilation, a Christian-Identity conference in Bakersfield, California, where one of the featured speakers (along with Klansman Louis Beam) was California State Senator Don Rogers, who has donated thousands of dollars to the anti-immigrant Proposition 187 (S.O.S.) campaign.

There has been an ongoing pattern around anti-immigrant work, of extra-legal violence, white-supremacist involvement, and governmental approval. This suggests the outlines of a progressive, anti-racist agenda in relation to immigration issues —it must not only take on neo-nazi violence, but also challenge public racist anti-immigrant organizing, and oppose human rights violations and brutality by the Border Patrol and other state agencies. Our work must be based on solidarity in particular with the Mexican people on both sides of the border.

American Spring reflected its origins among the racist bully-boys of Tom Metzger's WAR (White Aryan Resistance) and its spread through the neo-nazi network of the Populist Party and the Liberty Lobby. But it was also built on the momentum generated by the well-financed activities of more "respectable" anti-immigrant groups like the Federation for American Immigrant Reform and the English Only movement, both of which have served as a conduit for hard-core racists and fascists to influence broader sectors of public opinion. The ties of English First, U.S. English, and FAIR to openly nazi groups based on Hitler's eugenics theories of aryan supremacy are well documented. So are the ties of the "America First" Populists and other hard-core anti-immigrant groups to the American nazis and the Ku Klux Klan.

American Spring was also significant because it provided ideological cover for and incitement to the Border Patrol and individual racists to carry out brutality and violence against undocumented migrants in particular, and Mexicans and other people of color in general. The recent killing and beatings of Mexican migrant and documented resident workers in San Diego, the high-speed chases by the Border Patrol that resulted in five deaths in Temecula, the human rights violations in the border region documented by Americas Watch, are the bitter fruit of the racist hysteria fomented by the racist right through actions like American Spring and the earlier Light Up the Border rallies.

When Michael Elmer, a Border Patrol agent in Arizona with a history of beating and shooting immigrants, shot a migrant worker twice in the back, left him for dead, and admitted falsifying his reports to

174

cover the killing up, the government was forced to prosecute for a change. Yet despite his admissions, and the testimony of his partner, who couldn't stomach the killing and the cover-up, the Border Patrol agent's lawyer was able to successfully argue to the jury that the border was a war zone where any violence by agents was justified, and to win an acquittal for his client on all counts, even the confessed false reports. The similar acquittal of the cops who beat Rodney King drew worldwide attention and protest; the acquittal of this Border Patrol agent for a cold-blooded killing barely made the papers in California. Elmer still faces a possible federal civil rights trial, and additional assault charges for an unrelated incident in which he is alleged to have fired automatic weapons at a group of 30 unarmed undocumented immigrants, wounding one. A 1991 audit by the INS showed that one-third of weapons use by Border Patrol agents violates policy. Yet the agency has resisted calls for a civilian review board.

Since the late '80s and throughout the early '90s, vigilante action, white-supremacist organizing, police violence, and Border Patrol repression of undocumented immigrant workers have formed a potent and potentially explosive mix in the canyons where Tijuana meets San Diego, and elsewhere along the long border that stretches through Arizona, New Mexico, and Texas. It is this reality, substantially unchallenged by the white left, which made possible an event like American Spring, in which dozens of open nazis rallied at the border. Numerous homicides and shootings of Mexicans and other migrants have taken place in the area for the last several years.

One white San Diego resident was recently convicted of raping a Mexican woman at knife-point after she had car trouble while driving to Mexicali. Another was convicted of "false imprisonment" in 1991 for beating and handcuffing a Mexican man as he looked for work. After binding Candido Gallosa's mouth and hands with duct tape, Randy Ryberg had dumped him in a field near a store with a sack over his head reading "*No Mas Aqui.*" Over the past two years, a large number of Chicano transvestites and pre-op transsexuals have been killed in San Diego, but this has generated none of the media hysteria that greeted other serial killings in that city.

In one 1992 incident, a Mexican migrant worker was chased down in a car and shot to death; later in the year, an encampment of Mexican and Central American laborers, some of whom were legal, documented residents, was attacked and beaten brutally by a gang of white men with baseball bats. It is this reality which formed the backdrop for American Spring. Yet unlike Germany, where people of goodwill have turned out in the hundreds of thousands to counter such a campaign of racist, anti-immigrant terror, opposition to the nazis and racist violence has been centered in this country almost entirely in the Chicano community. Only a scattering of white anti-racists, for example, attended the counter-demonstrations against American Spring in 1992 and 1993, or the pro-active, pro-immigrants' rights rally held on August 20, 1994 in San Diego to counter the planned, but aborted, anti-immigrant rallies.

At least some of the killings may be the work of organized white supremacists. Doug Seymour, a police reservist who infiltrated Metzger's grouping in the early '80s when it still called itself the California

Klan and was affiliated with David Duke, reported that several members boasted of having killed and decapitated Mexican migrant workers, but police ignored his reports. The so-called Heavy Metal Militia, a group composed mostly of white teens, went out into the desert outside outside San Diego for weapons training and shooting practice in 1990–91. The semi-clandestine group reportedly also included off-duty San Diego police officers. The group was videotaped harassing Mexican migrant workers, and the youthful leader, 17-year-old Jason McAllister, was eventually convicted of harassment and extortion.

Another vigilante activity was "Light Up the Border," organized by the widow of a Border Patrol agent and promoted by former San Diego mayor Roger Hedgecock on his radio show. It drew hundreds of white San Diegans to the border with their RVs and four-wheel-drive vehicles to direct their headlight beams at possible immigrant crossing areas.

This in turn helped to legitimize Tom Metzger's White Aryan Resistance (WAR), which leafleted a call to nazi skinheads to "wage war" against illegal immigrants and against the counter-demonstrators who have turned out to protest the vigilantes. Death threats were sent to Roberto Martinez of the American Friends Service Committee for organizing the counter-demonstration. Meanwhile, the Border Patrol itself installed several permanent floodlights and deployed portable lights to augment them. The new head of the INS at the time, commissioner Gene McNary, went to San Diego to promise increased enforcement efforts against those crossing over without documents. INS apprehensions in the area began averaging over 1,300 a day, up more than 50% over the previous year.

This is a classic case of blaming the victims. Undocumented workers have consistently been the target of violence by individual racists, neo-nazis, police, INS, and predatory smugglers who take advantage of their vulnerability. This violence inevitably spills over into the larger society. For example, a group called the Holy Church of the White Fighting Machine of the Cross issued a 30-day ultimatum in early 1991 calling for the repeal of laws against hate crimes and demanding the militarization of the border. In a message to a San Diego TV station, the group hinted that it was responsible for bombing the Federal Building in that city. Several white men in military-type outfits were seen laughing and running from the scene shortly before the 1991 explosion. The FBI investigated the blast. The White Fighting Machine did not explicitly claim responsibility for the bombing, but said it "cannot guarantee there will not be injuries in the future." The group called for the mobilization of the National Guard to seal off the border, and demanded new trials for those incarcerated for hate crimes. An associate of Metzger's was eventually charged.

This racist group also sent death threats to Roberto Martinez. Their letter to Martinez addressed him as a "dirty f-king spic greaser" and a "beaner," and warned him to stop "criticizing the Border Patrol and the whites who are trying to save our white country from the jews and goy stooges." The letter concluded, "We are going to choke all you pachookos, vato maricone. White power is going to get you." Martinez believes Light Up the Border and similar

178

campaigns cannot escape some of the blame for legitimizing such racist violence and harassment.
"Directly or indirectly, [it] is attracting fringe groups,"
he says. Martinez has received other threatening letters and calls, including one addressed to "the
American Friends Beaner Committee," which
appeared to come from nazi skinheads.

Muriel Watson, who initiated the Light Up the
Border campaign, told the press in San Diego, "I'm
sorry for Mr. Martinez, but when you stick your neck
out and you take a stand, this is part of the heat."
Ex-Mayor Roger Hedgecock, who used his radio
show to promote the Light Up the Border protests,
claimed that the threats did not come from within
the campaign, and said he had personally received
similar letters "from the same guy. They appear to
come from the same typewriter." The effect of
Hedgecock's comments were to trivialize the death
threats against Martinez, and provide continuing
cover for the racists involved with the anti-immigrant
campaign.

Light up the Border was called off for a while by
its organizers after WAR began circulating its threats.
The numbers participating had dwindled, after two
months where counter-demonstrators from Chicano
civil rights groups and immigrant support organizations turned out in response to the vigilante action,
and exposed its racist connections. With mirrors,
they shined the headlights back at the drivers. Muriel
Watson, who started the action, expressed satisfaction that the Border Patrol and the police were stepping up their presence in the area. San Diego P.D.
Chief Burgren announced the deployment of a number of SWAT team members in a special Border

Crimes Intervention Unit, to develop joint actions with both the INS and the Tijuana police.

However, there is as much justifiable skepticism and fear in the Mexican and immigrant communities about the police as well as "La Migra" (the Border Patrol/INS) as there is of the vigilantes and racist terrorists. Martinez, for example, also chaired the Coalition for Law and Justice, which represented a group of Chicano residents in El Cajon, who charged they were victimized and mistreated by police using racial slurs. At least one such beating resulted in the hospitalization of the victim of the police attack. The police chief of El Cajon acknowledged that there had been a pattern of "sustained misconduct" against Hispanics by several officers. The chief pledged to work with the Coalition to develop training for the police, and to improve the process of taking citizen complaints, particularly from non-English speaking residents. The Coalition was also instrumental in the adoption of civilian review agencies for both the San Diego city cops and county sheriff's deputies. They urge a similar review agency for the Border Patrol itself.

The San Diego cops have been involved in numerous shootings, including two recent cases where Hispanic men "armed" with baseball bats were shot by the police. Also, San Diego has a very negative history of border enforcement activities. Its first special Border unit became the subject of a book by Joseph Wambaugh, *Lines and Shadows*, charging the cops with hooliganism and racism. In January of 1989, a second such "crime prevention" unit, which included Border Patrol agents, was disbanded after having killed 19 people. But Audrey Bergner, testifying on behalf of an anti-immigrant group called Americans for Border Control (ABC), put the blame for the violence on the undocumented immigrants themselves, and reiterated her call for "an impenetrable physical barrier" on the border. Her group, ABC, was originally set up by then INS Western Regional Commissioner Ezell to help promote an anti-immigrant hysteria. It led to the passage of the Immigration Reform and Control Act (IRCA), authorizing legal sanctions against employers who hired undocumented workers and massive increases in Border Patrol enforcement efforts.

Then-State Senator Art Torres summed up the feelings of many observers when he declared that "law enforcement is not the solution to this long-term problem" [of violence on the border]. "Peaceful development and economic improvement to the south" is necessary, he said. The so-called North American Free Trade Agreement (NAFTA), for which President Bush railroaded authority through Congress, which he signed shortly before leaving office, and which Clinton then championed, winning ratification, will not solve the problem. By deepening U.S. domination and exploitation of Mexico, it will exacerbate it.

Yet opposition to the pact has not centered on solidarity with the struggle of the Mexican people to overcome this domination and exploitation. Instead, demagogic politicians like Ross Perot exploited the same anti-Mexican scapegoating about job losses to Mexico and increased immigration that the racist right uses to fuel its xenophobic campaign. Again, this is similar to the situation in Germany, where all the mainstream parties are trying to amend the constitution to restrict refugee rights as the "solution" to the problem of nazi violence against refugees, immigrants, and Germans of foreign extraction.

The Free Trade pact, like the so-called "amnesty" before it, underlines the economic and political causes of the immigration issue. The U.S. effort to drive migrant workers out through economic pressure, by drying up jobs through onerous documentation requirements and penalties against employers, appears to have failed. Even in economic hard times, with high unemployment, low-wage immigrant labor is essential to the U.S. economy and its "global competitiveness." This is why we have not yet seen the massive deportation sweeps that occurred in earlier downturns like the Great Depression. Immigration activists have long maintained that the U.S. has never been interested in stopping the flow of migrant labor, but only in increasing its exploitation and the profit extracted from it by making it illegal. The parallel war on drugs that has also been used to justify the militarization of the border is a similar sham. Criminalization in both cases only serves to increase victimization, and thereby profitablity. It doesn't stop the importation of drugs or labor.

This cynical reality has in turn fed the racist right groups which have made anti-immigrant organizing one of the centerpieces of their outreach in southern California and elsewhere around the country. It allows the racist groups to present themselves as "populists" or anti-establishment, even as they are doing the dirty work of the economic elite that benefits from the importation, oppression, and exploitation of the immigrants. In Texas and Georgia, and elsewhere in the south and southeast, the KKK has been promoting a similar anti-immigrant and anti-Mexican hysteria. NAFTA exposes the sham which the militarily imposed border represents. *Sin Fronteras* is not merely a slogan of the Chicano movement. Both capital and commodity-labor are meant to move relatively freely across the border, subject to no law but that of the market. The Border Patrol and the neo-nazi violence only further exploit these realities, while trying to suppress the struggles of the immigrant and migrant workers for justice.

At the same time, in the context of ongoing economic contraction, larger sectors of the population, and not only whites, have bought the idea of blaming immigrants for their economic and social woes. Rather than confronting the system as a whole, they are looking for a convenient, vulnerable scapegoat. This pattern, though related more to issues of capital and consumer goods export than labor import, has also been played out around Japan. Instead of blaming U.S. economic problems on Japanese competition, or scapegoating Japanese Americans or other Asian Americans for the job losses that have resulted from American economic mismanagement and intentional deindustrialization, we should be seeking real solutions to our own economic woes. Instead, U.S. political leaders engage in Japan bashing that encourages anti-Asian violence in this country.

One prime example of the connection between hard-core fascist groups and the anti-immigrant movement that has been legitimized by high-ranking public officials, is the national campaign going on to make English the official language. This campaign has functioned in several states and on a national level in much the same way that Light Up the Border in San Diego served as a kind of united front of conservative office holders, right-wing vigilantes, and open white supremacists.

Like the overall anti-immigrant strategy of the racist right, the English Only campaign has had great impact and increasing success. The radical and racist right has been able not only to shape the national debate on this issue, but to draw massive popular support. Initiatives and laws sponsored by the English Only movement have carried the field in state after state, winning legislatures and large popular vote majorities. The issue is currently on the center stage in Georgia, with the only major opposition centered on fears that adoption would have a negative impact on the Olympics scheduled for next year in Atlanta.

U.S. English and English First are the two national organizations that are leading the effort to adopt state initiatives compelling the use of English as the official state language. They advocate adoption of a similar constitutional amendment on a national level. The two groups, which provide the main organizational infrastructure for the movement popularly known as English Only, are deeply rooted in racist and fascist elements of the U.S. and international right wing.

An examination of the network of organizations and activists involved with the English Only movement makes this racist and fascist orientation clear. It explains why even some establishment conservative figures like Linda Chavez, the former head of U.S. English, have backed away from the movement. But in the absence of public exposure of these links, the English Only forces are building strength and mass support. They are a fascist wedge into the body politic comparable to the victory of Klan leader David Duke as a Republican candidate in Louisiana, and his subsequent senatorial, gubernatorial, and presidential campaigns. Duke too, sought to use anti-immigrant sentiment to drape his campaigns in patriotism. Pandering to similar sentiment is one way Pat Buchanan stole Duke's thunder and took a third or more of the vote in some Republican primaries.

U.S. English was the brainchild of Dr. John Tanton, who also founded the Federation for American Immigration Reform (FAIR) and a network of other anti-immigration and zero population growth groups. Until 1988, U.S. English was part of a nonprofit group called "U.S. Inc.," which also bankrolled such entities as FAIR and Americans for Border Control. ABC, not the grass-roots group it claims to be, was set up as noted earlier by then INS Commissioner Harold Ezell, before passage of the Immigration Reform and Control Act, to pressure Congress to give greater powers to the INS. Similarly reflecting the symbiosis between the repressive state apparatus and the mass anti-immigrant groups, FAIR bankrolled Proposition 187 author Alan Nelson, former head of the INS. FAIR seeks not only to stop illegal immigration, but to severely limit legal immigration as well.

The roots of U.S. English, FAIR, and others of Tanton's groups, as well as those of English First, become clear when we examine the major sources of funding for the groups beyond Tanton's own resources. Key funding for FAIR has come from the Pioneer Fund, a little known foundation dedicated to eugenics as a means of "racial betterment." Pioneer was created in 1937 to support what it called "applied eugenics in present-day Germany." This was a reference to Hitler's Nazi program of forced sterilization of those judged to be "feeble-minded" or "inferior." (And remember, Hitler's program was modeled on previous legislative efforts in the U.S.) By 1937, the violently racist, anti-semitic nature of the Nazi regime was already clear. So Pioneer's claims to support only scientific, non-racist research is simply diversionary.

Pioneer has always been linked to the hard right in the U.S. Directors included Rep. Frances Walter of the House Un-American Activities Committee (HUAC), and die-hard segregationist Sen. William Eastland. In the 1970s, Pioneer funded the racist "genetic" research of William Schockley and Arthur Jensen, which purported to prove that Blacks have hereditarily lower IQ scores than whites. Jensen served on the advisory board of *Neue Anthropologie,* a German neo-nazi publication of the time.

In addition to Tanton's groups, Pioneer also funded the work of Roger Pearson, the author of *Eugenics and Race,* a book which promoted the "Aryan superiority" theories of Hans Gunther, a racial theorist acclaimed in the Third Reich. Pearson, who had a history of racist activity going back to 1956, later became a national and international leader of the World Anti-Communist League (WACL), an amalgam of U.S. and European nazis and neo-nazis, Latin American death squads, and Asian dictatorships.

Pioneer's support for FAIR and Tanton's other groups, which are unrelated to genetics, expose the racist thinking behind the fund. John Trevor, an officer of the Pioneer Fund, testified in Congress against repealing the racial preferences in U.S. immigration law (enacted in the 1920s at the height of Ku Klux Klan influence and anti-immigrant organizing). Trevor warned that eliminating the preference for Northern Europeans would produce "a conglomeration of racial and ethnic elements" and "a serious cultural decline."

The other principal funding source for U.S. English has been Cordelia Scaife May, an heiress to the Mellon family fortune. She has poured at least $2.5 million since 1980 into U.S. English, FAIR, Immigration PAC, and other Tanton groupings. Her racist thinking is evident in the sponsorship by her Laurel Foundation of the book *The Camp of Saints.* This racist, futuristic fantasy, in which Third World immigrants invade Europe and destroy its civilization, was virtually required reading among staffers at U.S. English. Even Linda Chavez, when she was titular head of U.S. English, called the book "sickening...racist, paranoid and xenophobic." She was disturbed by its popularity among staff members of the English Only group, and this may have been a factor in her resignation. The book is currently being distributed in the U.S. by National Vanguard Books, run by William Pierce, author of the nazi genocide-fantasy *The Turner Diaries.*

The Mellon family fortune, based in Gulf Oil, Martin Marietta, (a major defense contractor), and Colt Industries (the firearms and weapons manufacturer), has been a key source of funding for the entire New Right since the 1960s. Richard Mellon Scaife has provided more than $150 million over the years to the Heritage Foundation and a host of other right-wing groups. In this way, U.S. English is hooked into the network of right-wing single-issue organizations that also include the "right to bear arms" (anti-gun control), "right to work" (anti-union), and "right to life" (anti-abortion) movements. Colt, for example, tried to stop the California ban on assault weapons developed after the attack on Indochinese children in a Stockton, California school yard by racist Patrick Purdy.

English First, the other principal organization behind the English Only movement, is involved in a similar network. It is, if anything, further to the right than the Tanton nexus, or at least more open about its rightist orientation. Larry Pratt, the national head of English First, is a former right-wing Virginia legislator and officer of the Council on Inter-American Security (CIS). This hard-right think tank was the author of most of Ronald Reagan's Latin American policy and repeated the favor for George Bush.

Pratt runs an assortment of far-right outfits out of an office in the Washington, D.C. area, including Gun Owners of America and English First, and has ties to anti-abortion groups as well. In a bizarre footnote to the beating of Rodney King, Pratt suggested in a letter to the *New York Times* that King would have fared better had he been armed to defend himself. Pratt recently exposed the racist character of his leanings by participating in a gathering called by the Christian Identity "Reverend" Pete Peters of Colorado to organize support for white supremacist Randy Weaver who was arrested after a shoot-out with federal marshals in Idaho.

CIS is extremely paranoid about the revolutionary potential of Latin America. The group defined Sandinista Nicaragua as "the fuse" leading to "the bomb" of Mexico. This hostility extends to Hispanics inside the U.S. In a paper called "Creating a Hispanic America: Nation Within a Nation?", the CIS virtually equated bilingual education and services with terrorism. "Bilingual education," it declared, "has national security implications." The paper compares the U.S. southwest to French-speaking Quebec, with its potential for separatism. It sees the Chicano and Spanish-speaking population as in themselves a threat to U.S. national security and unity.

The paper also indulges in more blatant racism. It describes the Indian ancestors of Latinos as "uncivilized barbaric squatters" with "a penchant for grotesque human sacrifices, cannibalism, and kidnapping women." This is the ideology that guides English First leader Pratt in his fund-raising appeals for the English Only cause. In one letter soliciting potential donors, Pratt claimed, "Many immigrants these days are encouraged not to learn English. They remain stuck in a linguistic...ghetto, living off welfare and costing working Americans billions of tax dollars."

The CIS, which is a key force in the English First constellation, has extensive ties to the Rev. Sun Myung Moon's Unification Church, a cult-like, anti-democratic religion which seeks political influence within the right-wing movement internationally. CAUSA, a funding arm of the Moonies with big economic interests in Latin America, is one important link between the two. The CIS also includes in its ranks reactionary Christian rightist Pat Buchanan (the former member of the Nixon and Reagan White House teams who ran an anti-gay, anti-woman, anti-immigrant campaign for the presidency against George Bush). Adolfo Calero of the Nicaraguan

Contras, and retired Gen. John K. Singlaub, head of the World Anti-Communist League, now renamed the World League for Freedom and Democracy, are also in the CIS. This brings us full circle, back to the milieu funded by Pioneer, Tanton's "eugenicist" supporters.

This network of funding is no coincidence or matter of guilt by association. Tanton wrote a memo for a group he participates in called WITAN, Old English for "Council of Wise Men." In it, he clarified the basis of his fears about immigration and language issues. "Can 'homo contraceptivus' compete with 'homo progenitiva' if the borders aren't closed?" he wondered. Among the problems he detailed as arising from a growing Hispanic population are "the tradition of the 'mordida' (bribe); the lack of involvement in public affairs," Roman Catholicism, low educability, and a high drop-out rate. His fears were directed at Asians as well. "Keep in mind that many of the Vietnamese coming in are also Catholic," he says, and therefore more likely to have large families and to be less assimilable to the U.S. (white Protestant) culture.

"This is the first instance in which those with their pants up are going to be caught by those with their pants down," Tanton wrote. "As whites see their power and control over their lives declining, will they simply go quietly into the night? Or will there be an explosion?" This is exactly the scenario drawn by Tom Metzger in his prognostications of a coming race war. Tanton's anti-Catholicism is reminiscent of the nativist, anti-papist Ku Klux Klan of the 1920s.

Such sentiments proved so embarrassing in their frankness that after they were made public,

Tanton was forced out of the group he founded, as he had previously been kicked out of Zero Population Growth. His exit did not cleanse U.S. English, however; even after his departure, Linda Chavez, the titular head—probably chosen for the combination of her Spanish surname with Reaganite views—decided that she could no longer stomach the scene and resigned. Chavez is herself a rightist with quite a tolerance for discrimination—as a Republican nominee, she used lesbian-baiting attacks in her campaign against Democratic Rep. Barbara Mikulski for the vacant Maryland U.S. Senate seat in 1986.

Other more liberal members of U.S. English, like Walter Cronkite, have also jumped ship. Gore Vidal, the novelist, disavowed ever having taken a position on the national board of the group, despite having been listed by the group on its stationery. "Obviously, this amendment is out to get Hispanics," he said, in disclaiming membership, "and I can't support it."

However, these defections have done little to stop the English Only movement. In California, U.S. English and English First have jointly funded a parent–teacher group called LEAD (Learning English Advocates Drive) which opposes bilingual education and has tried to get several teacher unions including the United Teachers Los Angeles to oppose bilingual instruction. Affiliates of the English Only movement in several states have continued to push successfully for adoption of "English as the official language" amendments to state constitutions, either by legislative or initiative action, getting such measures approved in Arizona, Florida, Colorado, and other states. Since the adoption of such an initiative in

California, they have been involved in attempts to ban non-English signs on businesses in several cities.

The English Only campaign has its antecedents in the Nazi drive to power in Germany, and in the infamous Nuremberg laws which codified Hitler's ascent and the Nazi program. One of the key provisions of these laws, which institutionalized Nazi control of German society, was the suppression of "ethnic" languages, including Yiddish, Romani, and the Slavic tongues spoken by minorities. The laws elevated German as the official language of the new Reich. In a similar way, the South African apartheid regime attempted to impose "Afrikaans"—the settler version of Dutch—on the African people.

The U.S. is particularly paranoid about Spanish, because in many areas of what is now the U.S., including Florida, California, Texas, and the southwest, Spanish was spoken before English ever arrived. Treaty obligations, in fact, specified respect for the language rights of the Spanish-speaking residents of some of these areas when the U.S. seized them militarily. Like the treaties with the Native American nations, these have generally been ignored. The U.S. withheld statehood status from areas like New Mexico and Arizona until a white English-speaking majority was in control. The U.S. also tried unsuccessfully for three generations to eradicate Spanish in Puerto Rico, which it has colonized since 1898.

Today, as the Europeans unify while speaking more than a dozen different languages, the paranoid and xenophobic nature of the English Only movement should be apparent. However, the movement is succeeding in winning adherents to its hidden agenda by hammering away at its theme of patriotism and national unity. John Tanton made it clear how much the movement feared exposure of its true nature. "The issues we are touching here must be broached by liberals," he wrote in the memo which led to his downfall. "The conservatives simply cannot do it without tainting the whole project.... People might think that your public spirited rhetoric is a mask for intolerance."

The anti-immigrant hysteria is not restricted in fact to immigrants, but is a justification for broader racism. All Asians, all Latinos, become targets. For example, widespread discrimination against workers who appear or sound "foreign," or who are not U.S. citizens, has resulted from the penalties enacted in the Immigration Reform and Control Act (IRCA) against employers who knowingly hire undocument-ed workers or who fail to obtain and maintain proper documents of their workers' eligibility for employ-ment in the U.S. This was shown in a study conducted by the General Accounting Office (GAO) to evaluate the impact of the employer sanctions.

Francisco Garcia, immigrants rights director of the Mexican American Legal Defense and Education Fund (MALDEF) declared that the Latino community would not stand for this "intolerable level of discrimi-nation," and his group and others are lobbying Congress to repeal the sanctions. But despite protes-tations to the contrary, this is exactly the impact the regulations were designed to have. They were meant to drive the undocumented further underground, to try to drive a wedge between older residents and more recent arrivals, and to make all immigrant workers, and all people of color, more easily exploited.

The GAO research for its report also included sending out teams of men, one of whom looked and sounded Hispanic and one who appeared Anglo, to major employers in the Midwest and Southwest. The Latino applicants were one third less likely to be interviewed and less than half as likely to get hired. Yet the promoters of anti-immigrant hysteria always try to use the excuse that immigrants are "taking our jobs." In fact, according to the GAO, almost 891,000 employers have begun discriminating as a response to the law. The pattern of job bias was the strongest in states like California, with a large Asian and Hispanic population.

The fact is that, like David Duke's code words about white rights, opposition to affirmative action, and denunciations of welfare, the theme of protecting American jobs is a flimsy pretext and excuse for the anti-immigrant campaigns. Scratch an "anti-immigrant" activist and you will often find a racist. That's why Tom Metzger actively directs recruiting efforts towards the anti-immigrant movement, and the anti-immigrant wing of the environmental movement. He believes he will find a receptive audience for his propaganda about "mud people" and preserving "white heritage."

Although the sponsors of Prop. 187 and others fomenting the anti-immigrant hysteria claim they are only opposed to illegals, the facts show otherwise. For example, Prop. 187 would require teachers to ascertain the citizenship or residence status of the parents of their students, even if the student is a citizen, and report it to the INS if there is a suspicion of illegal immigration. Negative Population Group, which picks up where ZPG leaves off, calls for a to beat them and arrest them. As in Orange County, most of the charges were eventually drastically reduced or dropped. As in Orange County, a charge of "lynching" is still pending against at least one striker. In California, the lynch law makes it a felony to take someone from police custody and is commonly used against demonstrators who help people escape police clutches.

Meanwhile, however, the Immigration and Naturalization Service entered the picture. Although drywall and other construction trades in southern California have long been a magnet for undocumented workers, it is only with the advent of the strike and the workers' unprecedented solidarity and militance that the INS began a crackdown. The agency moved in to screen 134 of those arrested in Orange County, and placed immigration holds on 86 of them (meaning that if they are released from police custody, they would be sent to INS detention). Eventually, the INS initiated deportation proceedings against 57, of whom 38 agreed to accept voluntary departure and were returned to Mexico. "If this were a group of white workers, the question of how many were undocumented would never even come up," says Miguel Caballero, legal director of CIWA, the California Immigrant Workers Association/Asociacion de Trabajadores Latinos, an associate union membership program of the AFL-CIO, which supported and provided legal assistance to the strikers.

But the strikers themselves had a simple explanation for their success. "We are a family," says Arcadio Rios, an undocumented striker and father of six, of his co-workers in Orange County. "I watch over them and they watch over me. That's the only thing we have going for us." Gloria Romero, chair of the Hispanic Advisory Committee to the L.A.P.D., said the employers were "using the police as strike-breakers" and called on new chief Willie Williams to uproot "the culture of violence and racism" still plaguing the department. A spokesman for Williams said that the new chief and the police commission would investigate the incident and examine depart-ment policy in labor disputes generally.

But in fact the drywallers' strike, and an earlier strike by janitors, showed clearly that the essence of the L.A.P.D. and INS policy towards immigrant work-ers is to function as strike-breakers and enforcers for the employers. Three years ago in an unprovoked and unexpected police riot, the L.A.P.D. attacked a group of 500 striking janitors and supporters inside Century City. They were marching through the area in what was supposed to be an authorized demon-stration against building owners who refused to negotiate. The brutal attack, in which a pregnant marcher lost her baby, horrified office workers who witnessed it and people who saw the beatings on the evening news shows. It probably served to draw new support to the striking janitors, mostly all Salvadoran refugees, some of whom risked deporta-tion by participating in the strike. The janitors filed a $10 million claim against the police and the city, eventually won their strike and a series of contracts, and came out in large numbers to support the dry-wallers in their similar struggle. They are currently engaged in a similar organizing drive in downtown highrises, and for public employees in Pasadena.

The "Justice for Janitors" campaign, and the drywallers strike, give the lie to the racist organizers restriction on legal immigration to the total number of U.S. citizens who emigrate to other countries each year. The L.A. County Board of Supervisors recently criminalized the act of standing on the street soliciting work, no matter what the legal residence status of the offender.

Treatment of Arab Americans during the Gulf War is another example of the anti-immigrant hysteria that is being used to fuel reaction after the death of the Cold War as an excuse for repression. FBI agents interviewed Arab Americans across the country with the approval of the National Security Council, in a move designed, according to an FBI assistant director, "to ratchet up" awareness of a terrorist threat. The FBI visits were concentrated in Southern California and Detroit, because of their large numbers of residents of Arab descent. The move was condemned by even the most mainstream Arab American spokespeople.

At this writing, the U.S. is actively seeking to deport two long-standing legal residents for their political work in support of Palestinian rights, in the case known as the "L.A. Eight." Similar repression and detentions are taking place in other parts of the country. The L.A. Eight uncovered immigration documents detailing "contingency plans" for the massive round-up of resident immigrant populations under the context of a "war emergency," and their detention in camps in Louisiana and Texas.

Khader Hamide, one of the L.A. Eight Palestinians whom the INS and FBI are trying to deport, saw the FBI attack on the Arab American community during the Gulf War as "part and parcel of the same situation" that faced him. "It's an attempt to silence the Arab community, to frighten us away from exercising our first amendment rights. The scariest thing about the current situation," said Hamide at the time, "is that they might actually move to implement that contingency plan. The FBI maneuvers increase the hype that the whole Arab community is suspect." In its dealings with Arab immigrants, we see the same continuity between the government and its repressive apparatus and the neo-nazis that is evident in other aspects of immigration policy.

The FBI claimed that its visits were designed to assure Arab Americans that the FBI would protect them from violence in the event of an "ignorant backlash" from military action in the Gulf. But the agency asked for leads and assistance in identifying "terrorists," with the result that they helped to fuel stereotyping of and attacks against Arab Americans, who were hit by a massive wave of hate crimes during the war. Albert Mokhiber of the American Arab Anti-Discrimination Committee (ADC) said the visits took us "back to the World War II Japanese American concentration camps," fomenting "suspicion of Arab Americans." At this writing, even while condemning Israel's expulsion of Palestinians, the U.S. is still actively trying to deport the Palestinians of the L.A. Eight for exercising their free speech. The hysteria was renewed in the wake of the World Trade Center terrorist bombing.

Asian and Pacific Islanders have been another target of anti-immigrant hysteria, both around the language concerns of English Only and in bloody anti-Asian violence around the country. In attacks similar to the "Paki-bashing" by nazi boneheads in England, East Indians have been the target of "dot-busters" in New Jersey. Vietnamese have been targets in Texas and California. The racism which finds all Asians indistinguishable has resulted in killings of Chinese whose attackers call them Japs. The anti-Asian mentality has been fed by Japan-bashing in high places, just like the other forms of anti-immigrant hysteria.

Nor are such sentiments restricted to whites. Anti-immigrant feelings have been involved in inter-ethnic conflict and tensions between Blacks, Latinos, and Asians in L.A. and elsewhere. Robert Brock, a Black man who works closely with white racists, has attempted to make unity with neo-nazis around themes of anti-Jewish, anti-Latino, and anti-Asian prejudice. Continued violence against Asian Americans has been a key feature in the growth of hate crime.

Yet another target of the anti-immigrant hysteria has been labor organizing. In California and elsewhere, immigrant workers, Chicanos, and Central Americans, even when undocumented, have become among the most militant and successful union organizers. For example, a four-month-long strike by 4,000 to 5,000 drywallers, construction workers who cut and install sheetrock in residential and other buildings, was met by a wave of police harassment and arrests across a six-county southern California region in 1992. Yet in the face of felony arrests, beatings, and deportations, the striking drywallers, mostly Mexicano men, maintained their struggle and their demand for decent wages and benefits and union recognition. They finally won a union contract from building contractors and sub-contractors in the area, except in San Diego.

197

Strikers were arrested at pickets in San Diego, San Bernardino, and Riverside. Some of the most dramatic and highly publicized incidents took place in Orange County and Los Angeles. On July 2, 1992 a massive picket line at a construction site in Mission Viejo was broken up by police after contractors claimed that strikers had invaded the jobsite and physically removed non-striking workers. The incident resulted in the largest mass arrest in the history of Orange County. One hundred and fifty-three striking workers were arrested and charged with felonies as serious as kidnapping. They all refused to plea bargain, jamming up the courts for weeks, while other strikers, their families, and supporters had two large, noisy demonstrations outside the county courthouse in Santa Ana. Eventually, all charges were dropped against 67 of those arrested, and most of the remainder pleaded guilty to infractions or misdemeanors.

In a similar incident at a construction site in Hollywood on July 23, 1992, sub-contractors and private security guards pulled weapons, including a shotgun, on picketers. When the strikers remained defiant, and one shook the fence, shouting, "Go ahead, shoot me!" the builder called in the L.A.P.D. About 20 cops were already nearby in five police cars, and they detained several strikers inside the work site. The workers were chased by the pursuing police towards the Hollywood freeway, where their path was blocked. In desperation, they ran up the on-ramp and across both the southbound and northbound lanes of the freeway. But when they climbed over the retaining wall on the opposite side, they were confronted by still more police, who began to beat them and arrest them. As in Orange County, most of the charges were eventually drastically reduced or dropped. As in Orange County, a charge of "lynching" is still pending against at least one striker. In California, the lynch law makes it a felony to take someone from police custody and is commonly used against demonstrators who help people escape police clutches.

Meanwhile, however, the Immigration and Naturalization Service entered the picture. Although drywall and other construction trades in southern California have long been a magnet for undocumented workers, it is only with the advent of the strike and the workers' unprecedented solidarity and militance that the INS began a crackdown. The agency moved in to screen 134 of those arrested in Orange County, and placed immigration holds on 86 of them (meaning that if they are released from police custody, they would be sent to INS detention). Eventually, the INS initiated deportation proceedings against 57, of whom 38 agreed to accept voluntary departure and were returned to Mexico. "If this were a group of white workers, the question of how many were undocumented would never even come up," says Miguel Caballero, legal director of CIWA, the California Immigrant Workers Association/Asociacion de Trabajadores Latinos, an associate union membership program of the AFL-CIO, which supported and provided legal assistance to the strikers.

But the strikers themselves had a simple explanation for their success. "We are a family," says Arcadio Rios, an undocumented striker and father of six, of his co-workers in Orange County. "I watch over them and they watch over me. That's the only thing we have going for us." Gloria Romero, chair of the Hispanic Advisory Committee to the L.A.P.D., said the employers were "using the police as strike-breakers" and called on new chief Willie Williams to uproot "the culture of violence and racism" still plaguing the department. A spokesman for Williams said that the new chief and the police commission would investigate the incident and examine department policy in labor disputes generally.

But in fact the drywallers' strike, and an earlier strike by janitors, showed clearly that the essence of the L.A.P.D. and INS policy towards immigrant workers is to function as strike-breakers and enforcers for the employers. Three years ago in an unprovoked and unexpected police riot, the L.A.P.D. attacked a group of 500 striking janitors and supporters inside Century City. They were marching through the area in what was supposed to be an authorized demonstration against building owners who refused to negotiate. The brutal attack, in which a pregnant marcher lost her baby, horrified office workers who witnessed it and people who saw the beatings on the evening news shows. It probably served to draw new support to the striking janitors, mostly all Salvadoran refugees, some of whom risked deportation by participating in the strike. The janitors filed a $10 million claim against the police and the city, eventually won their strike and a series of contracts, and came out in large numbers to support the dry-wallers in their similar struggle. They are currently engaged in a similar organizing drive in downtown highrises, and for public employees in Pasadena.

The "Justice for Janitors" campaign, and the drywallers strike, give the lie to the racist organizers who blame deteriorating working conditions and labor weakness on undocumented and immigrant workers. In fact, in the face of repression and exploitation and repression, such workers have been the most militant and successful labor organizers in recent history. A report by the Center for Third World Organizing shows that organizing drives and strike actions are twice as likely to be successful if the work force involved is at least half people of color than if it is predominantly white. Recognizing the vital contribution of immigrant workers to organized labor and the defense of all workers' rights, the unions have been in the forefront of organized opposition to the Prop. 187 anti-immigrant initiative in California.

In the face of continued neo-nazi agitation around the immigration issue, progressives must come up with a pro-active policy around immigration issues. Otherwise, as in Germany where the mainstream political parties have allowed the nazis to define the terms of the struggle as to how much and how best to limit immigration, the fascists will carry the day.

Immigration rights activists believe that the problems will never be solved so long as repression and economic underdevelopment drives Mexicans and Central Americans north, and the U.S. labor market simultaneously seeks such low-waged workers. Therefore, the only solution must be predicated on support for the democratic and anti-imperialist struggle in Mexico. The Zapatista uprising in Mexico in the wake of the implementation of NAFTA means that there is an armed revolutionary insurgency inside the economic/juridical borders of the

American empire itself.

Our position must be that the border is the illegitimate result of military conquest. "We did not cross the border," say the Mexicans, "the border crossed us." As NAFTA extends that imposed border to Chiapas and beyond, we must build a solidarity and progressive internationalism that can counter the racists, the multi-national corporations, and the government.

Because an attack against one is an attack against all, we must defend the language rights and the job rights of all immigrants, with or without documents. We must build an active solidarity with the struggle of the Mexican people on both sides of the border.

We must expose the continuum from government repression to anti-immigrant organizing to racist violence by individuals and organized nazi elements against Asians and Pacific Islanders, Mexicans and other Latinos, Arab Americans, and others. We must oppose constitutional amendments like English Only and the attempt to strip the citizenship protections of the 14th Amendment. We must dispel the anti-immigrant racism of sectors of the environmental movement. We must identify the liberatory potential for everyone of the national liberation struggles like that of the EZLN in Mexico, and the labor struggles like those of the janitors, the garment workers, and others inside the imposed borders. And in so doing, we must build an anti-racist movement as massive as that which swept Germany following neo-nazi anti-immigrant violence there, but with the revolutionary potential to reshape this entire society.

Was Hitler an Ecologist?

Racism, Environmentalism, and Environmental Racism

It is undeniable, by anyone but the most self-deluded mouthpieces for multinational industrialists, that the world faces a growing environmental crisis, a threat to the ecosystems of the planet caused by human activities. In response, an environmentalist movement has grown up, and governments around the globe have been forced to set up agencies chartered with protecting the air, water, and land. But the nature and extent of this environmental crisis, its causes and cures, are the subject of intense political struggle. This is a contribution to that struggle and debate, in the hopes of helping to expose the connections between the environmental problems that face us, and the issues of racism and colonialism. We need to expose and derail the efforts of forces on the racist and fascist right to broaden their appeal by seeking influence and adherents in the environmental movement.

Racist "Environmentalism"

European racists and fascists have been out in front of their U.S. counterparts in seeking to portray themselves as environmentalists and to penetrate and influence the "green" movement with racist pro-paganda. *Searchlight* magazine, a British watch-dog of the racist right, has documented how Michael Walker, an activist with Britain's neo-nazi National Front, relocated to Germany and began publication of *Scorpion,* a magazine that attempts to link the greens to rabid nationalist groups. Walker has co-sponsored a series of annual conferences in England that bring together hard-core anti-Semites, "Odinists" who link white supremacy to a pagan earth-religion, and some environmental activists.

According to *Searchlight,* the British National Front itself tried to establish a front group called Greenwave in 1989, which they attempted to portray as a new formation created by green activists frus-trated by existing groups. They used the Greenwave name to run one of their members for Parliament in a by-election, and sought to establish links with the British Green Party and Friends of the Earth. After the group was exposed as nazi front, organizers for Greenpeace, who had previously registered the name Greenwave, threatened to sue the neo-nazis to force them to stop using the name.

The National Front attempted to deny its involve-ment in the group, but the national coordinator of the group was exposed as a German woman living with a "former" local leader of the National Front. That NF leader had previously attempted to set up the National Socialist Workers Initiative, yet another British neo-nazi formation. Such tactics have paid off. The National Front, which links "ecology" to racism and anti-immigrant hysteria, in 1993 won its first local election to a council seat in England, beat-ing the Labor Party candidate by a slim margin.

Was Hitler an Ecologist?

Here in the U.S., one of the strongest proponents of an alliance between racists and Greens has been Tom Metzger, former head of David Duke's Ku Klux Klan in California and founder of White Aryan Resistance (WAR). Metzger devoted a recent issue of his white-supremacist tabloid, *WAR*, to racist environmentalism.

As early as 1983, in the first issue of his Klan publication after renaming it *WAR* (then *White American Resistance*), Metzger reported favorably on the German Greens: "In Bavaria and Nuremberg, there are party cells which certain kinds of nazis took over, not militarist nazis but "folkish" nazis, to preserve forests and water, preserve old "folk" culture, plus save the Aryan race....They are pro-local police, want non-white immigrants and migrants repatriated." Metzger blames environmental problems on "over-population" by "racially inferior" groups, non-Aryans whom he refers to as "mud people" or the "mud flood."

The Aryan Women's League, a WAR off-shoot whose logo is a women's fist symbol over a swastika, proposed in the pages of *WAR* that racists have "a duty to restore the world back to its original balance alongside with our ultimate goal...of preserving the pure Aryan race." Monique Wolfing of the AWL chapter in San Francisco wrote, "The way to do this is to make ourselves known as environmentalists and wildlife advocates. There are many groups out there helping wildlife and the environment. They are not necessarily white power advocates like ourselves, but if we make contributions to these groups, we achieve two things, 1) we break out of our media stereotype...and 2) we gain recognition."

In a series of articles in *WAR*, Metzger declared his support for Earth First! Metzger identified the beginnings of the ecology movement with the "green" policies of Hitler's regime, citing well-springs of the Nazis and Hitler youth in outdoors hiking clubs in Germany under the Weimar Republic. He recalls that an American racialist, Madison Grant, a major proponent of "manifest destiny" as pre-ordained white rule over North America, was the founder of the Save the Redwoods League. Identifying Earth Firsters who were set up and imprisoned by FBI operatives as similar to "white separatists" who suffered similar setbacks, Metzger said, "Race first, but are we able to separate the race from the earth? The label 'earth first' may rub some racial separatists wrong, but upon a closer look, where is the Aryan Race without a healthy earth?" Metzger, who promotes the "Third Position" ideology that communism and capitalism are equally bad, blames corporate damage to the environment on the Jews.

In a subsequent article headlined "Ecology is for Aryans, Too," a Metzger follower says, "Don't you think, my Aryan comrades, that it's time to start using any and every means to put a stop to the capitalist and other scum who are raping our mother earth to the point of her extinction?" Such anti-capitalist rhetoric is consistent with Metzger's viewpoint that capitalism and communism are both Jewish plots to control the white man.

Another strong U.S. advocate of painting the white racist movement green has been Gary Gallo, a neo-nazi who runs an outfit called the National Democratic Front. Gallo devoted a part of his newspaper *The Nationalist* to a section titled "On the

Green Front." Like Metzger, he attributes the origin of the ecology movement to the original Nazis, Hitler's National Socialists.

Referring to a sympathetic account of the life and views of Walther Darre, Hitler's minister of agriculture, Gallo says the book *Blood and Soil: Walther Darre and Hitler's Green Party* has been ignored because it shows "the National Socialist roots of the Green Movement." Gallo credits Darre with inventing the slogan "Blood and Soil" in his effort to rejuvenate the "Nordic sub-race," declares him to be an early proponent of the "small is beautiful" theory, and attributes to him the origination of the term "organic farming" to apply to growing food without pesticides and chemical fertilizers.

Gallo, like Metzger, seems to propound an "Aryan environmentalism," based on the idea that Aryans are the founders of agriculture and all other forms of civilization. Gallo says Darre was not an extreme "Nature-before-man" ecologist, but believed that "man had to live close to nature to counter the malevolent effects of civilization and its domestication of man.... Man had to use reason...to guide and direct the relationship between man and nature for the benefit of both."

In an article for *WAR* called "Is Mother Nature a Racist?", Wyatt Kaldenberg, one of Metzger's chief lieutenants, echoes these views. "The churches, schools, and mass media have all dumped the blame for the Third World's lack of development on the shoulders of the White male....But why is it that the White man is always above the mud, looking down?... The Aryan create(d) a high agricultural civilization in the Northland.... By 5000 BC the Aryan had developed the big 7 (species): ducks, chickens, sheep, goats, cattle, pigs and horses...the White man invented wind and water mills...the ancient Aryan built Stonehenge and the Egyptian pyramids."

Since the racists hold to this (historically inaccurate) view, their solution to the spread of industrialism and the havoc it has wrought is depopulation of the planet by elimination of the inferior races. Metzger reports, favorably, that "Earth First leaders have made logical statements that AIDS is a positive trend in world population control." (Metzger and other white racists like J. B. Stoner consider AIDS as God's gift to the white man in eliminating homosexuals, Jews, and "non-Aryans.") Metzger goes on to say, "This raised the ire of Jewish con-artists who plague sincere environmentalists."

German neo-nazis involved in or close to the Green movement have expressed similar ideas. Hoimar von Ditforth, a German neo-Malthusian who believes population control is the essence of environmentalism, has said, "Today alone, forty thousand children will die—one every two seconds. They will starve. Horrible? But what would be much worse would be if these children did not die from starvation...but survived...to have children themselves. Then the catastrophe would be enormously greater."

One of the founders of the German Green movement was Herbert Gruhl, a far-right politician who left the ruling conservative Christian Democrats after chairing the party's working group on the environment in the Bundestag. Angered that his Green Action Future grouping was marginalized by the Green Party, which adopted a center-left orientation, he split to form the Ecological Democracy Party

Was Hitler an Ecologist?

(OPD), becoming its chairman. When the OPD refused to follow his leadership into an open alliance with Germany's electoral neo-nazi parties, the NPD and the Republikaners, he split again, forming a new group in 1989 which called for ending immigration to Germany (supposedly on "ecological grounds"). Even while still leading the ODP, Gruhl had appeared as a guest speaker at neo-nazi gatherings and "historical revisionist" conferences (which claim Hitler's genocide is a hoax perpetrated by Jews).

In a move similar to the efforts of right-wing conspiracy theorists and racists in the U.S. to infiltrate the left, Gruhl's old party, the ODP, joined a coalition of mostly progressive groups opposing the Mastricht Treaty for European unification. At the same time, the ODP, which has never repudiated Gruhl or his ideas embedded in their party platform, has attempted to make itself the political voice of the German equivalent of the "right to life" movement. Their environmentalist, anti-abortion, and anti-immigration arguments are expressly based on a defense and glorification of the German "volk." With the support of the ODP and of some Greens, Gruhl was awarded a Federal Service Cross by the government. Gruhl defines the alternative to people perishing because of the results of over-population as "precautionary reductions" of non-Western peoples who "flood the earth like a sinister natural catastrophe."

Gruhl is not content to let starvation solve the problem. After all, those starving may prove a threat. "Societies of culture [which he defines as racially pure] are always threatened from without, since their standard of living arouses other peoples' envy.... So these peoples [of the West] have a more

209

urgent need for armed forces for their defense than poor tribal peoples have." Gruhl says that only two alternatives remain: "to perish, or to take precautionary reductions." Since "most of the peoples of the world are not capable of behaving in a rational way," these precautionary reductions must be carried out among them by force.

Such ideas have also been promoted in such books as *The Camp of the Saints*, widely popular in the anti-immigrant and English Only movements, which portrays white civilization threatened by the population "explosion" in the non-white, and therefore unproductive and inferior, Third World. Here in the U.S., John Tanton, a eugenicist and recipient of funding from a number of nazi-oriented groups, who professed similar views, was on the board of the mainstream group Zero Population Growth until his evident racism became an embarrassment. Negative Population Group, an even more blatantly anti-immigrant organization, advertises regularly in the pages of the Sierra Club's magazine.

Mainstream Environmentalist Racism

Such racist arguments have made other inroads into the mainstream environmental movement. Early proponents of "deep ecology" in Earth First! were guilty of openly racist theorizing. Some welcomed AIDS as a potential decimator of unwanted populations. Groups like the Sierra Club have flirted for some time with the ideas that are galvanizing an anti-immigrant hysteria, a large-scale version of the NIMBY (not in my back yard)/"close the door after me" mentality that has plagued environmental activism. Environmentalists of color have been sharply critical of mainstream environmental groups and the government agencies they work with for ignoring the "toxic racism" that makes communities of color disproportionately victims of environmental degradation and toxic waste dumping.

A national study has shown that areas with the highest levels of air pollution are disproportionately those where African Americans and Latinos live. This racial disparity is true not only in relation to white people, but even in relation to all poor people. A majority of Blacks and Latinos in the U.S. live in areas where two air pollution standards are violated, compared to only a third of whites, or of all poor people. Study after study has also shown a clear pattern of hazardous and other waste facilities most commonly being located in existing African American, native and Chicano communities. In Houston, Texas, for example, all the municipal landfills and six of eight incinerators were placed in Black neighborhoods between the 1920s and the 1970s. From 1970 to '78, three of four privately-owned landfills were also placed in the African American community; with 28% of the population, they had 82% of the trash. The same pattern holds true in rural areas nationally as well.

Such problems are not coincidental. A 1984 study prepared for the California Waste Management Board on how to site trash-burning power plants identified poor Black and Hispanic areas as likelier candidates for successful siting. It contrasted the higher level of political involvement and power in white areas with a lower degree of political participation in communities of color, which were also considered likelier to accept the "development" opportunity of incinerators out of economic necessity. However, over the last few years, outraged and militant communities of color have given the lie to this cold-blooded racist analysis.

Blacks, native people, and Latinos fighting toxic racism are now one of the strongest forces in the environmental struggle. This is because they face some of the greatest environmental problems, due to racism. A recent study by the NAACP and the United Church of Christ showed that Blacks are 50% likelier than whites to live near a commercial toxic waste facility. Not only that, but the level of such concentration was worse in 1994 than it had been in 1980. Once again we see operating a key aspect of domestic colonialism—immiseration and deterioration of conditions for people of color while conditions are supposedly improving for society "at large." Mainstream environmental groups must shake off their torpor, ignore the siren songs of racism from the right, and join the movement for environmental justice that is challenging such colonial realities.

Radical Right Pseudo-Environmentalism

Falling somewhat closer to the mainstream than the "green racists" like Metzger, is another tendency that puts a radical-right spin on environmental issues. This tendency seeks to expropriate reactionary concern over ecology policy into a pro-active front of hard-right struggle along with a panoply of issues including gun rights, anti-abortion action, and opposition to "special rights" (a code-word for anti-gay, anti-Indian, and other racist and sexist politics). Most of these groups fall under the rubric of the so-called "Wise Use" movement, right-wing activism on environment issues. The movement grew out of the backers of Reagan's notorious Secretary of the Interior, James Watt, including the Mountain States Legal Foundation. At a 1988 conference in Reno, Nevada, as the transition from Reagan to Bush was taking shape, the movement was formalized under the leadership of the Center for the Defense of Free Enterprise. More than 500 groups nationally now back its "Wise Use Agenda," which holds that the environment must be allowed to be exploited for human use, subject only to the constraints of the capitalist market economy.

The executive vice-president of the CDFE, and a chief theoretician of the Wise Use movement, is Ron Arnold, a former board member of the Pacific Northwest chapter of the Sierra Club. Arnold is fond of describing the environmental movement as "a watermelon—green on the outside and red on the inside." As the right groped for new enemies and causes in the wake of the collapse of the "evil empire," environmentalism came to the fore as one contender (supplementing, rather than competing with, other such targets, like abortion, gay rights, affirmative action, and immigration). Arnold has been involved with the Washington chapter of the American Freedom Coalition (AFC), a merger of the fundamentalist "Christian Voice" with the Rev. Sun Myung Moon's CAUSA organization. He foresees the mission of the Wise Use movement as "wiping out" and replacing all other environmental groups.

The other major leader of the CDFE, which ran another Wise Use conference in Nevada in the summer of 1992, is Alan Gotlieb, its president. Gotlieb came out of the Young Americans for Freedom, the

William Buckley–inspired arch conservative campus group, to become a top fund-raiser, through direct mail, for Ronald Reagan's presidential campaigns. He himself focuses less on the environmental issues than does Arnold, continuing to use the CDFE as a mechanism for raising and distributing large amounts of money for the far right, particularly the gun-rights advocates. He and the CDFE are partners in a number of TV stations; he owns a radio station and publishing houses, printing and publicizing the books that come out of Wise Use. The Moonie-influenced AFC rents space from him in the Liberty Park office complex in Bellevue, Washington which also houses the CDFE.

An example of the bizarre twist the Wise Use movement gives environmentalism is its call for the passage of a "Global Warming Act." This bill calls for the "conversion" of all decaying and oxygen-using forest growth in the national forests into "young stands of oxygen-producing, carbon-dioxide absorbing trees to help ameliorate the rate of global warming and prevent the greenhouse effect." In other words, to prevent global warming, clear-cut the forests! No wonder the Wise Use movement has won the support of corporations like Louisiana-Pacific Lumber; Honda, Kawasaki, and Yamaha sit on the board of its constituent Blue Ribbon Coalition, which won passage of a law calling for the establishment of off-road motor-biking trails in federal land-holdings. Coors, a backer of many far-right-wing causes, has supported the Mountain States Legal Foundation.

The CDFE also advocates expanding economic concessions in all the national parks and turning them over to Disney and other amusement companies; as well as opening all public lands, including the parks, to mineral and energy production. It specifically calls for oil exploration in the Alaska National Wildlife Refuge. Far from going away with the transition to the Clinton administration, the Wise Use movement has stepped up its organizing and fund-raising efforts, using Clinton and Gore's identification with environmental concerns as a focus.

Some of Clinton's taxes and land use fees particularly aroused their ire. Bruce Babbitt, Clinton's Interior Secretary, was forced to abandon most of the mineral extraction and grazing fees proposed for federal land. The Wise Use groups are active in "state's rights" struggles in the western states which are also drawing the participation of paramilitary survivalists and militia proponents. California State Senator Don Rogers, a backer of the "10th Amendment Resolution" opposing federal mandates on the states in environmental and other areas of law, participated in August 1994 for the second time in the "Jubilation" conference of the racist, anti-Semitic *Jubilee* Christian Identity newspaper. Rogers' fellow speakers included Louis Beam, "former" head of the KKK and Aryan Nations in Texas, and John Saunders III of the anti-gay, anti-abortion Chalcedon, Inc., which called for imposing a Christian theocratic state.

Under the guise of "State Sovereignty," a slogan which is advanced by many white supremacists as well, the Wise Use groups are promoting the idea, which has won support from the Supreme Court, that environmental regulations of private land use are an unconstitutional "taking" of private property. This must be countered with something other than corporate liberalism, because the corporations stand to gain untrammeled rights to put profits ahead of all other considerations under such formulas. In fact, Clinton's "compromise" on the old-growth forests of the Pacific northwest, as well as his decision to allow the Liverpool incinerator to proceed, show that he is hardly the friend of the environment he claimed to be. To oppose the corporations and the racist right around these issues, we cannot rely on the regulatory bureaucrats or establishment politicians.

Colonialism, Racism, Environmental Destruction

The environmental movement can effectively address and help overcome the crisis facing our planet only if it understands that the problem is rooted in the history of white supremacy and global conquest that proceeds from the era of Columbus and the European penetration of Africa, Asia, and the Americas to the present day. The struggle to save and restore the environment must be a struggle against racism, imperialism, and colonialism, or it is doomed to failure. The advent of industrialism was founded on a world system of enslavement and land theft, and today this triad of exploitation threatens the existence of human life, perhaps all life on the planet.

In the light of this understanding, we need to examine many of the old dichotomies. The problem is not only in the corporations which defile the air and water in the name of profit; it is also in a way of life that denies both individual and collective responsibility to live in harmony with each other and the world. The U.S. learned its land hunger from a European culture that had deforested most of a continent in the rush to enclose, as private agricultural property, the lands that had once been held in common. In a few generations, our country has also destroyed most of the forests that were not merely maintained but cultivated for millenia by the indigenous people of this part of the continent. In the last few large forested areas, such as the Pacific northwest, we are continuing to do the same, as satellite photos clearly show how little has been done by Forest Service regulation to preserve the forests. Sadly, Clinton's new "compromises" have apparently persuaded major sectors of the mainstream environmental movement to embrace this fiction of preservation.

We must mend our ways, but to do so we must challenge the "American dream" and the "American way of life," as well as the material power of the corporate elite that has defined these deadly ideals. Only a continuing struggle against racism will give us the clarity of vision and purpose to do so.

We can hardly be surprised that, after propagandizing the American way of life in every corner of the globe, and helping erect a system of resource extraction that touches the most remote communities we are being emulated in deforestation from the Amazon to Asia. Environmentalists who blame the problems on overpopulation have blinded themselves to the genocidal depopulation of Africa and of the indigenous peoples of the Americas that is still being carried out. It is the resource-hungry corporations of

217

the advanced industrial countries that are placing the greatest burden on the planet.

When Gandhi was asked what he thought of Western civilization, he replied that he thought it would be a good idea. The superstructure of class society erected by the European powers and their settlers has lost track of the essential understandings of native peoples and most life forms—that you don't shit where you eat, you don't piss where you drink, and you don't mess with mother nature.

At a recent California conference which attempted to generate a dialogue between environmental and ethnic groups, one environmentalist pointed out that there was not enough food in the world to feed everyone the North American diet. This of course does not mean that there are too many people or too little food. It means that the North American diet is part of what is killing the planet. Vast areas of the planet have long been turned over for unsustainable monoculture, to raise beef, sugar, coffee, tobacco, coca, in an attempt to satisfy the seemingly insatiable appetites in the metropolitan centers of the empire. The very survival of the people indigenous to those colonized lands has mattered only insofar as their labor has been needed to exploit them.

But colonialism is not simply something that great powers like the U.S. visit on the far corners of the globe. It is a system which exists within daily life inside the U.S. itself. It is reproduced not only in the conditions of existence in the inner cities, the farmworker shanties, the colonias on the U.S. side of the border with Mexico, the Native American reservations, but in the totality of the economic and social system. Thus, wealth is extracted from internally colonized peoples and wastes are dumped on them. To sustain benefits for the few, the system must loot from the many, from the planet, from the future. This cannot go on much longer. The lesson could have been learned earlier; perhaps when, after stealing Oklahoma from the indigenous people, the Euro-Americans cleared the forests, stripped the topsoil and turned a paradise into a dust-bowl through a self-induced drought. But it must be learned now.

Vigilante Attacks on Environmentalists

One of the most important aspects of an anti-racist, anti-colonialist approach to environmental issues is that it identifies much more clearly the nature of the enemy and the opposition we will face if we seek to cleanse the environment. Colonialism and racism are not simply bad ideas or practices; they are economic, political, and social relationships which are enforced when challenged. Environmentalists of color are much more aware than many in the mainstream environmental movement of the life or death stakes involved in the environmental struggle. The repressive power of the state, the corporations, and the racist right will be directed against environmental activists or any dissidents who pose a serious challenge to the powers that be.

Over the years, attacks against several environmental activists have made national headlines. But these have been taken up as scandals, rather than as an aspect of the system. The mysterious death of Karen Silkwood, involved in exposing irregularities in handling nuclear materials by Kerr-McGee, eventually became the subject of a Hollywood film. The assassination of Chico Mendes, the defender of the

Amazonian rain forest, has received similar treatment.

The case of Judi Bari and Darryl Cherney, activists with Earth First! and the IWW (Wobblies), also achieved great notoriety. The victims of a 1990 bombing of their car after having received numerous death threats for their work around Redwood Summer, Bari and Cherney were further victimized by a government attempt to portray them as terrorists responsible for the bombing themselves. The FBI was never able to discover or develop any evidence to justify the charges (which were eventually dropped). Photos of the damage to the car, recently obtained through the Freedom of Information Act, show clearly that the bomb went off under the front seat, with Bari and Cherney as the targets, not in the back seats.

Although Bari and Cherney had previously been driven off the road by a logging truck, and although they continue to receive death threats, law enforcement has never gone after the real perpetrators of the attack. Bari, who was a leading proponent of allying the environmental movement with forestry workers who were being victimized by the corporations, and Cherney, who has been a clear voice within Earth First! repudiating racism and sexism, were clearly targeted for their politics, both by the attackers and later by the FBI. Meanwhile, unresolved, their case has been the focus for charges and counter-charges that are having a very negative and divisive effect within the environmental movement and the left in northern California.

Judi Bari has made clear that she believes the attack was motivated by hatred of her as a woman and a feminist, as much as by her environmental activism. This is often the case. A TV news-magazine last year detailed a series of attacks, including rapes, abductions, and physical assaults that were carried out against a group of Florida neighbors, mostly women, who had been trying to deal with environmental problems in their community. Stephanie McGuire and the other women involved in that situation believe their attackers were goons who were probably working for Procter & Gamble, the company responsible for the water pollution plaguing their area.

Dolores Huerta, a leader of the United Farm Workers Union, which has been involved in protecting farm workers and their communities from pesticides and other environmental toxins released by agri-business, was the victim of police brutality in San Francisco, in a beating that destroyed her spleen. The rise of eco-feminism and the development of grass-roots environmental groups among people of color, often led by women, means that this radical environmentalist leadership coming from women will increasingly be the target of the defenders of the status quo.

These cases are only the most publicized of a string of such incidents. The pattern they establish, of an intersection of racism, sexism, and state repression with a violent defense of corporate interests against environmental activism, are all too common. Chicano activists in Colorado annually mark the anniversary of the 1972 murder of Ricardo Falcon, a leading activist in their movement who was killed (by a white racist supporter of George Wallace) while on his way to a conference linking land and water rights struggles in Mexico and the

U.S.

Activists in Puerto Rico and in Hawaii who have protested the role of the U.S. military in environmental destruction have similarly become targets of repression. Angel Rodriguez Cristobal, a Puerto Rican activist who tried to stop U.S. Navy bombing of Vieques, a Puerto Rican island whose ecosystems are being obliterated by its use as a military base, died under mysterious circumstances inside a U.S. mainland prison. Native Hawaiians challenging the despoiling of their land and seas have similarly been harassed and imprisoned. But the tactics used to maintain this kind of colonial domination inevitably are also reproduced within the U.S. itself.

Some examples:

- The Arkansas home and office of a director of Greenpeace USA's Toxics campaign, Pat Costner, was destroyed in an arson fire. Costner's irreplaceable 30-year collection of material about toxic contamination of the environment was destroyed in the fire.

- Betty and Garry Ball of the Mendocino Peace Center were physically attacked by The Stompers, a racist hate group that supports the timber industry. The Stompers, also involved in threats against Judi Bari, tried to overturn the car the Balls were sitting in.

- Karen Pitts, a whistle-blower at the Rocky Flats nuclear plant in Colorado, one of the worst contamination sites in the U.S., has been the victim of a shooting and an attempted arson. Her husband, who continued to work at the plant, was the target of ongoing harassment. Another whis-

222

tle-blower there, Jackie Beafer, became the victim of blatant sexual harassment at the plant. They believe the union was part and parcel of the attempt to isolate them. The union local president was hired as a manager by the company.

- Native American activists attempting to defend their land and environment have often been the victims of violent racist attacks. In Wisconsin, the Menominees and others have been targeted by PARR (the misnamed "Protect American Rights and Resources"), which has hooked up with the Populist Party, Posse Comitatus types, and other shadowy groups that have shot at and attacked native people engaged in treaty-protected fishing.

- Lisa and Gene Lawhorn, environmental activists in Oregon, were also the victims of vigilanteism and harassment. Gene, a worker in a forest products mill, was the target of threats, harassment, and violence at both work and his union for opposing the clear-cutting of ancient forest lands. Lisa, with a bumper sticker on her car reading "Justice for Judi Bari," was twice driven off the road by logging trucks.

- Marlene Stevens and Terri Johnson, involved in fighting a toxic waste incinerator in Phoenix, Arizona, were the victims of police abuse after they resisted being barred from a public hearing on the project. They were zapped three times with stun guns, and driven out into the desert for several hours in the back of a paddy wagon before being taken to the police station and booked.

The Highlander Center in Tennessee, an organizing institute with a 60-year history of involvement in labor, civil rights, and environmental struggles, has agreed to serve as a clearing-house for reporting threats and violence against environmental activists. A conference held there on the subject laid the groundwork for an environmental harassment support network. For more information, contact the Highlander Center, 1939 Highlander Way, New Market, TN 37820; tel.: 615-933-3443.

To develop the strength to withstand such attacks, it is necessary to develop an environmental politics that unites with the people who daily contend with such circumstances of repression and environmental degradation. Hopefully, it is not yet too late to learn the lesson, to embrace an economics, politics, and ecology of de-colonization that can liberate the colonizers as well as the colonized, and the earth itself.

This requires more than half-measures or simply stronger regulations. It means that environmentalists must embrace the cause of self-determination and recognize the leading role and clearer insights into the system being put forward by people of color, for whom the environmental struggle is part of an encompassing liberation movement against the totality of oppression.

The despoiling of the environment would have been impossible without the power relationship of the dominator and the dominated. It cannot be overcome without breaking that relationship, by empowering the oppressed to control their own lives and nations, and by stripping the unjust power from those who seek power over others and over nature.

Racist, Sexist, Anti-Gay

The Convergence of the Racist Right and the Christian Right

T he Nazi mass murder of homosexuals in the death camps of the Third Reich, symbolized by the pink triangle assigned to gay concentration camp inmates by Hitler's regime, is fairly well known. Less widely discussed, outside of gay liberation circles, is the fact that a flourishing gay rights/gay liberation movement existed in Germany prior to the rise of fascism. Along with Jews and Romani, and along with activists in the German feminist, socialist, and anarchist movements and other advocates of free thought and social transformation, the organized gay movement was one of the targets of the growing power of Nazi ideology and repression. The books which the Nazis burned included gay literary efforts and studies, along with the works of Jewish authors and scientists, and communist writings.

The parallel to current political developments is more than disturbing. The Nazis, like the new right today, waged a fierce ideological struggle against feminism and women's rights. Hitler outlawed abortion and criminalized gay sex, and proposed the slogan "Kinde, Kuche, Kirche", (children, kitchen, church) as the correct parameters for women's role. The Nazis portrayed open homosexuals as key examples of the "decadence" destroying Aryan purity through the efforts of Jews and Bolsheviks.

The Nazis, then as now, did not spring forth without antecedents or roots. Nazi views are extreme expressions of the repressive forces and tendencies of the pre-existing society. It's important to understand the growing convergence of the Christian right with openly racist and fascist forces in campaigns against gay and women's rights, and the troubling consequences this trend foreshadows. This is not in the expectation that such exposes will bare the Christian rightists as "un-American radicals" who will then be rejected by the population at large, but in the hope that such an understanding will arm a movement for social change with weapons of cultural and political criticism. In the same regard, it's also necessary to examine some of the negative effects of racism in shaping the predominant response of the gay movement to these realities.

Today, we tend to demonize and exceptionalize the Nazis because of the horrors they caused. But by doing so, we fail to understand them or how they must be combatted. According to extensive research into the membership files of the German Nazi party, the early Nazi party members, from the '20s until Hitler came to power, were sociologically almost indistinguishable from the rest of German society. They included blue-collar workers and rural and

urban small property holders, and they were, if anything, somewhat more rooted in their communities
than the general population. We sometimes talk of
the "good Germans" as the ones who did nothing to
oppose fascism; but in fact, many of the "good
Germans" were right there in the party from the
start, building fascism.

Hatred of homosexuals did not distinguish the
Nazis from many other Germans; neither did anti-
Semitism nor anti-communism nor national chau-
vinism nor a desire to see Germany take its "rightful
place" among the imperial powers. All these aspects
of the Nazi program were also put forward by other
parties and were shared by broad sectors of the
German population. What distinguished and built
the Nazis was their will to power and their willingness to use force, violence, intimidation, and other
extralegal activity to put their program into practice,
even before they achieved state power.

The Nazis combined the hooligans (disciplining
their thuggishness with uniforms and titles) with the
respected and respectable bigots. Thus, they were
able to build a mass base, align themselves with
anti-democratic forces within the German state itself,
and win the backing of big financiers and industrialists. In the anti-gay campaigns that have revitalized
the radical religious right, providing openings at one
and the same time into both racialist groupings and
mainstream electoral activity, we see the danger of a
repetition of this process in the U.S. today.

For example, acts of homophobic, racist, and
anti-woman violence are on the rise in the L.A. area
and around the country, and the government can't
or won't stop it. According to the 1994 report of the

L.A. County Human Relations Commission, hate crimes last year against gay men, particularly physical assaults, exceeded all other categories, even against Blacks, who have always previously been the predominant victims. An unholy alliance of racists, right-wing religious fundamentalists, and reactionaries in various levels of the government are making common cause around such issues as AIDS, abortion, and opposition to so-called "special rights"— that is, to laws preventing discrimination against gays and lesbians. The public proclamations of neonazis like Tom Metzger of WAR, neanderthals like Congressman Bob Dornan, and "stealth" fundamentalists like Rev. Lou Sheldon and Pat Robertson, are being put into practice in the form of gay-bashings, clinic attacks, and racist violence. These developments have been validated by high-ranking military officers and leading senators and members of Congress.

An examination of anti-gay and anti-woman violence in the U.S. would begin most pertinently not with marginal groups of nazi skinheads, but with the U.S. military. The Tailhook incident in the Navy is too well known to chronicle here, as is the vigorous and outspoken opposition of top military brass even to "don't ask, don't tell" as a policy on gays. This attitude by their military leadership, as well as by the Senate and Congressional leadership who blocked any reform, was not lost on the enlisted ranks. Three U.S. Marines were recently acquitted of brutally beating a gay man, a civilian, in a gay bar. A gay U.S. sailor was killed by his shipmates, one of whom attempted to plead guilty to lesser charges to circumvent a trial. Last year, three sailors beat up a gay man in Ventura County in an unprovoked gay-bashing. In Fayetteville, North Carolina in August 1993, an Army sergeant shouting his opposition to gays in the military went on a rampage, killing four people. Sergeant Kenneth Junior French, armed with two shotguns and a rifle, opened fire apparently at random in a restaurant, striking 11 people before he was wounded and captured. A waitress who escaped said, "He was shouting 'I'll show you, Clinton. I'll show you about gays in the military.'"

Nor can we expect protection from law enforcement agencies, even when they claim to allow or even welcome openly gay cops. The L.A. sheriffs, for example, carried out a vendetta against AIDS activists. An ex-CIA operative on the San Francisco P.D. was recently found to have passed confidential information on members of ACTUP and other progressive groups to a private spy operation. In Texas, state anti-sodomy laws are used to keep gays and lesbians off the police force in Dallas, which uses lie detectors to screen them out. Attitudes within law enforcement, like those within the military establishment, propagate the oppression of lesbians and gay men.

For example, the controversy around the L.A.P.D. that erupted following the videotaped beating of Rodney King included evidence of police homophobia and religious fundamentalism in the top ranks. Then Assistant Chief Robert Vernon came under criticism from the City Council after a local newspaper released transcripts of tapes by Vernon, circulated by a local church, in which Vernon denounced homosexuality, called for women to be submissive to their husbands' "leadership," urged parents to discipline their kids "with a stick" to save them from hell, and referred to police as "ministers of God" who are allowed to use deadly force.

Vernon had issued a memo in 1975 which was L.A.P.D. policy for 17 years, though a statement saying that no discrimination will be tolerated finally replaced it. Vernon's earlier memo stated that "there is no area sacred from the homosexual when it comes to furthering their insurgent ideas.... Homosexuals have a corrosive effect on their fellow employees because they attempt to entice normal individuals to engage in perverted sexual practices.... The disqualification of applicants based on homosexual conduct must be continued."

Critics at the time also questioned then Chief Daryl Gates's ability to determine Vernon's fitness, and whether his religious views had affected his job, noting that Gates's wife attended Vernon's church, as did many police officers. At least two cops charged that they were coerced into attending, with the threat of being frozen out for promotions. It was also disclosed that prior to carrying out orders to arrest Operation Rescue blockaders who were shutting down a women's clinic, Vernon had consulted with elders of his church to seek their permission.

Such views of top leadership were apparently reflected in L.A.P.D. activity at the street level and within the precinct houses. Jon Davidson, the senior staff counsel for gay and lesbian rights at the local ACLU, said that "lesbians and gay men have been among those singled out for assault and unequal enforcement" by the L.A.P.D. Roger Coggan, the legal services director at the Gay and Lesbian Community Services Center, reported that the agency had received 60 reports of police misconduct against lesbians and gays during 1991–92, almost one in every six of the anti-gay hate crimes reported to them over that period. Gay and lesbian activists also testified harshly about police practices to the Christopher Commission formed in the wake of the King beating to investigate police abuse and how the department and the city handle it. The Commission documented numerous homophobic, anti-woman, and racist attitudes expressed by L.A. cops over their patrol-car computer terminals. Fights between gay men, for example, were called "NHI"—No Humans Involved.

The department was also successfully sued by a former officer, Mitch Grobeson, who claimed he was harassed internally so severely after he was "outed" as a gay man by a sheriff's deputy, that he had been forced to quit the L.A.P.D. despite having been once personally commended by Chief Gates. Grobeson blamed the department's homophobia on the Chief and Vernon. In refusing to recruit open gays to the force, Gates was quoted as saying, "Who would want to work with one, anyway?" Shortly before retiring, Gates told another local police chief, head of the neighboring Monterey Park force, that "gays are evil, and do evil."

In his law suit, which was joined by several anonymous officers, Grobeson charged that the department allowed both harassment of gay cops and police brutality against gay and lesbian civilians that was covered up with complicity from the top. Grobeson sought to expose the brutal beating of a gay man by a cop in a mixed Latino and gay area east of Hollywood, at a 1985 street fair that had become an annual event to promote understanding in the diverse neighborhood. He told the press that Vernon "instructed the L.A.P.D. to destroy evidence against the officer" involved. Grobeson recently won his suit against the department in 1993. Yet as this book was being prepared, the L.A.P.D. was once again being sued for harassment by several other gay officers, one year after it responded to Grobeson's lawsuit with promises of non-discrimination.

Since the cops can be part of the problem, the targets of racist, sexist, and homophobic attacks must begin to rely on our own efforts, unite our forces, establish our own political momentum and agenda. The racists and reactionaries already have a broad social and political agenda, and they are uniting and recruiting. In San Diego, for example, Rev. Dorman Owens, the same fundamentalist minister whose group buzzed the Gay Pride parade with an airplane two years in a row, was convicted in a bombing conspiracy against a women's clinic. In Simi Valley, the same white supremacists who tried to mobilize around the Rodney King beating were also associated with nazi boneheads involved in fag-bashing and attacks on immigrants and Jews. According to the Bay Area Coalition for Our Reproductive Rights, the Evangel Christian Fellowship, one of the chief organizing centers for Operation Rescue of California, was also heavily involved in the racist anti-immigrant state ballot initiative, Prop. 187 on the November 1994 ballot, designed to deny all medical care and education to so-called "illegals," and to turn all teachers and health care providers into agents of the INS. So this convergence is taking place across a spectrum of issues, but anti-gay activity remains one of the strongest unifying factors.

Anti-gay rhetoric and organizing leads to anti-gay violence. Several activists in the 1993 March on

232

Washington for gay and lesbian rights and liberation returned to their cities of origin to find their homes vandalized or torched. In Washington,D.C. itself, several gay activists were accosted at gunpoint after the end of the march. In San Diego, dozens of Mexican immigrants, many of them transvestite male prostitutes, have been killed or attacked in the past two years. In Oregon, during the campaign around the anti-gay Ballot Measure 9, an arson fire set by nazi skinheads took the lives of a Black lesbian and a gay man. In Hartford, Connecticut in August 1993, two "straight" men, brothers Johnny and John L. Pittman were convicted of a hate crime for raping a gay man out of bigotry against gays (!). In Los Angeles, a group called the Blue Boys (apparently for wearing Dodgers caps and colors) terrorized a gay neighborhood for several months three years ago, attacking gay men with baseball bats. In 1992, the name resurfaced at Cal State Northridge, in an L.A. suburb, in a series of anti-gay flyers that promised rewards for physical assaults on gays.

Such phenomena are international in scope. Gays were among the first targets of nazi bonehead groups in England and Germany. In Brazil, official figures show one homosexual being killed every five days. Luiz Mott of the Gay Group of Bahia says gay rights activists have identified a dozen "extermination groups," including a nazi skinhead gang that wears t-shirts reading "Death to Homosexuals." A U.S. judge recently ruled that homosexuals were a persecuted group in Brazil and granted a gay Brazilian man asylum in the U.S. because of a well-founded fear of oppression in his homeland.

Despite such horrors, significant sectors of the

U.S. state and society continue to uphold anti-gay positions. Two openly gay teachers were forced to resign from a Burbank, California junior high at the end of the 1991 school year, and when queer activists protested, some local residents screamed at the demonstrators that the nazis hadn't gone far enough. Subsequently, the Citizens for Excellence in Education, a group which attempts to get Christian rightists onto school boards, has been organizing in the city. They tried to make abortion an issue in the school board election and opposed the provision of supportive counseling for gay students.

In New York City, Pat Robertson's Christian Coalition has more openly been trying to take control of local school boards by allying fundamentalist Protestant churches, the Catholic Church, and some conservative ministers around a common opposition to a curriculum that included tolerance of gays. Robertson's coalition was able to take control of a handful of local school boards (although openly gay candidates and liberal supporters of the "Rainbow Curriculum" were able to win in a number of others.) At this writing, two-thirds of the U.S. Senate voted in favor of a rightist amendment to an education bill that would deny federal funds to any school district that supported a positive view of homosexuality.

Unchallenged, in fact encouraged by political and religious leaders, anti-gay attacks become more widespread and affect general attitudes. Polls have shown, for example that as hysteria over AIDS diminished in the general population, attitudes actually hardened against people infected with or suspected of HIV—so-called "high risk groups" like gay men and inner-city drug users.

Meanwhile, various white supremacists and Christian radical rightists have seen in the gay issue a chance to legitimize themselves through association with more mainstream "conservatives." On the same day in the fall of 1992, David Duke, the "former" Klansman and Nazi turned perennial candidate, and Randall Terry, the anti-abortion extremist who runs Operation Rescue, declared their opposition to allowing open gays in the military. In August 1994, a Christian Identity conference in Bakersfield, California featured Louis Beam of the KKK, John Saunders III (stage name John Quade), anti-gay, anti-abortion supporter of Christian Reconstructionist J. R. Rushdoony, and right wing California State Senator Don Rogers. In their wake, even more openly racist and violence-prone figures have also been riding the wave.

Consider these recent developments:

- In Oregon, the Coalition for Human Dignity and other progressive groups have repeatedly documented the links between the Oregon Citizens Alliance (OCA)—until recently, the official state affiliate of Pat Robertson's National Christian Coalition, and the driving force behind the state's anti-gay electoral activity—and more nakedly racist and anti-Semitic groups. The OCA has received money from the Christian Patriots, a Christian Identity–oriented group (Christian Identity preaches that Jews are Satan-spawn, that people of color are pre-Adamic [sub-human], and that Aryans are the true Israelites, with America their promised land). The leader of the Christian Patriots in Oregon is a supporter of "Bo" Gritz and notorious for his anti-Semitic views.

WHITE LIES • WHITE POWER

According to the CHD, the featured speaker at an August 1993 Portland conference of the Traditional Values Coalition (headed by a former OCA leader) was David Barton, a Christian Reconstructionist who calls for the death penalty for gays and has appeared at Christian Identity gatherings along with such open and violent racists and anti-Semites as Texas Klan leader Louis Beam. The CHD also reports continuing harassment of lesbian activists in Portland by nazi skinheads from the American Front. Lesbians' home addresses have been made public by the Gay Agenda Resistance computer bulletin board system, which features messages from anti-gay, racist, and anti-semitic users.

Opponents of Christian/racist right attacks on gay rights have been targeted for violence. Organizers of the "No on Ballot Measure 9" campaign reported numerous instances of cars with "No on 9" bumper stickers being driven off the road. In September 1992, at the height of the campaign, the home of a Black lesbian and a gay man, Hattie May Cohens and Brian Mock, was firebombed by neo-nazis, in an attack that combined racism, homophobia, and oppression of the disabled. In June 1993, Sean Edwards, Leon Tucker, and Phil Wilson, all in their 20s, were convicted and sentenced for the murder and arson. Edwards, who received the longest sentence, 25 years, had previously been convicted for racist vandalism of a cemetery and possession of a sawed-off shotgun.

• In 1994, after Oregon OCA leader Lon Mabon traveled to Nevada in an unsuccessful attempt to put a similar anti-gay initiative on the ballot in that state, nazi bonehead Justin Slotto was arrested for stabbing to death gay rights leader William Metz.

236

Police testify that Slotto, a white supremacist, stabbed Metz in the back, cut him more than 20 times, and tried to carve a swastika on him.

- In Colorado, Christian Identity leader "Reverend" Pete Peters was found liable for violating fair election practices laws for putting money raised by his "church" into anti-gay electoral campaigns. Peters, some of whose followers were involved in the execution-style slaying of Jewish talk show host Alan Berg after he criticized Peters' guest, Jack Mohr of the Christian Patriots, has been a leading backer of "Bo" Gritz, the former Green Beret who ran for President on the Populist Party ticket.

Another open racist involved with the Colorado "Family Values" campaign to adopt an anti-gay initiative (which succeeded where Oregon's failed) was white supremacist Richard Barrett. Barrett, whose Mississippi-based "Nationalist Movement" has provided paramilitary training to nazi skinheads, set up a Colorado chapter which made the anti-gay referendum its top priority. Local Klan leader Shawn Slater, a "former" nazi skinhead who claims to have abandoned violence since joining national KKK leader Thom Robb's Knights, has also tried to associate himself with the anti-gay cause. In the summer of 1994, Slater split from Robb and aligned with a more militant Klan faction.

As in Oregon and Nevada, such anti-gay organizing has led to violence. Ruth Williams, a psychotherapist who had displayed a pro-gay rights bumper sticker on her car, was beaten unconscious in her office. Crosses were cut into her skin and Christian slogans spraypainted on the walls of the office, which was ransacked. The head librarian at Colorado College, who had displayed a "Vote No on 2" placard in his yard, had his tires slashed, windows smashed, and a shot fired into his car. A book seller involved with the Citizens Project, a main group opposing the anti-gay initiative, had his business repeatedly vandalized. As in Oregon, cars with pro–gay rights bumper stickers were run off the road. In one Colorado case, the driver of the other vehicle held up a sign reading "Lesbo" at the woman he had forced off I-25. Practically everyone who wrote letters to the editor of local papers opposing the anti-gay initiative received harassing, anti-gay calls, sometimes death threats.

- In California, the Rev. Lou Sheldon's Traditional Values Coalition has also served as a conduit for linking the Christian Right with the Christian Patriots and Christian Identity racists. When Sheldon condemned the first Orange County gay pride parade several years ago, a number of nazi skinheads showed up and attempted to physically attack marchers. Nazi skinheads have also been seen participating in Operation Rescue–led clinic blockades in Orange County. According to Marta Collier of the Women's Health Action Movement (WHAM!), the head of OR was seen and overheard giving instructions to several nazi skins at a clinic blockade this summer. (He was telling them to be careful not to associate themselves openly with OR.)

California was out front in racist-oriented attacks on gay rights. In the 1980s, neo-nazi Lyndon LaRouche's organization spearheaded two separate ballot drives to attempt to quarantine people with AIDS, and LaRouche's paper provided political justifications for nazi skin attacks on gays. In 1986, at the height of his

group's electoral success, LaRouche backers
formed PANIC (Prevent AIDS Now Initiative
Committee) and twice succeeded in putting measures on the state ballot, though both were
defeated.

A 1987 article in LaRouche's newspaper *New
Solidarity,* signed by LaRouche himself, reported
favorably on "the probability of widespread lynchings
of homosexuals and drug-users by AIDS-terrorized
teenagers.... The potential for violence is brought up
to lynch moods by powerful fears...in which images
of death are linked to sexual imageries. Patterns of
lynchings occur only if the lynchers see themselves
as instruments of popular justice, acting [in the
event of] lawful agencies of government having failed
to deal with a fearful threat."

Other neo-nazi groups also seized on the AIDS
epidemic as a centerpiece for their organizing.
Convicted Birmingham church bomber J.B. Stoner
came to California in the fall of 1987 to preach his
gospel that AIDS is God's gift to the white man, eliminating Jews, Blacks and Hispanics, and homosexuals. He attracted a small crowd, mostly of nazi boneheads, to a speech in Glendale, where his supporters
were far outnumbered by counter-demonstrators
drawn out by PART's first action. It was in this period that a big increase in gay bashings, particularly
by nazi boneheads, was first noted. These brutal
beatings are still continuing. In one recent case in
Orange County, an Asian man was kicked and
stomped nearly to death by nazi boneheads who had
gone to a beach area known to be frequented by
gays, looking for a target for a "queer-bashing."

More recently, the racist Jewish Defense League

Several JDL members came out to an L.A. protest in
August 1993 of the Pope's visit to the U.S. (the JDL
wanted to voice opposition to the beatification of
Pope Pius XII, who never condemned the
Holocaust). But the JDL ended up spending most of
its time screaming anti-gay curses and threats at
the other demonstrators, who were opposing the
church's stands on abortion, gays, and condom use.
Subsequently, the local head of the JDL called the
ACTUP-L.A. hotline, shouting additional curses and
obscenities.

Irv Rubin, the national leader of the JDL, put a
message on his group's telephone hate-line. "ACTUP
is a turn-off.... Earl Krugel, L.A. city chairman of
JDL, told them off in no uncertain terms.... If it's
coming from anti-Semitism, if it's coming from
ACTUP, or neo-nazis, or Blacks, or whatever the
animal may be, they have to realize they have run
into a new Jew in town.... Let every stinking liberal
out there know that ACTUP and all the gay cru-
saders who believe it's in accordance with Judaism
to strike out against the enemies of gay people, that
that's not necessarily true." So along with Blacks,
Arabs, and Jews who don't toe their line, the JDL
has apparently added lesbians and gays to its enemies list, not surprising in that the JDL often seems
to mirror the nazis it claims to oppose.

Progressives must do more than simply expose
and oppose the growing alliance of racist and reactionary forces of all stripes that has been forming
around common anti-gay politics. There is a need
for pro-active support, and a thorough-going critique of the sexual politics of white and male
supremacy. Lesbian and gay liberation are crucial

components of a politics that seeks human liberation, equality, and justice. The right to be free to love and to express one's affections in a non-exploitative way, without repression by the state or society, is vital to everyone, no matter what our sexual orientation or inclinations.

The hostility towards same-sex expressions of desire is rooted in a rigid thought system of sexual differentiation. This ideology in turn is meant to uphold a power differential. A sharp and mutually exclusive line is drawn by male-dominated society between men and women. That in turn supports the notions and practices of male supremacy. Men's definitions of women as "other" are similar to the dehumanization and prejudice that were made necessary by the practice of race-based chattel slavery. Because the biological underpinnings of sexism (again, like those of racism) are actually weak, the fierce institutional suppression of any alternatives is required. Loving relationships and sex between individuals of the same gender have existed in all human societies (and throughout the animal kingdom); but the system of male supremacy has dictated that they be deemed "unnatural" or "sinful."

"Manhood" and "womanhood" are in fact social, cultural, and political constructs erected above the continuum of the biological differences among people; they vary widely from culture to culture and at different points in history. These concepts have been used as a torture rack to force individuals to fit the mold required to maintain white and male supremacy and class society. The identification with the oppressors produced in men because of our complicity in the exploitation of women is one of the system's key support mechanisms. This identification subverts the capacity of the oppressed and exploited, women or men, to struggle creatively and collectively for a better world. At the same time, the mechanisms of "male bonding" function as an effective substitute for human solidarity, thus allowing the creation and maintenance of hierarchical institutions.

We live in one of the most powerful empires in the history of humanity. Its power structures have extended their tentacles not only into every corner of the globe, but into our own beings and consciousness. Yet a chain is only as strong as its weakest link. Love is a tremendous threat to a system based on hate, alienation, and exploitation. Love is the basis for the solidarity and sacrifice that are essential to overcome the exploiters. That is why the system tries so hard to limit, define, and shape our experience of love. This process occurs to those defined as heterosexuals as much as to so-called homosexuals.

It is interesting to note that those terms, when first coined, were both meant to refer to compulsive sexual deviations. The idea that one can or should only love the "opposite sex," is based on the separation of humanity into two sexes, each opposite to the other—that is, one superior and the other inferior. The ability to love regardless of gender is thus an implicit challenge to male supremacy.

However, what is implicit must be made explicit. Gay men are not exempt from complicity in male supremacy, and certainly not from racism or white supremacy. We all, men and women, are capable of internalizing and accepting our own oppression. Many of us identify with our oppressors, granting

them legitimacy and power, and seeing their interests as our own. There is no clear-cut hierarchy of
oppression, no linear ladder on which only those at
the top are guilty of screwing over everyone neatly
ranked beneath them, and thereby benefiting only
themselves. Sexism, homophobia, and sex-role
oppression intersect with other forms of oppression
and exploitation. Male supremacy may predate class
society, private property, and the family. But the
current world historic order dates from the
Columbus era of European invasion and conquest
of the other lands and peoples of the world. It oper-
ates on the basis of white supremacy, incorporates
male supremacy, and functions to allow whole
nations to exploit and oppress other nations.

At the same time, a relatively fluid class structure allows room for individuals from any oppressed
group to attach themselves to and enforce the mechanisms of such power. Individual closeted gay men
have always been welcome within the power structure; a gay movement which seeks only equal rights
for openly gay men to do the same will be succumb-
ing fatally to the white-supremacist status quo.
What's more, it will be doomed to failure. It's impossible to end homophobia and sex-role oppression without rocking the boat, yet the predominant tendency
in the gay movement seems to want to do just that.
The misguided notion of making "gays in the military"
a central strategy and demand of the gay movement
is the clearest recent example of this tendency.

Sam Nunn, Colin Powell, and the Joint Chiefs
of Staff may have been more clear-thinking on this
issue than gay activist spokesmen, who wanted to
drape themselves in the flag and pretend that every-

thing could go on just as it had been if closeted gays in the military were allowed to express themselves. Maybe we should believe Senator Nunn, General Powell, and the brass when they say that the U.S. military (unlike the Canadian, the Dutch, or even the Israeli), cannot accommodate open gays. Given the role of the U.S. military as a prop for world domination and a bulwark of state power domestically as well, with militarism reaching into the schools and shaping our economy and values, the goal of allowing open gays in the military is laudable only to the extent that it would actually do what its governmental and rightist opponents fear—diminish the military's aggressive war-making capacity.

Racist, homophobic, and anti-woman terror must be stopped. We need to build an activist anti-racist, anti-sexist movement; learn more about how we can defend ourselves against these predators; alert the community to neo-nazi propaganda and violence. To do so requires a broad and encompassing, but essentially revolutionary, politics of personal and social transformation.

Front Man for
Facism

"Bo" Gritz and the Racist
Populist Party

Lie down with dogs, get up with fleas. "Bo"
Gritz and his supporters must know the
truth of this bit of country common sense.
Despite the growing body of evidence of Gritz's
deep and enduring links to the white-supremacist movement, some people on the left continue
to pay rapt attention to the former Green Beret
and Populist Party presidential candidate, and to
provide him with air time, coverage, and credibility. Yet as this book is being prepared for publication, Gritz's lieutenants are beginning the
process of organizing his followers and trainees
into Green Beret–style A-teams and B-teams,
surveying them as to their previous military
experience in order to best assign them in Bo's
white citizen's armed forces.

It's necessary to document Gritz's own racist
positions and affiliations, to clarify the neo-nazi
nature of the Populists and Gritz's other affiliations in
the Christian Identity movement, and to expose the

dangerous paramilitary survivalist network of "white state citizens" that Gritz is currently building through his "SPIKE" training (Specially Prepared Individuals for Key Events).

In 1988, Bo Gritz (rhymes with Knights) briefly accepted the nomination to run for vice-president of the United States on the Populist Party ticket; that year the party ran "former" nazi and Ku Klux Klan Imperial Wizard David Duke for president. Gritz had the good sense to resign from the ticket and run for Congress from Nevada in the Republican primaries instead. But he was hooked up with Duke long enough for publicity photos to exist of the two of them together. In 1992, Bo ran as the Populist Party candidate for president himself. Even as neo-nazi David Duke parlayed the credibility he got from his Populist presidential run into electoral success in Louisiana as a Republican, Gritz attached himself ever deeper to the Populist Party and to a network of racist Christian Identity and Christian Patriot groups around the country.

In recent years, Gritz has been trying to re-establish the credibility he lost after his naked self-promotion in the '80s for an abortive "raid" on south-east Asia. He claimed he was going to find and free MIAs supposedly still held captive, and portrayed himself as the model for "Rambo." Then, Gritz directed most of his fund-raising efforts at stalwarts of the Hollywood right, like Clint Eastwood and William Shatner. He also had dealings with Texas billionaire Ross Perot, who was later to swamp Gritz's third party presidential candidacy. But more recently, Gritz has focused some of his speaking and fund-raising activities in California and elsewhere around the country at progressives and others who were concerned about George Bush and the New World Order, trying to tie them in to his "America First" Coalition, along with the Populists and various neo-nazi elements. He continues to get air-time on some alternative radio stations.

Gritz has spoken out about his discoveries of CIA involvement in heroin trading in southeast Asia and his awareness, while heading Green Beret counter-insurgency efforts in Latin America, of similar Agency involvement in cocaine dealing. As a result, he has developed an audience, and to some degree a following, among opponents of U.S. intervention in the Third World, leftists, and even pacifists, who would otherwise be extremely suspicious of his militarism. Representatives of groups such as the Christic Institute once made joint appearances with him. Although some, like Christic, repudiated and denounced his associations with racist extremists, Gritz continues to distribute tapes of their appearances at his Center for Action. Meanwhile, KPFK radio's "Roy of Hollywood" has persisted in allowing Gritz to peddle his apologies for racism unchallenged.

Gritz continues to distribute material from the Christic Institute, John Stockwell, and others as covers for his own views, along with tracts by the anti-Semitic Eustace Mullins. He has made his SPIKE training in ten cities a recruiting ground for the so-called State Citizenship movement, which preaches that the only true citizens are those whose citizenship predates the 14th Amendment (whites), while considering "14th Amendment Citizens" (Blacks and others) to be aliens naturalized by the District of Columbia, which they consider a "foreign power." This is only a slightly more polite version of the epithet for the federal government used by the Order and Metzger: "ZOG" (for Zionist Occupied Government).

Gritz has moved from his former base of operations in Nevada up to Idaho, where his Populist candidacy drew its strongest support, particularly among the ranks of survivalists, retired cops, and Aryan "pilgrims" who have been moving to that state. Gritz is establishing a "Christian Covenant community" there on land purchased on a Native American reservation, as a headquarters for his paramilitary SPIKE teams. He has set up three such communities, known as "Almost Heaven," to opposition from some other local residents.

People drawn to Gritz should be aware that the Populist Party, in spite of its friendly, democratic-sounding name, was an amalgamation of "former" Klansmen, nazis, and other racist far-right-wingers cobbled together in 1984 with the support of Willis Carto, long considered an anti-Semite and Hitler apologist, and his Liberty Lobby. Carto has been involved in a leading role with groups that claim that Hitler got a bum rap for his role in defending "Western civilization," and with one that planned the repatriation of American Blacks to Africa. He was a member of the Populists' National Executive Committee at its inception and for many years thereafter, repeatedly coming out on top in power struggles, though he has had a falling out with Gritz and the current national leadership of the Populist Party, as well as with the holocaust-revisionist Institute for Historical Review.

Let's review the historical record of the modern Populist Party, which twice nominated Gritz for national office. The Populist Party's first presidential candidate in 1984, Wheaties athlete Rev. Bob Richards, virtually ceased campaigning in embarrassment over the racist nature of the party apparatus. Duke, its 1988 nominee, of course had no such misgivings. The party's first chairman, Robert Weems, a former Mississippi KKK leader, described its strategy: "We Populists have adopted a tri-partisan approach...we share with Lyndon LaRouche...within both major parties and through the Populist Party itself." (Lyndon LaRouche is another neo-nazi political figure also backed at one time by Carto, who is now on parole from federal prison.)

Carrying out this strategy, the KKK/Populist David Duke ran in the Democratic Presidential primaries, then in the general election as a Populist, then in a special election in Louisiana as a Republican. He used the notoriety, name recognition, and national fund-raising base he built with the Populists to win a seat in the Louisiana state legislature and espouse his "sanitized" racism. Even after winning office as a Republican in 1989, Duke met again with the Populists, including such stalwarts as Chicago neo-nazi leader Art Jones. Jones later followed Duke's lead and ran in the Republican primary for Congress from Chicago with the backing of Willis Carto's Populist Action Committee (a new grouping, separate from the Populist Party, that Carto established after his falling-out with party leadership).

Ralph Forbes, who ran Duke's Democratic primaries presidential campaign, is another "ex"-nazi and "ex"-Klansman, who later switched parties to run for office in Arkansas as a Republican. While flirting with the Populists, he ran a Christian

Identity–oriented radio ministry called "The Sword of Christ." He recently filed suit to prevent a medical school in his state from teaching about abortions. Forbes continues to be closely associated with Knights of the Ku Klux Klan leader Thom Robb, who recently declared that the KKK intends to train "one thousand David Dukes." Robb himself was forced off the Republican ballot in Arkansas after filing for their nomination to Congress.

Gritz himself has been following this same multi-party strategy. Even after he resigned from the Populist ticket with Duke in 1988 to run in the Republican primary in Nevada, he wrote to the party, "I intend to offer the Populist Party platform in my campaign, and carry it forward in public office." Luckily, he lost in the primary. After the initial disclosure by People Against Racist Terror (PART) and others of his party's nazi links, he suggested his candidacy was run by the America First Coalition, of which the Populists were only a part.

What is the Populist Party platform and who are the Populist leaders? Racism and racists, only thinly disguised. Don Wassall, the Pennsylvania state chairman who became National Executive Director and for now has won a power struggle with Carto—the latest in a series of faction fights over control of party finances—used the party's newspaper, the *Populist Observer*, to reprint explicitly racist material from the National Democratic Front, an avowed white-supremacist group based in Maryland.

Van Loman, who chaired the Ohio chapter of the Populist Party, and ran under its banner for the Cincinnati City Council, was formerly the Grand Dragon of the Ohio Knights of the Ku Klux Klan.

Loman participated in the national Populist gathering which David Duke attended after he won office as a Republican in Louisiana.

Jerry Pope, once the Populist state chair in Kentucky, was an organizer of the National States Rights Party, the segregationist, anti-Semitic grouping led by convicted Birmingham church bomber J. B. Stoner. (Interestingly, when Duke switched to the Republicans and won a seat in the Louisiana legislature, his opponent, endorsed by the "official" Republican apparatus from Reagan and Bush on down, had himself been a member of the racist NSRP.)

In Washington State, in 1989, the United Front Against Fascism (UFAF) held several successful demonstrations against the Populists, thwarting their efforts to obtain ballot status in one county. As a result, anti-racist organizers received death threats. The Christian Sons of Liberty (CSL), an "Identity" group central to the Populist organizing there, put out vicious red-baiting and anti-gay attacks on UFAF leaders. The CSL published home addresses of UFAF organizers, in a clear attempt to foment violence.

In the midwest, the Populists have sought and run candidates from PARR (Protect American Rights and Resources) and given an electoral forum to their effort to abrogate Native American treaty rights. In Oregon, the same Christian Identity and Christian Patriot forces that formed the backbone of Gritz's candidacy were involved in the anti-gay Ballot Measure 9 campaign. Rev. Pete Peters, a backer of Colorado's anti-gay initiative, dedicated his pamphlet "The Death Penalty for Homosexuals is Prescribed in the Bible" to his "friend the Colonel" Gritz.

In California, the Populist Party is cut from the same mold. California has always been one of the strongest state affiliates of the Populists. David Duke raised in California 11% of the funds for his Louisiana legislative race, much of it from among people who had backed his Populist presidential candidacy. Half the money for his gubernatorial campaign came from outside of Louisiana, much of it from California. Southern California leaders of the Populists have included former San Fernando/Simi Valley Klan leader Dennis Hilligoss, and Harbor-area nazi activist Joe Fields (an associate of Duke, local Nazi party chieftain Stan Witek, and Tom Metzger of White Aryan Resistance [WAR]).

Fields was, in fact, a member of the party's National Executive Committee. Fields and his Afrikaner (White South African or "Boer") wife were the two main guests at a neo-nazi gathering in South Central L.A. in February 1992 that nearly precipitated a riot. More recently, the Fieldses participated in August 1994 in a Christian Identity "Jubilation" in Bakersfield, California, along with Texas Klan and Aryan Nations leader Louis Beam, and Christian Reconstructionist philosopher John Quade, a.k.a. John Saunders III.

Behind the Gritz campaign, the Populists became the most active neo-nazi group in southern California, and successfully united a variety of racists in their ranks. Many of these same elements continue to coalesce for Gritz's SPIKE training, which has drawn upwards of 200 people at a series of training sessions around southern California. In 1991, the Populists sponsored several programs in Orange County, one featuring John Tyndall, leader of the neo-nazi National Front in England. Another spotlighted the impeached ex-governor of Arizona, Evan Mecham, whose reactionary forces have allied with fundamentalist preacher Pat Robertson to take over the Republican Party in his home state. Among the participants at that Populist parlay was Kim Badynski, head of the virulent Northwest Knights of the Ku Klux Klan based in Washington State. In Ventura County in southern California and up north in Alameda County, the California Populists have held party meetings to commemorate Adolph Hitler's birthday.

The Populists have a long-range goal, of unifying Christian rightists and Christian patriots, anti-abortionists and anti-Semites, into an apparatus dominated by neo-nazis. With Gritz, they had the added bonus at the same time of coopting or at least disarming progressive forces that would otherwise have exposed and opposed them. Gritz himself made and apparently canceled plans to run for governor of Idaho as his next electoral arena for consolidating his support. He is now focusing instead on the religous nature of his calling, preaching to his followers about visions of Jesus and the approaching end-times.

In a recent SPIKE Team training in Pasadena, Callifornia, Gritz drew nearly 200 people, including Birchers, gun enthusiasts, revisionists, and advocates of the white-supremacist doctrine of "state citizenship." A similar number attended a subsequent training session in the San Fernando Valley. At these SPIKE sessions, Gritz mixes training in weaponry and tactics with instruction on intelligence gathering, proselytizing for his version of Christian Identity, and selling freeze-dried food and other survivalist supplies like reloading equipment.

Gritz's Racist Views and Affiliations

In person, Gritz is a magnetic, charismatic speaker. He is short, barrel-chested, and graying, with the take-charge vitality that befits a man trained to the habit of command in a lifetime of highly-decorated service in the military. People who have gone to hear him speak, suspicious of his military background, have come away impressed by his exposés of government double-dealing and corruption. At a campaign appearance by Gritz in Simi Valley in 1992, he held his audience's attention with ease through more than two hours of off-the-cuff speaking. Gritz combines the political sophistication developed in a couple of decades of clandestine operations with a militant Christian fervor.

In Simi Valley, he lauded Oliver Stone's then-current film, "JFK," and promised to open the Kennedy assassination files if he was elected; he named names of top aides of then President Bush connected to the heroin trade. At the same time, Gritz predicted dire consequences if the U.S. lost its sovereignty and weaponry to the United Nations. He lectured his supporters about not expecting him to work miracles as President, but promised to entirely eliminate income taxation.

About 70% of the overflow crowd of several hundred seemed to be drawn from Christian right and Liberty Lobby circles, but a substantial minority were people who had heard Gritz a couple of nights before on Roy Tuckman's late night show on Pacifica Radio's progressive-oriented KPFK-FM. Many of them were unaware of the extent of Gritz's connections on the racist far right and of the history of the Populists. In his more recent SPIKE training sessions, Gritz has upped the ante considerably, making plans for conducting night landings in fields, air-drops, and a variety of other maneuvers for helping Christian fugitives evade capture by the authorities.

The problem with "Bo" Gritz's Populist candidacy was not one of guilt by association with neo-nazis. Gritz himself has embraced the Populists' politics of anti-Semitism, racism, anti-immigrant hysteria, and anti-gay bigotry. As criticism emerged of the Populists, Gritz claimed in his speaking engagements that he had "cleaned house" since the Duke days. But this was an outright lie, still being circulated by supporters who claim to be libertarians or even anarchists. Joe Fields, for example, the open neo-nazi who headed the Populists in L.A., was also a national officer of the party. What's more, Gritz's connections to racists and anti-Semites extend beyond the ranks of the Populist Party itself.

For example, Gritz was a member of the board of the Populist Action Committee (PAC), established by Willis Carto of the *Spotlight*. Although Carto is on the outs with the current leadership of the Populist Party, accusing them of financial mismanagement, he still publicizes the state affiliates of the Populists while attacking Wassall. He supported Duke's abortive presidential candidacy in 1992 more than Gritz's, and after Duke and Buchanan faltered in the Republican primaries, he backed Ross Perot. An article in *Spotlight*, Carto's paper, implied the Liberty Lobbyists became disgruntled with Gritz when he declined to follow their suggestion to run first in the Democratic primaries. Gritz claims that he only joined Carto's Populist Action Committee as a favor to Tom Valentine, the Liberty Lobby's radio host, and has never been actively involved with it, but he said he "doesn't care" if they wanted to continue using his name. He is no longer listed.

While many of Gritz's southern California public speaking appearances in 1992 seemed directed at progressives, the bulk of his organizing and speech-making since has been carried out through the apparatus of the Christian Identity movement, which preaches that Anglo-Americans are the true "chosen people" of the Bible, that Jews are satan-spawn, and that non-whites are "pre-Adamic," that is, sub-human. The Coalition for Human Dignity in Portland, Oregon has documented the involvement of so-called Christian Patriot and Identity churches in the Gritz campaign in that state, as well as participation by nazi skins. In January 1992 Gritz spoke at a dinner of the Christian Patriot Association in Oregon. His appearance drew an additional 250 people to hear him speak after the dinner, including nazi bonehead Bob Heick, leader of the American Front racist skins.

Gritz has been closely tied to the Rev. Pete Peters, a national leader of Christian Identity based in Ft. Collins, Colorado. Gritz has spoken at Peters' "Scriptures for America" Rocky Mountain Bible Retreat, also attended by such noted anti-Semites as "Colonel" Jack Mohr and by KKK defense attorney Kirk Lyons.

Lyons' Patriot Defense Foundation has represented nazi boneheads and the Order white-supremacy underground sedition defendants, and has coordinated Tom Metzger's appeal of his liability for the nazi skin killing of an Ethiopian refugee.

Lyons rushed to Waco, Texas to offer support to David Koresh in his stand-off with federal agents, urging the U.S. to allow someone like Gritz to negotiate a settlement, as he had in a similar shoot-out and stand-off in Idaho (see below). Gritz has spoken at similar Christian Identity gatherings in the northwest, in Nampa, Idaho, and the southeast, in North Carolina, where he has shared the rostrum with neo-nazis. A recent program in Montana in defense of a white-supremacist "tax resister," Red Beckman, included Gritz along with a Montana KKK leader who is active in the campus Young Republicans.

The connection of Gritz to Mohr and Peters is particularly striking because the two were part of the incident which precipitated the murderous birth of the Order or "Bruder Schweigen," a neo-nazi underground, in the mid-1980s. Richard Mathews and David Lane, the founders of this clandestine, paramilitary outfit, hooked up at Peters' La Porte–based "church." And it was the humiliation of Peters and Jack Mohr, a guest of Peters in Colorado, by Denver talk show host Alan Berg, which prompted the Order conspirators to execute Berg and initiate their reign of racist terror. Mohr, meanwhile, promoted the Populist Party from its inception, through his paramilitary network, the Christian Patriots Defense League.

Peters briefly denounced Gritz, as did Jack Mohr, after Gritz declared at a speech in L.A. that he would put himself in harm's way as President to defend the rights of gays. Carto has similarly criticized Gritz for telling *High Times* magazine that he would respect the decriminalization of marijuana on a state's rights basis. At one point, Gritz liked to use the example of his home state, Nevada, which has legalized gambling, and in many counties prostitution, as an example of the approach he would take for how the government should deal with sin, and this alienated some of his Christian supporters. Subsequently, beginning even during the campaign at an appearance in San Diego, and increasingly and more stridently since, Gritz has called for the biblical penalty for homosexuality (death). This is the theme of one of Peters' most important propaganda pieces.

In a speech to Peters' retreat as he began his presidential campaign, Gritz acknowledged that the crucial money to print his self-published autobiography, *Called to Serve*, came from Rev. Peters. *Called to Serve* spells out Gritz's own far-right views pretty clearly. He refers to the "Rockefeller/Rothschild" Federal Reserve system as being controlled by "seven Jewish families." This is not a momentary aberration or a slip of the tongue. At his Call for Action '90 conference in Nevada, Gritz featured the anti-Semitic views of Eustace Mullins in analyzing the Federal Reserve, and he distributes the works of Mullins, who was a supporter of Ezra Pound and the Italian fascists and believes the Reserve Bank is part of a Jewish conspiracy for world domination. Reflecting his Christian Identity beliefs, Gritz refers to America in *Called to Serve* as "the new Zion," and white Christians as "the gathering tribes of Israel."

As the heat increased on Gritz because of these racist beliefs and associations, he tried to distance himself from them. Gritz acknowledges that Mullins made "off color remarks about Jews" at Freedom Call '90. Gritz claims that he himself didn't hear the remarks, as if that absolved him of responsibility.

Front Man for Facism

He continues to circulate tapes of the speech and Mullins' book on the Federal Reserve system. In response to questioning, Gritz admitted that Peters "probably thinks white people are better than Black people and that most Jews are bad."

Gritz, when pressed, acknowledged problems of racism among the Populists. He recounted how at a national Populist convention in Orange County, where he agreed to accept the party's nomination, someone came up to him and asked, after seeing a photo of Gritz's Amerasian children, if they didn't want to go home. "I'm slow on the uptake and by the time I realized he meant my kids should go to Asia, he was gone," Gritz has said. He also talks about an incident that occurred while he was speaking at a Populist event in Florida. When "a Black Muslim stood up and asked how he could spread my message in his community," Gritz referred him to the Florida Populist leader, who said that Blacks would have to form their own party, because the Populists were for whites only. Gritz says that he disassociated himself from the Florida Populists as a result. But if Gritz divorced every racist state and national apparatus of the party, he would have to abandon the party entirely.

At his Simi Valley appearance, Gritz made much of his personal lack of prejudice as a soldier, having trusted his life to comrades in arms of all religions and nationalities. Gritz condemned David Duke for his nazi activities. He reminded his listeners that his own father had died fighting the swastika during World War II. Gritz said that his understanding of Christianity as the basis for America meant upholding freedom of conscience.

But even in supposedly moving away from the racists and Populists, Gritz has not really changed his spots. In Simi Valley, Gritz unveiled his new America First Coalition as the umbrella for his candidacy. His platform, labeled "the Bill of Gritz," supports only the Constitution and the Bill of Rights. The platform calls for rescinding any other amendments not consistent with the states' rights orientation of these documents, which Gritz calls "divinely inspired." Effectively, this means returning to the pre–Civil War form of government and society. For example, Gritz wants to rescind the popular election of U.S. Senators, making them representatives of and chosen by state legislatures, as they were originally. At the 1994 Bakersfield Jubilation put on by the Christian Identity *Jubilee* newspaper, the latest version of this theme appeared as a call for a "refounding" amendment, which in line with Gritz's thinking is designated as the eleventh amendment to the Constitution.

At Gritz's Simi Valley presidential campaign speech, there were newspapers on the front table from "The Sovereign Advisor," describing itself as a "political movement to restore states rights and state citizenship." This movement specifically distinguishes the "White citizens" of the states from the (African American) 14th amendment citizens of the federal government, whom it considered resident aliens. This continues to be one of the central aspects of Gritz's SPIKE training. At a July 1994 gathering, Gritz described with pride his daughter's interest in becoming a "State Citizen." Gritz couched his opposition to George Bush and the New World Order in the apocalyptic terms that are common on the Christian right. This is even more evident in his current attacks on Clinton. He sees the Universal Product Code and a recent L.A. decision to require micro-chip identification of pit bulls as the "mark of the beast" from the biblical Book of Revelations. He predicts that with the collapse of the Soviet Union, we are nearing a "synthesis" of capitalism and communism into a globalism that will usher in the rule of the anti-christ and the end times.

In opposing Bill Clinton's globalism, Gritz feels less need for a "progressive" cover than he donned against Bush; thus the increasingly open move towards paramilitary survivalism, anti-Semitism, and racism. He predicts, for example, that Clinton's health care reform will be the mechanism by which the "mark of the beast" micro-chips will be implant-ed in humans, calling forth the necessity for defen-sive violence by Christians.

Gritz depicted his own 1992 candidacy as the last peaceful chance to avert catastrophe. "The New World Order is like an onrushing train, but derailing trains is something I'm very good at," he declared to the strongest applause of the evening in Simi Valley. In 1992, he said he ran for office rather than fight guerrilla warfare, but he admitted even then that "honestly, I'd rather do it the other way, because that's what I've been trained for all my life and what I feel more comfortable with." He promised to give the constitutional, electoral route one last chance.

Asked whether his candidacy was serious, since he was only on the ballot in a few states, Gritz replied, "Dead serious. If we don't take Capitol Hill by the ballot in 1992, then by 1996 we will be defending our rights with the bullet against [the]

New World Order." With his SPIKE teams and training, Gritz is moving rapidly and effectively to put
this into practice. He is training people to view their
communities and surroundings as "terrain," and to
become couriers, fighters, suppliers, or auxiliaries
under his political-military leadership. He now predicts that Bill Clinton's 1996 reelection will be the
last constitutional election, conveniently pushing
zero-hour some six years into the future.

Racist views were also reflected and expressed
in Gritz's own campaign literature for his presidential candidacy, which were very similar to the
Populist Party positions he sometimes claimed to
disavow. In a four-page brochure signed and authorized by Gritz, the ex–Green Beret couched his program less in electoral than in revolutionist terms.
"We can, we will, we must oust 'the' government and
restore 'our' sovereignty. We need a second
American Revolution" [quotation marks in original].
The racist nature of this revolutionism is evident in
the rest of the platform he puts forward. Referring to
his enemy as "seditious bankers" and "satanic globalists," Gritz pledges to "derail their plans and send
them back into the abyss."

His platform was full of xenophobia and racism.
"It's time to return America to the Americans...halt
the legal and illegal immigration that is turning
America into a Third World country...end affirmative
action...end this country's decadent, degenerate
ways. I've spent my life fighting for America, and
now it's time to fight again. Will you be part of my
grassroots army?"

This militaristic rhetoric, wrapped in thinly-
veiled code-words for anti-Semitism, racism, sex-

ism, and homophobia, is an invitation to his followers to engage in cross-burnings, gay-bashings, and vandalism. Opposing legal immigration on racialist grounds is another kettle of fish even from demagogues like California Governor Pete Wilson, and justifies the charge of racism. Nor did Gritz really try to separate himself from the Populist Party as a whole. He specifically tried to develop "coat-tails" in his campaign literature, calling on his backers to support other Populist candidates for state and local offices.

In the midst of his campaign, Gritz injected himself into a stand-off in Idaho between federal marshals and white supremacist Randy Weaver, who refused to appear to face charges of selling illegal weapons to undercover operatives. Gritz revealed his true colors when he flashed the nazis' Hitler salute to a group of nazi boneheads and Aryan Nations sympathizers who had gathered to support Weaver. Gritz later chose to deny it on a subsequent appearance on Roy Tuckman's show on KPFK in Los Angeles. Gritz put himself forward as a "negotiator" because Weaver was a former associate of his in the Green Berets. He prayed with Weaver to his white-supremacist Christian Identity god, Yahweh, and arranged for him to surrender. Subsequently, Gritz has attempted to cloud his activity behind a facade of conspiracy theories, claiming on KPFK that Weaver was targeted by the government for what he knows from his Special Forces experience.

But Weaver was charged with criminal activity, selling sawed-off shotguns; whatever anti-establishment support he may enjoy in Idaho or elsewhere does not justify the way he endangered the lives of his family, or the deaths of his wife, his son, and a federal officer, which his actions and government counter-measures caused. The equally criminal actions of federal agents, which led to Weaver's acquittal, are to be condemned. But they shouldn't blind us to Weaver's, and Gritz's, racist politics.

Gritz has also been denying in radio interviews that he gave the nazi "sieg heil" salute, saying that he was only waving. But TV footage of the scene clearly shows Gritz giving the stiff arm salute to the nazi-skins, and he is quite audibly heard to say that "Randy" (Weaver) asked him "to give this salute and said that you would understand what it means." This was met with lusty cheers and returned salutes from the crowd. Gritz also defended the nazi-skins on the scene to reporters as misunderstood and well-meaning patriots. Gritz, who once proclaimed his opposition to David Duke for using the swastika, may be embarrassed by what he himself did in Idaho. But he only compounded his outrageous action by lying about it, in classic nazi style.

Gritz suffered a number of political setbacks as his affiliations became known, including the loss of the American Independent ballot line in California (which went to Howard Phillips of the U.S. Taxpayers' Party, another far-right grouping that has also been tied to the miltant anti-abortion movement and the state militia movement). There were two failed attempts by the Populists to gather up enough people at a rally in Oregon to qualify for the ballot in that state. He tried to parlay his high visibility in the Idaho incident into a boost for his flagging campaign, and apparently felt he had nothing to lose by more naked racism. His actions did

win the support of the Liberty Lobby and its newspaper, the *Spotlight*, which had been expressing
skepticism about his candidacy.

The Weaver incident, and subsequently the
similar stand-off in Waco, promoted much united-
front activity among various Klan, Identity, survivalist, and nazi factions. Gritz won his largest vote
totals in Idaho. In the wake of the election, a number of Gritz's more extreme Mormon followers were
excommunicated from or disciplined by the Mormon
Church. Meanwhile, he has continued to associate
with the Christian Identity movement. In March
1992, a Gritz appearance sponsored by the
Christian Patriot movement in Oregon was canceled,
and another Gritz "training seminar" in Portland
was picketed by the Coalition for Human Dignity.

Racist Populist Party Activity in Los Angeles

The Populists used Gritz's candidacy to step up
their racist organizing all around the country. L.A.,
with which I am most immediately familiar, will
serve as an appropriate case study, as it is one of
ten cities in which Gritz continues to actively conduct his SPIKE training and organization building.
PART, People Against Racist Terror, the group I
work with, learned about the Populists' L.A. organizing and its local anti-immigrant, anti-Semitic activities while distributing a leaflet headed "Bo Knows
the Truth About the Racist Populist Party," at an
appearance by Gritz at the L.A. airport Hilton.

Typically, that event was sponsored not by the
Populists themselves, but by a local "new age" bookstore, Mandala Books, which had been running a
conspiracy lecture series. They invited the Christic

Institute to have a table, after becoming worried about criticism of Bo's racist and rightist affiliations. But the Populists also had a table at the event, and were out in force. They began anti-Jewish harassment of the PART activist who was distributing the exposé of their racist nature, calling him alternately a Communist and an agent of the Mossad (Israeli espionage). Many of the several hundred people drawn to the event were evidently disturbed by the Populists' tactics, and questioned Gritz about his connections with them during the event. Gritz defended the party and was more open about his own rightist politics than he had been previously.

PART exposed and demonstrated outside a gathering of the Populists at the Hastings Ranch public library in Pasadena, California in September 1991. They were meeting to plan a "Borderwatch" demonstration for later in the month. They had a speaker, Ruth Coffey of Long Beach, from a group called Stop Immigration Now, which has been involved with "Light Up the Border" demonstrations in San Diego. Another planned speaker, an Arab doctor who went on a delegation to Jordan led by Nord Davis, a white racist from North Carolina who was opposed to the Gulf War, canceled after PART exposed the meeting and the racist nature of the Populists.

We expressed outrage that the Populists would be promoting anti-immigrant hysteria on the eve of Mexican Independence Day, and propagating anti-Semitism in the midst of the Jewish high holidays. The following month, the Populists met at the library again under heavy police guard. Five counter-demonstrators drawn by InCAR, the International Committee Against Racism, were arrested, and several brutally wrestled down and struck by police in riot gear. (PART wasn't involved in that demonstration.)

A contingent of about half a dozen Black men associated with the Self Determination Committee attended the Populist events in Pasadena. The Self-Determination Committee, run by a Black pseudo-nationalist named Robert Brock, has been prominently allying itself with white supremacists in southern California for several years. Brock's most notable association has been with Daniel Johnson, author of the so-called Pace Amendment to the Constitution, which would restrict U.S. citizenship to people of northern European extraction. Brock, at Johnson Associates, served as the local phone contact for Mississippi-based white supremacist Richard Barrett in his foray into Simi Valley following the police brutality acquittals in the beating of Rodney King. He spoke at the 1994 Jubilation in Bakersfield along with Louis Beam, and at this writing was headed for a speaking engagement in Germany before a neo-nazi outfit there.

The Populists have picked up members from the Pace Amendment Advocates, which closed its Glendale, California headquarters after Johnson moved temporarily to Montana to run for Congress. They also seem to be emphasizing the anti-Jewish and anti-immigrant aspects of their politics to cement an alliance of convenience with Brock's group. Fields tries to cite this opportunistic alliance to claim that the Populists are not racist. In March 1993, Fields and Brock appeared together on a segment of Geraldo Rivera's talk show that claimed to compare "black panthers" and neo-nazis. Fields claimed that there were "good racists" and "bad racists," and he was the former, because he only wanted to protect his own race's survival.

In 1991, told they had to put up a bond to cover the costs of police protection and that they could not exclude people from the library, the Populists, Fields, and Brock tried to meet elsewhere. In November 1991, Brock tried to sponsor a Populist-inspired conference at Pasadena City College featuring himself, Fields, a speaker from the American Independent Party (the right-racist group with ballot status in California which ran both George Wallace and unreconstructed white racist Lester Maddox for president), and a representative of Students for America, the youth group associated with Pat Robertson's Christian Coalition which has been trying to take over the Republican Party. The college canceled, evidently for reasons of security, after the nature of the gathering was exposed. (PCC students had been among those arrested at the library demonstration.) The Populists then tried to secure the meeting hall of the American Friends Service Committee in Pasadena under false pretenses. The AFSC also canceled when they were informed of who was actually trying to rent their facility.

The youth group that was scheduled with the Populists in Pasadena, Students for America, is also organizing on at least one other campus in this area. Students for America (SfA) was set up by Ralph Reed of the Christian Coalition. Although not organizationally affiliated with the Populists, SfA is symptomatic of the dangerous success Gritz and the Populists are having in trying to put themselves at the center of a united front of various right-wing

Christian and Christian Identity group, gun groups, and other fringe groups that they try to influence towards their politics.

The SfA chapter at Cal State University in Northridge, scene of several recent hate incidents directed against lesbians and gays, Jews, and Mexicans, planned to bring embattled L.A. police chief Daryl Gates to the campus to speak in November 1991. Gates canceled at noon on the day of his scheduled appearance, supposedly because of fears of security problems, after students from the BSU, MEChA, and SQUISH, a lesbian and gay group, planned to demonstrate. Stefan Khachaturian, who described himself as a regional coordinator for Students for America, vowed that Gates would come to speak to a private, closed meeting of the group. Students for America is also reportedly organizing in the "Inland Empire" area of Riverside and San Bernardino counties, east of Los Angeles.

In December 1991, Brock was finally able to hold a gathering at PCC which brought Libertarians, Birchers, and others together, and he turned the podium over to Fields to conduct a Populist Party meeting. In February, Brock sponsored an event in south central L.A. at which he claimed to be bringing together Dr. Leonard Jeffries, a Black CCNY professor, and LeGrand Clegg, a Compton office holder and Black activist, with Willis Carto himself, along with Joe Fields' wife Dierdre, Hans Schmidt (the former Hitler Youth member who runs the German American National Political Action Committee), and Mark Weber of the Institute for Historical Review (a former associate of William Pierce, the National

Vanguard leader whose book *The Turner Diaries*, served as the inspiration for the white-supremacist underground, the Order).

In fact, despite Brock's provocative lies, which were taken at face value by the ADL and the JDL, who denounced the event as a hate fest of "Black nazis and white nazis," none of the supposed Black speakers had ever agreed to come. Clegg, who had never even received an invitation, denounced the program and threatened to sue Brock. The Malcolm X Grassroots Movement, supported by PART, held a demonstration that denounced the neo-nazis and "historical revisionists" who did attend, basically Joe Fields and his white South African wife, two of their associates from the IHR, and a distributor of Willis Carto's *Spotlight*.

In April 1994, Gritz himself returned to Pasadena City College to conduct a series of seminars as part of his SPIKE training. Many of the same groupings and individuals were on hand again.

Joe Fields: The Face of the Populists

The head of the L.A. County chapter of the Populists when Gritz ran for President, also then a member of its national executive committee, was Joe Fields. One Joe Fields in national leadership is more than enough to discredit any political formation, and Fields is typical, not exceptional, in the ranks of the Populists. Fields has been a nazi activist of long standing in the L.A. Harbor area. He also became a national "footnote" to the story of David Duke's campaign for governor of Louisiana, after a tape-recorded interview with Fields and Duke was widely circulated. On the tape, made at a gathering of Carto's revisionist Institute for Historical Review, Fields openly asserted his nazi identity and beliefs, such as that the Jews deserve "everything they get, even extermination," while Duke admonished him to be more discreet.

It's ironic that Fields, who boasts on the tape that he would "never deny" he is a nazi, now is denying it, having taken Duke's advice to heart. Fields specifically opposes democracy on the tape, noting that it allows "anything that can claim to be human to vote." His interview is riddled with references to "kikes" and "niggers." Now Fields professes to be a supporter of the Bill of Rights, but on the tape he declares matter of factly that he would suppress any speech that he deems not in the interest of the white race. He ran for State Assembly in 1992 on the American Independent Party ticket (the group that achieved ballot status running George Wallace for president, and which gave its ballot line to Duke and the Populists in 1988). As this book is being prepared for printing, Fields is the American Independent Party candidate for U.S. Congress from the same vicinity.

Like David Duke, Fields has, since his youth, been centered on neo-nazi politics. On the tape he expresses the admiration he has had for Hitler and the nazis ever since he saw war movies as a little boy. While a student at L.A. Harbor College, Fields ran a series of articles in the student newspaper calling the Holocaust a hoax, some taken without attribution from right-wing publications. He was disciplined for meeting on campus with Tom Metzger to plan the distribution of "holo-hoax" material.

Later in the mid-'80s, openly acknowledging his

271

nazi affiliation, Fields joined three other Nazi Party members in wearing swastikas into an Oktoberfest celebration at a German restaurant in Torrance, California. The nazis were expelled after refusing to remove the nazi regalia (and because the bathroom had been vandalized with nazi grafitti on a previous visit). The nazis were verbally abusive to a Black employee of the restaurant. Yet Fields sued, represented by the ACLU, and won. (On the tape, Fields refers to his defenders as the "ACL-Jew.") One of Fields' co-plaintiffs in the swastika case, Nazi Party chieftain Stan Witek, was convicted on weapons and assault charges and more recently for conspiracy for burning three crosses in L.A. along with Tom Metzger during this same period of time. Another, Carter Loven, also stood trial for the same cross-burning along with Richard Butler, head of the Idaho-based Aryan Nations. Fields himself got into a brawl with Jewish activists at a City Council action in 1988 on the swastika case.

After "leaving" the nazis, Fields was closely associated with the Institute for Historical Review. He married a white South African woman he met through the IHR. Like David Duke, who underwent plastic surgery, Fields has changed his appearance; he has trimmed down from a weight that once exceeded 300 pounds. But neither man has changed his white-supremacist politics. After PART began exposing Gritz, Fields, and the Populists, I became the target of harassment by Fields's supporters. Two of the neo-nazis visited my home with a Fields placard, far outside the south bay district where Fields ran on the American Independent Party ticket for the state assembly. Subsequently,

272

PART received a series of calls threatening to hold meetings of the Populists and white nationalists at my home, to track my children at school, and similar threats.

Fields himself, while staging an anti-abortion protest at an October 1992 pro-choice rally in Westwood, accosted me and told me the Populists knew where I lived. The harassing phone calls have continued up to the present. Fields and/or his cohorts shared the information with Tom and John Metzger, who put my home address on their telephone hate-lines, urging their followers to visit and discuss "racist terror" with me. Fields has also hooked up with Mississippi-based white supremacist Richard Barrett, holding joint anti-immigrant activities with Barrett's local lieutenant, Jim Jones, most recently a 1994 gathering at the Torrance library.

"Progressive" Apologists for Gritz

Despite this continuing history of white-supremacist involvement by both Gritz and the Populists, Gritz's material has been reprinted and promoted by the progressive-oriented conspiracy catalog from Prevailing Winds Research in Santa Barbara. The Prevailing Winds promo for Gritz's literature includes a pamphlet by long-time anti-Semite Eustice Mullins. Craig Hulet, a.k.a. K. C. DePass, urged leftists to unite with Gritz against Bush and the New World Order. Today, Hulet denounces Gritz as "a clown." Yet in 1992, when it was vital to expose Gritz's racist beliefs and affiliations, Hulet urged the left to disregard or mute criticisms of Gritz, claiming such criticisms really come from George Bush and the "globalists." Gritz returned the favor by promoting a Hulet meeting in Seattle in October 1991.

An earlier draft of this exposé criticized the Christic Institute for allowing itself to be used to give Gritz credibility, at the same time that it presents itself as an anti-racist organization. Subsequently, Christic disassociated itself from Gritz and his Populist candidacy. On a radio appearance on KPFK, Father Bill Davis of Christic credited material they had received from PART with helping to alert them to the problem. Fr. Davis says he nearly walked out of Gritz's Freedom Call '90 program, and in retrospect is sorry he didn't.

In another example of the cooptation of the left by the racist right, progressives associated with Vox Populi, an attempted anti-intervention coffee-house in the Venice area, helped a local activist who calls himself "Tom Reveille" to start up a "pirate" radio station, a mini-transmitter not covered by the FCC. Reveille turned out to be a follower of Willis Carto. He received funds with which to continue broadcasting from Carto, and devoted his air time to questioning the Holocaust. Reveille has admitted meeting with Joe Fields and with open members of the Nazi Party.

The FCC shut down Reveille's station last year, and the ADL has protested some allegedly anti-Semitic programming on KPFK to the FCC (resulting in a decision by the station to cancel some Black programming while leaving Gritz's acess to airtime untouched). PART does not support either of these moves; the FCC doesn't protect free speech, but only enforces corporate control of the airwaves.

The "new age" movement is another area where

Gritz, the Populists, and other racists have been recruiting. The Alexandria II bookstore in Pasadena has held a book-signing party for Gritz to peddle *Called to Serve*. It has distributed *Phoenix Express,* a bizarre "new age" publication with supposedly "channeled" writing from space aliens that support Gritz and have regurgitated the vicious anti-Semitic forgery *Protocols of the Elders of Zion.* We have heard of this paper, now renamed *Phoenix Liberator,* being circulated in the San Francisco area and in Madison, Wisconsin to new age and left bookstores. Mandala Bookstore in Santa Monica, despite expressing misgivings about the Populists, continued to sponsor Gritz and other similar speakers, mixed in with John Stockwell or Daniel Sheehan as if there were no distinction. George and Deseree Green, of the *Phoenix Liberator* have run into trouble with the law in Nevada, where a series of dummy corporations they set up were accused of defrauding investors who turned to the Greens for fiscal advice from the alien Commander Hatonn. Green appeared with Gritz at a 1994 Montana conference along with a broad array of racists from the northwest. And Green, too, has gotten air-time on KPFK's news broadcasts for his bizarre economic views.

Another area of intense Gritz/Populist recruitment is among "conspiracy buffs." The *Spotlight* crowd, through Carto's Noontide Press, has always mixed claims of CIA double-dealing with theories about Jewish/Masonic domination. Thus Willis Carto has promoted his attorney Mark Lane's conspiracy theories about the Kennedy assassination and Populist Action Committee member Fletcher Prouty's "insider" exposés of the CIA; Craig Hulet relies on Anthony Sutton, whose books are mainly marketed by neo-nazis, for a critique of the Trilateral Commission. Some people are swallowing this bait, and getting hooked for the rest of the Populist politics. Prevailing Winds Research's catalog continues to offer Gritz's material without any disclaimer or warning, as if it were equivalent to the anti-imperialist analyses of Michael Parenti or the anti-fascist exposés by Russ Bellant which they also offer. Groups in Portland, Colorado, San Francisco, and L.A. are marketing video and audio tapes of Gritz and/or Hulet on a similarly co-equal basis with those of anti-war and anti-imperialist speakers. This is highly irresponsible. Many groups that promote a kind of channel surfing approach to conspiracy theories have given very favorable coverage to Gritz, Metzger, and other racists, portraying them as simply daring anti-establishment figures.

Gritz never represented a serious electoral threat to capture the White House for the racists. But his electoral work with the Populists has led into an even more dangerous phase of paramilitary organizing through his SPIKE organization. Gritz has been conducting SPIKE training sessions throughout the northwest and southwest, with the support of Christian Patriot ex-cop Gerald "Jack" McLamb. The duo are setting up what they call Christian Covenant Communities as a key aspect of strategy to build a base and organization. The SPIKE training sessions, another vital component of the strategy, include both ideological orientation and weapons training. SPIKE training sessions have been held in Texas, North Carolina, Utah, Arizona, California, Idaho, and Florida.

Front Man for Facism

In Montana, Gritz has been involved in the setting up of a similar white-supremacist-type com-
pound by "Constitutionalist" Martin "Red" Beckman.
The Constitutionalists are Montana's version of the
Christian Identity/Christian Patriot movement. Gritz
participated, along with Beckman, McLamb and Rev.
Pete Peters, at a conference in Billings, Montana that
tried to portray Beckman as a tax protestor being set
up for the next "Waco-style" assault by the feds.
Other participants reportedly included Rudy "Butch"
Stanko, a convicted seller of tainted meat to the U.S.
Army who briefly headed the neo-nazi Church of the
Creator, and John Abarr, head of the Knights of the
KKK in Montana. When Abarr was with the KKK in
Montana, he ran the Congressional campaign of
Daniel Johnson, former head of the Glendale,
California–based League of Pace Amendments
Advocates, which would restrict U.S. citizenship and
residence to "Aryans." Abarr is apparently now the
vice president of the campus Young Republicans at
Eastern Montana College.

Also at the conference was George Green of
America West Distributors and the *Phoenix Liberator
Express,* which purports to be the racist, anti-
Semitic transmission of an extra-terrestrial space
fleet commander, channeled through Green's wife.
The Greens are facing charges of fraud and money
laundering in Nevada for setting up a pyramid of
phony corporations apparently designed to evade
taxes and fleece followers who come to them for
"extra-terrestrial" investment advice. The Greens'
material was distributed at a Populist Party gathering in Pasadena during Gritz's campaign.

Central to Gritz's approach to the SPIKE training is his attempt to impart and apply his Green Beret training and operations methods to organizing a militarily capable white Christian resistance movement. The training at Pasadena City College concentrated on getting people ready to be organized into A-, B-, and C-teams, or into auxiliaries that would function under these teams' command. The A-teams, modeled on the Special Forces, incorporate 12 people responsible for personnel, intelligence gathering, transportation, logistics and supplies, communications (with other teams and operatives), and civil/governmental liaison. They are meant to be well-trained militarily. Every five A-teams are responsible to a B-team; every five B-teams to a higher-ranking C-Team. Gritz himself leads the central, national command, out of Almost Heaven in Idaho. The teams are all meant to lead a much larger cadre of auxiliaries and sympathizers (also drawn from the SPIKE trainees, but less suited for combat-type conditions).

Gritz is teaching weapons handling and fabrication, how to produce your own ammunition, and battle-field medical procedures. He is teaching helicopter and small plane operations, and inculcating in his followers a perspective on this country as terrain for a coming apocalyptic conflict. He is training his followers in intelligence gathering, secure communications, carrying out night landings and air drops, and other more openly military activities and skills, such as rappelling and gun-fighting. He provides lessons in picking locks and sells the lock-pick kits to go along with it. As the stages of the training progress, they include field-stripping weapons, reloading ammunition, and other aspects of military self-sufficiency. Gritz personally lectured on how members of his teams and their auxiliaries could function to help protect white survivalist fugitives from illegitimate government authority.

In addition to charging for the training, Gritz and his colleagues are peddling videos, survivalist gear, training manuals, even freeze-dried food. He is no doubt turning a pretty penny, but his primary motive is not financial but political. The two cornerstones of his operations are the Christian Identity religion and the State Citizenship/State Sovereignty philosophy. Though Gritz himself is nominally a Mormon, his key supporters and associates are advocates of Christian Identity doctrine, which preaches that the 10 lost tribes of Israel are the northern Europeans, and that America is their biblically-promised land. Identity preaches that Jews are the spawn of Satan, and that non-whites are "mud people," pre-Adamic creations (sub-humans) which God evidently botched before getting it right with the white man. Christian Identity provided the main forces that established the neo-nazi underground Order in the 1980s, from the Idaho compound of Richard Butler, and the Colorado encampment of Pete Peters.

Despite this history, Peters today is remarkably enjoying increasing acceptance in the broader Christian right community. He has been aired on the same Christian broadcast network as Falwell and Robertson, despite his patently heretical views, his open racism, and his virulent homophobia. Peters was guilty of election finance law violations for using "church" funds to support anti-gay ballot measures in Colorado. He is the author of a booklet calling for the death penalty for gays.

The other element of Gritz's SPIKE/Christian Covenant program is State Sovereignty. This innocuous sounding movement contends that only white citizens are true, "state" citizens, whose rights are superior to even the Constitution. Others (Blacks and non-white immigrants) are considered to be "federal citizens" of the District of Columbia, not the states, and therefore aliens. These "aliens" were granted their rights after the Civil War by the 14th Amendment (which the State Citizens do not recognize). State Citizens claim to have no obligation to pay federal taxes or file income tax returns; they refuse to use zip codes or social security numbers, or sometimes even to carry driver's licenses, which they believe serve to establish state ownership rights in your vehicle.

Another aspect of Gritz's politics is a not-very-covert anti-Semitism. In his monthly newsletter, Gritz preaches that current Israeli leaders and other Jewish notables are paving the way for the anti-Christ (apparently still Mikhail Gorbachev, despite the fall of the Soviet Union). He blames the Rothschilds for most of the economic problems in the U.S. It is curious and short-sighted in this regard that establishment Jewish organizations spend most of their time publicizing and condemning Louis Farrakhan, even after he expelled Khalid Muhammad, and almost none casting public light on Gritz and his network.

Gritz has solidified his anti-gay posture since establishing SPIKE. In a recent issue of his *Center for Action* newsletter, he reported favorably on a "study" which showed that such calamities as hurricanes, earthquakes, and economic disruptions coincided with Gay Freedom Day marches on the anni-

versary of the Stonewall rebellion, which he inter-
preted as a sign of God's displeasure with gay rights
activists. He reasoned that the punishment was
directed at God-fearing straights who were foolishly
allowing gays to continue their abominations.

Gritz is devoting a lot of energy to both northern and southern California. He is apparently setting up one of his Christian Covenant communities
near Paradise, California. Controversy erupted there
after Gritz ran a SPIKE training session at a school
up there, and gave away a semi-assault rifle as a
door prize. SPIKE teams have been formed in 10
cities, including Dallas and Phoenix. The phenomenon is related to others pushing the formation of
state "militias" as quasi-governmental bodies, a
kind of rightist dual-power. Militias are currently
actively being organized in Montana, with KKK
involvement, in Wisconsin, with participation of the
Posse Comitatus, and in North Carolina, where former members of the Klan and the paramilitary
White Patriot Party are involved.

Gritz has his struggles with some of these other
formations. In the May 1994 issue of his *Center for
Action* newsletter, he harshly criticized Linda
Thompson, who has claimed that 80,000 Chinese
troops under UN command are poised in Montana,
and has called on all militia members to arm themselves and march on Washington, D.C. the second
week of September 1994, if Congress does not repeal
the 14th, 16th, and 17th amendments, GATT,
NAFTA, and the Brady Bill. Though his own beliefs
are almost as bizarre, Gritz is nobody's fool. He shot
down Thompson's paranoid ranting because he
doesn't want his cadre to waste themselves in suici-

dal gun battles with federal troops or agents while his movement is still in the building and preparation stage.

But he is deadly serious about building a white fighting force that can contend for power militarily in the coming years. He's laying the groundwork for a white Christian war of "resistance" as the century draws to a close. Gritz has begun predicting that the biblical end times are approaching, on an approximately seven-year timetable and countdown related to Israel's reaching peace treaties in the Middle East. He is urging his followers to prepare, and to hasten the apocalyptic return of Jesus (by not eating pork or shellfish, among other methods).

Progressives and anti-racists must draw a clear line that exposes and condemns Gritz and his racist and neo-fascist allies in the Populist Party, SPIKE, and other such formations. Recognizing freedom of speech puts no affirmative obligation on us to promote or uphold such racist views. Unifying with Gritz would inevitably discredit the white left with the movements for immigrants' rights, Black empowerment, Native sovereignty, women's liberation, and gay and lesbian dignity. No one concerned about conspiracies and the abuse of government power, about spiritual development or the survival of the planet, should offer Gritz or the racist and fascistic-oriented Populist Party a shred of acceptability. The Populist Party and SPIKE or similar "state militias" are only the latest hood these night riders of the Ku Klux Klan have put on, to mask their identities so they can win support for carrying out their racist terror. DON'T BE HOOD-WINKED!

The Klan Behind the Camera

Racist Mobilizing on Broadcast and Cable TV

You're relaxing on the couch, finishing a cold one. The game's over early, and you punch buttons idly on the remote control, channel surfing for something to watch. What's on? Newt Gingrich, talking to no one about nothing in particular. Must be C-SPAN. MTV's got the same old same old, a new music video with soft core s & m. HBO has a rerun of "Last Action Hero." Wait a minute—what's this? Looks totally bizarre. The screen shows a benevolent looking guy, a real straight arrow in a hairpiece and a three-piece suit, sitting there with two rough looking skinheads in metal studded black leather jackets. The camera pans in on the straight dude. In a well-modulated, slightly smarmy voice, he intones:

"Welcome. The show is 'Race and Reason,' and I am your moderator, Tom Metzger."

Through the looking glass. The skins proceed to talk about racial purity and the gripes of white youth with this old guy who might be a skinhead himself, except he's wearing a rug.

283

What is this show? They may call it "Race and Reason," but "Racist Outrage" could be closer to the mark.

In fact, this is no ordinary talk show, cultivating controversial guests for the ratings, and Metzger is no ordinary talk show host—he's the former Grand Dragon of the Ku Klux Klan in California. He now heads White Aryan Resistance (WAR), which produces the show. He's been convicted in Portland, Oregon for fomenting some of these nazi skins to kill an Ethiopian immigrant. He's been convicted for a triple cross-burning in L.A. along with the Klan, the Nazis, and the Aryan Nations.

His TV show, "Race and Reason," has put the white-supremacist movement into living rooms throughout America on cable-TV community access channels in California, Oregon, Washington, Texas, Georgia, Pennsylvania, and northern New York State. Most recently in 1993–94, the show has aired on cable in Simi Valley in Ventura County and on an Orange County cable system. Metzger's show has been met by protests everywhere it airs. Fifty demonstrators picketed Chicago's Channel 19 when "Race and Reason" debuted there. According to Larry Duncan of the Committee for Labor Access, which produced the "Labor Beat" weekly on Channel 19, Chicago Access Corporation, the franchise holder for several cable channels, had guidelines prohibiting all producers from using obscene or libelous material. "We told them this was libel against entire communities. What could be more obscene than fascism?"

But most cable managements maintain they are required by law to air the show. Metzger claims first amendment protection for his show. He says that the right of free speech allows him to air his "racial nationalist" views. "Race and Reason" is lower key than most of the propaganda from WAR, and is carefully designed to legitimize Metzger. While he avoids the open advocacy of race war and racist revolutionism that marks his newspaper, *WAR*, and his telephone hate line, Metzger doesn't moderate his racism and anti-Semitism for "Race and Reason."

He calls it "a white man's talk show." Having traded in his robes for a business suit over a decade ago, when he ran for Congress from San Diego, winning the Democratic nomination, Metzger has been reborn as the white supremacist's Donahue. He is able to get his message out to the folks he wants to reach in the privacy of their homes. He has taken a page from Falwell, Swaggart, and the other TV preachers, using TV, computers, and telephone hot lines to project a 21st century Klan.

On his show, Metzger elicits similar racist and sexist views from his guests. These have included the bodyguard for the late neo-nazi leader George Lincoln Rockwell, Mike Brown; the late Ben Klassen of the Church of the Creator, who told Metzger that he supported "having any white nation cleansed of alien or mud races"; and Greg Withrow, then head of the White Student Union (WSU). Withrow applauded the white high school student in Sacramento, California who stabbed a Vietnamese youth to death, as the "highest example of white manhood." Withrow was later crucified to a wooden plank by nazi skins loyal to Metzger's son John, who took over the WSU and turned it into WAR Youth after Withrow had a change of heart.

285

Metzger hit on TV as the best way to maintain a public presence for the racist right wing in a period in the '80s when public Klan activity was on the decline. The subsequent resurgence of neo-nazi and KKK activity may be based in no small part on that strategy. Cable TV casts a broad net that draws in new followers and potential sympathizers without exposing them to public identification or attracting much attention from potential opposition. Yet everywhere the show has aired, it has also led to an upsurge in racist violence. In Sacramento, for example, the nazi skinhead who carried out a reign of racist terror during the summer of 1993, bombing the NAACP, a synagogue, and several Asian-American targets, first came in contact with Metzger through a TV show, called his hate-lines, ordered WAR, and proceeded to put Metzger's preachings into practice.

From his home base in southern California, Metzger has complemented the cable shows with participation in the Aryan Liberty Net, a computer bulletin board founded by the Idaho-based paramilitary Aryan Nations. This computer system provides telephone access numbers in the midwest, four other regions of the U.S., and in Canada. It has several levels of password security codes through which the initiated can communicate. Metzger's newspaper is distributed to white supremacists nationally. Now, Metzger also runs a network of telephone answering messages, dubbed "hate-lines" by his opponents, around the state of California, and throughout the country, by piggy-backing onto a commercial "voice bulletin board" system which uses digital technology to take messages and store them as computer data. Other racist groups are now following his lead using the same type of system to transmit their racist and anti-Semitic diatribes. Through these high tech means, he urges racists to form cells to carry out "leaderless resistance"—race war violence for which Metzger himself cannot be held personally liable.

The image of a responsible advocate of a minority opinion protected by free speech rights that Metzger presents on cable and broadcast TV is only one face that the neo-nazis, the KKK, and white supremacists turn towards the media. The other is perhaps best exemplified by an incident in Huntington, West Virginia in May 1986, at the same time that Tom Metzger was defending his right to produce "Race and Reason" on the campus of California State University at Fullerton using a publicly-financed production facility. In Huntington, WOWK-TV was knocked off the air in what then station manager Leo MacCourteney described as "an act of terrorism," half an hour before the station was to air an exposé of hate group organizing in the state.

Just before the scheduled broadcast of the first part of an Action News series called "West Virginia: Haven for Hate?", the station's main cable was slashed with an ax, disabling its network satellite dish. At the same time, someone scaled a security fence, climbed onto the roof of the station, and took out the microwave dish that linked the production facilities to WOWK's transmitter in Barker's Ridge, West Virginia. Restored to the air the following day, the station, then affiliated with ABC, aired a five-part segment on the Ku Klux Klan and other hate groups operating in the state. A threatening note was received at the home of a station official, but police and the FBI were unable to identify a suspect.

That attack is not an isolated phenomenon. More recently in Los Angeles, a west-side cable TV system has been the target of repeated vandalism. During one incident, the system's transmission of a football game was interrupted and replaced with a long and mocking diatribe against Jewish control of the media. The Pacifica Foundation radio station in Texas, dubbed "free speech radio," was the target of repeated bombings of its transmitter. Suspicion fell on followers of paramilitary Ku Klux Klan leader Louis Beam.

What is the relationship between Metzger's use of cable TV, broadcast talk shows, and "tabloid TV" to seek a sympathetic audience for the KKK and other white-supremacist groups, and the use of anti-Semitic and racist violence against broadcast media? According to a number of experts, shows like Metzger's are directly linked to a growth in racist violence in the communities where they appear. Trella Loughlin, a college teacher and community access cable producer in Austin, Texas, where "Race and Reason" has aired, supported community efforts there to keep Metzger's show from being cablecast. Noting an increase in attacks on Black people in the city after Klan marches held in the Texas capital, she said, "I wouldn't have put Hitler (on cable) in 1937, and I wouldn't put the Klan on now."

"Race and Reason" is central to Tom Metzger's sophisticated strategy of using various electronic media, including both cable and broadcast TV, telephone message hate lines and computer bulletin boards, as well as distributing audio and video cassettes, to build a base for WAR with relative secrecy and with little recourse for effective opposition. Although "Race and Reason" has provoked heated opposition where it airs, the only focus for outraged community protests has been the cable broadcasters who are forced by their licensing to make common cause with Metzger in claiming first amendment guarantees for his show.

By finding one local supporter sympathetic to his racist views, Metzger is able to fish in troubled waters by getting the show placed on local cable community access channels, which must air anything brought in by local subscribers. For example, "Race and Reason" was put on the cable system in Simi Valley after the acquittals there of the cops who beat Rodney King. The airings coincided with a series of campaigns by white supremacists based outside the area to hold rallies and garner support in Simi.

The success of Metzger's approach has not been lost on other neo-nazi and KKK organizers. In a period when the number of open Klan members was declining steadily, and most KKK groups turned away from making public appearances in their robes and hoods because they were out-organized by anti-racists, often taking embarrassing drubbings despite heavy police protection, Metzger hit on TV as the best way to maintain a safe, sanitized public presence for the racist right wing. He aided the distribution of his own show with widely publicized appearances on tabloid TV talk shows like Geraldo Rivera and Oprah Winfrey, along with his son John and the neo-nazi skinheads they were beginning to cultivate.

For Metzger, TV has proven the ideal vehicle. It casts a broad net that draws in new followers and potential sympathizers, without exposing them to public identification or active opposition. Following his lead, others are undertaking similar ventures. Louis Beam, former head of the KKK in Texas, a leader of the Aryan Nations, acquitted of federal charges of seditious conspiracy, has run video training seminars for white supremacists. K. A. Badynski, a neo-nazi in the northwest, produces his own cable TV community access program.

Perhaps the white supremacist who has proven most adept at exploiting TV coverage for his own purposes is David Duke, who gave out his address on several nationally broadcast interviews following his election to the Louisiana legislature and parlayed the financial support that came rolling in, into a race for the United States Senate and a run for governor. Duke found the first paying job of his life after a career of supporting himself through the white racist movement—as a radio talk show host on a small station north of New Orleans. After that show was canceled, Duke turned to selling insurance, but is now planning a run for Congress or governor in Louisiana.

In Kansas City, after the local Klan was unable to get "Race and Reason" aired because it was not produced locally, the KKK started their own show as well, called "Klansas City Kable." When a majority of the City Council proceeded to eliminate public access programming on the city's cable service rather than allow the Klan to broadcast, it provoked a furor over free speech issues. But the nature of Klan "speech" became evident when several KKK members were arrested immediately after a taping session, while carrying weapons, for harassing Black passersby on the street outside the studio.

The San Francisco Bay Area, long thought of as a liberal, progressive community, serves as a clear case study of the potential for the growth of deadly racist violence in the wake of neo-nazi cable and broadcast TV and radio organizing. In 1984–85, "Race and Reason" began to appear on cable channel 25, Viacom Cablevision in San Francisco. It was met with a series of protests and demonstrations. Simultaneously with the TV show, WAR established a local telephone hate-line. Messages advertised the show, called for the removal of Blacks from "Aryan territory," accused Jews of carrying out "genocidal abortions of white babies," and demanded the death penalty for homosexuals. WAR began to leaflet and sell its newspaper on college campuses.

The growth of WAR dovetailed with an increase in racist violence in the Bay Area. In February 1985, a man claiming to be from WAR called in a bomb threat to the Ethnic Studies Department at Cal State–S.F. In May, a live bomb was discovered in a Black Studies classroom, set to detonate while classes were in session. Later that year, when rock music impresario Bill Graham, whose mother and sister were killed in the Auschwitz concentration camp, organized a protest of Reagan's trip to the S.S. cemetery at Bitburg, his office complex was burned to the ground. Neo-nazis claimed responsibility. In September, several pipe bombs with anti-Semitic messages were found. Coy Ray Phelps, arrested for setting the bombs, had Aryan Nations and other racist literature and more explosives in

291

his home.

Charles Miller, local WAR leader at the time, disclaimed any involvement with Phelps and said his actions were "ineffective." The kind of action WAR did support, he explained, was the Order. The Order was a paramilitary racist underground group involved in the slaying of a Denver radio talk show host, Alan Berg.

War and the Order

The connection of Metzger and WAR to the Order, a clandestine, neo-nazi terrorist group also called the Bruder Schweigen (Silent Brotherhood) and the White Aryan Bastion, is particularly significant in light of Metzger's claims to first amendment protection for his show. Among the crimes for which more than two dozen members of the group have been imprisoned is the "execution" of Berg, after the Jewish radio moderator had verbally savaged several white supremacists he had on his talk show as guests. The Order also plotted to kill TV producer Norman Lear, founder of People for the American Way. Free use of the media is guaranteed, in the twisted logic of these racists, only to Aryans; for their "racial enemies," the price of access is death.

According to FBI testimony at a lengthy conspiracy trial of Order members in Seattle, and depositions from a captured member, loot from the group's multimillion-dollar Brink's and bank hold-ups was distributed to public white-supremacist chiefs like Metzger and Beam, and Aryan Nations head Richard Butler, all of whom are now involved in TV production and computer networking. Did the Order's loot finance the white supremacists' advance into the era of electronic communications? Most of the public neo-nazis deny the charges, although one Christian Identity leader returned some of the funds to the Feds. A federal grand jury in San Diego investigated Metzger's possible connections with this money, most of which has never been recovered.

Although Metzger makes no bones of his support for the Order—he proclaimed its imprisoned members as "prisoners of war" in every issue of his tabloid—he has tried to downplay his personal involvement by saying, "I've always had informal associations with any group in the country that is pro-white and racialist. We don't sit in judgment of any other group. [Each] does what it feels best, and that's the way we leave it." This "live and let live" approach is denied both by Metzger's fierce polemics with most other racist groups and leaders, and by his close association with the Order at its very inception. He participated in December 1983 in a triple cross-burning and unity rally of the KKK, nazis, and Aryan Nations in Los Angeles. Four of the other participants at this event, which in retrospect appears to have cemented the southwestern anchor for the Order, became federal fugitives in the Order case. They were eventually captured in Missouri and Arkansas, fleeing to other white-supremacist paramilitary compounds.

In his broadcast appearances, Metzger is usually more circumspect about his political support of and possible involvement in the Order than he is in the pages of his own newspaper, where he often extols their battle against "ZOG," the Zionist occupational government. But occasionally he lets down his guard on the air. When Barbara Jackson, a Bay-

Area anti-Klan activist, confronted Metzger on a radio call-in show about whether he knew the whereabouts of Frank Silva, former KKK leader in L.A., guest on "Race and Reason" and at that time a fugitive from federal conspiracy charges against the Order, Metzger replied that if Jackson gave him her home address, he would try to see that Silva obtained it.

The Young and the Racist

Over the years, Metzger has used his own show, his appearances on radio and TV, and his sale of racist music videos and cassettes by mail order through his newspaper as a principal means to reach out to and mobilize young people to his racist cause, including but not limited to nazi skinheads. Richard Butler, head of the Aryan Nations, said after his appearance on "Race and Reason" that it resulted in a 400-500% increase in phone calls. "It's a good way of communicating because it's the only thing young people are accustomed to these days." Metzger knows that getting into the mix of programming on TV is an avenue to the consciousness of the channel-switching cable TV generation.

On his own show, Metzger has repeatedly featured youthful racists. He interviewed Greg Withrow, founder of the White Student Union, before Withrow had a falling out with Metzger's son John, who took over the WSU. On both his own program and on TV talk show appearances with his son, Metzger projected Bob Heick, then a leader of the Metzger-affiliated neo-nazi American Front skins in the S.F. Bay Area.

Joe Mazella, another Metzger crony who appeared on his show and on the Oprah/Geraldo/

Donahue circuit with WAR, was a key youth organizer for Metzger. Mazella, who was vice-president of WAR Youth behind Metzger's son, was organizing nazi skinheads in Portland to the WAR banner, appearing on local TV talk shows in that city last year. The immediate result of his TV campaign to legitimize white racism and mobilize white racists was the murder of an Ethiopian refugee by some of the very nazi-skins he was organizing. Mazella had been staying in the apartment of one of the killers. In the aftermath of the slaying, Mazella, who had been a fixture on Portland TV for several weeks, was picked up on an outstanding warrant for racist vandalism in California and extradited. Eventually, he testified against the Metzgers in a civil lawsuit over the death of the Ethiopian, Mulugeta Seraw.

Not all of the people associated with Metzger through his TV and electronic outreach activities have turned away from the racism he draws them into. Geremy "von" Rineman, a nazi skin who appeared with Metzger on a TV show with L.A. investigative reporter Harvey Levin, was later arrested by federal agents for his involvement in the Fourth Reich skinhead illegal arms conspiracy. The Fourth Reich skinheads were also convicted on pipebomb charges and for plotting attacks on Jewish and Black leaders, including a plan to assassinate Rodney King. In Sacramento in 1993, a racist reign of terror took place, including the bombings of a synagogue, the NAACP, the Japanese American Citizens League, a Chinese American city councilman, and a state office building. Threats were also sent to a gay and lesbian center. Credit was claimed by a so-called Aryan Liberation Front.

The prime mover, facing trial as this book is being prepared, was a teenager who was first exposed to Metzger on a TV talk show appearance, liked what he heard, became a faithful caller to Metzger's phone hate-lines, and a reader and distributor of *WAR*, Metzger's paper. As Metzger promoted his new concept of "leaderless resistance," to avoid any culpability for his followers' violence, this young man apparently put it into practice. Although he is the only one arrested or charged in the case, his defense was that he did not act alone, and did not himself throw the fire bombs. As this book was being prepared for publication, he was convicted of a number of charges but won a hung jury on the most serious felonies, including attempted murder.

Metzger has taught his followers well in the techniques of exploiting the media's cravings for ratings and sensationalism to build their organizing and outreach. After the notorious clash between Metzger's son John and a Black guest on the Geraldo show, in which host Rivera's nose was broken, John Metzger appeared on a local morning talk show in L.A. The show purported to analyze the role of sensationalism in TV talk shows by inviting the two participants in the brawl to watch it repeatedly on video monitors and say how they were feeling at the time. Any serious discussion of the contents of Metzger's racist message was explicitly squelched by the host. Instead, Metzger was allowed to depict himself as an injured innocent, and to win sympathy from the audience's hostility to Rivera.

On the air, the younger Metzger openly admitted that the relationship between WAR and the media was one of mutual exploitation: "They use us to get ratings," he said, "and we use them to get our message out to the public." The problem is that both the message and its consequence is growing racism and violence. Figures obtained through the civil suit in Portland showed that cash donations to the Metzgers and WAR always swelled after their TV appearances. Sometimes, the benefits provided by the media are even more immediate in fulfilling the neo-nazis' purposes. In 1994, an L.A. radio station, KFI, which airs a number of "mainstream" racist and rightist talk show hosts, flew John Metzger and a racist associate to Germany on a Holocaust anniversary, allegedly to expose him to the crimes committed by Hitler. This obscene effort to hype the station's own ratings potentially provided Metzger with an international audience. Luckily, the German government expelled the neo-nazis upon their arrival in Munich, preventing them from cementing their contacts with local racists.

With his own show, the older Metzger has even more latitude than the easily exploited talk show hosts grant him. There, Metzger is in complete command; he runs the show, produces it, hosts it, often puts words in the mouth of his guests. He uses the program not only to organize viewers but as a means to unite other white supremacists nationally behind his leadership. He brings them on the show for interviews, he uses them to sponsor the show on local cable access channels in their areas, he even has them produce their own versions or segments, as was done by Ray Frankhauser, a Pennsylvania Klansman close to Metzger who was eventually sent to prison for his involvement in the schemes of neo-nazi Lyndon LaRouche. In Florida, a locally produced version of

"Race and Reason" has run as a weekly live call-in show.

Whether "Race and Reason" received financing from the ill-gotten gains of the Order is still an open question. What is known is that for several years, Metzger produced it with the aid of Group W (Westinghouse Broadcasting) in studios at the broadcast journalism department of Cal State Fullerton. Eventually, this activity was exposed by a staff person at the college who could not stomach being used to propagate Metzger's racist views, leading to a series of demonstrations on the campus. Production of the show was moved to Group W's own facilities in Fullerton; now Metzger handles all the production himself and is insulated from public pressure. The other known source of funding for "Race and Reason" was former co-producer and co-host Bill Padgett. Padgett was involved in a massive fraud with former financial whiz kid Barry Minkow and his "ZZZZ-Best" Carpet Cleaning Company. While Minkow was draining money from the fraudulent company and using it to bankroll, among other things, the racist Jewish Defense League, Padgett was doing the same for WAR and the Metzgers. Metzger and Irv Rubin, head of the JDL, each knew the other was milking the same cow. Despite their professed enmity—they have come to blows during one of their many joint appearances on the Wally George show on TV in Orange County—the two seemed quite content to share the wealth. We should note that the L.A.P.D. took seriously Minkow's claims that a lot of the money that passed through ZZZZ-Best was being laundered for the mob.

There has long been an odd symbiosis between the media-hungry Metzger and Rubin. When anti-

The Klan Behind the Camera

Klan activists in L.A., seeking to organize against the planned cross-burning which drew together Metzger's WAR, the local nazi party, the Klan, and the Aryan Nations, appeared on a local TV show, "Mid-Morning L.A.," in the early '80s, the program producers set them up by arranging for the first call-in to be from Irv Rubin. Rubin, instead of attacking the nazis, directed all his hostility at the anti-Klan organizers. Rubin and his JDL thugs later physically attacked a picket line protesting plans to give the KKK a fire permit for the cross-burning.

Metzger and Rubin continue to cross-promote each other through their joint or rival TV appearances. When Whoopi Goldberg wanted to draw ratings for her late night TV interview show, the first guest she scheduled was Metzger, at whom she lobbed a series of polite, conversational, soft-ball questions that did nothing to expose his hard-core racism. But when the show received a slew of protests and complaints for its kid glove treatment of Metzger, providing him with a virtual "infomercial" to sell his racist wares, the Whoopi show's response was to bring on—Irv Rubin. Rather than correcting the problem, Goldberg compounded it by providing Rubin in turn with a gracious free forum to spout the JDL's anti-Black and anti-Arab racism (and in the bargain, rerunning clips from the Metzger interview).

Despite all the disclosures of Metzger's deceitful free-speech-to-promote-race-war strategy, despite the repeated evidence of the undeniable connection between neo-nazi organizing on the air-waves and racist violence in the streets, the media are still open to exploitation by Metzger and the KKK. In

Pulaski, Tennessee, when the whole town closed up shop and turned their backs to protest a rally by the Aryan Nations, the only people who were there to greet the racist marchers and record their ceremony honoring a Confederate veteran were the reporters with their TV cameras. Today, the Klan and similar groups are broadcasting their message through interactive computer messaging services like Prodigy, Compuserve, and the Internet. Holocaust revisionists, supporters of Populist presidential candidate "Bo" Gritz, and other, more hard-core and open racists have turned to e-mail and faxes as new tools in their organizing repertoire. But TV coverage remains a principal goal, because of its reach into the nation's living rooms.

If any of the media attention involved a real exposé of the neo-nazis, their sources of funding, their plans for race war, or their allies in high places, the coverage might be justified. In the current circumstances, in which the white supremacists are taken at face value and allowed to set the terms of their appearances, it is complicity in the campaigns of the supremacists. As one outraged member of the studio audience told Oprah Winfrey when she repeatedly had Metzger and his nazi-skin thugs on her show as guests: "You're giving them a million dollars worth of free publicity." Metzger and the others, particularly the nazi-skins, don't expect to be embraced by the majority of viewers. They are quite content to use the shows to pick up contact with a rabid minority attracted to their openly racist views. Any opposition they neutralize by appearing respectable or within the acceptable spectrum of views that get aired is simply the icing on the cake.

300

The Klan Behind the Camera

TV producers and hosts often seem to feel that they are performing a public service by giving the nazi-skins the opportunity to "hang themselves" by advocating violence. This was the strategy followed by Montel Williams' show, which twice had nazi skinheads for long, vitriolic, and unopposed appearances. On the second one, Williams had on Thom Robb of the KKK along with his family, as well as a crew of Christian Identity skins from Las Vegas who had converted their mom to racism. He allowed Robb to play good cop-bad cop with the nazi skinheads, attempting to make himself appear as the moderate or rational one. He allowed the Christian Identity skins to poison the airwaves with their threats to exact vengeance when they came to power.

This author, scheduled for a separate, countervailing segment of the show to provide an anti-racist perspective, was never allowed on the air; instead, Williams ran out the clock, his juices flowing with the red meat the nazi-skins were happily providing. So his viewers were left unaware of the violence of Robb's closest associates, the affinity between the Klan and the nazi-skins, and other vital information. Both Robb and the Christian Identity skins were able to project exactly the image they wanted, unchallenged.

A similar philosophy guided the producers of a recent Fox-TV special, "Facing the Hate." To spice up the studio audience segment of the show, wrapped around pre-taped components focusing on the Museum of Tolerance and other attempts to reduce prejudice, the producers salted the audience with a phalanx of nazi skinheads from around southern California, hoping to get some audience-generating histrionics. As an anti-Klan activist, I was also brought in to the audience, and invited to bring anti-racist skinheads from SHARP (SkinHeads Against Racial Prejudice) with me, which I did. But we were not informed that we were being set up as "opposite numbers" for the racists, to provide in-studio drama. We were moved out of camera range and our comments excised from the show, when the producers apparently found them too politically provocative. The racists, of course, had their views aired in full.

The mass commercial media, corporate controlled, generally allow for a very narrow spectrum of opinion acceptable to the big business interests. FAIR (Fairness and Accuracy in Reporting) and other groups have repeatedly documented the absence of even liberal or labor voices, let alone left, grass-roots, or radical groups and individuals. Yet the racist right, advocating white supremacy, race war, and even genocide is not merely given access but actively courted and promoted. David Duke and Tom Metzger can find a comfortable niche as radio or cable talk show hosts when the air-waves are dominated by the blusterings of Rush Limbaugh. This must stop. The media themselves must become a focus of anti-racist activism and protest against this behavior.

Wolves in
Peace Clothing

Racist Right Infiltration and Disruption of the Peace Movement and the Left

Several groups on the racist right wing made opposition to the U.S. military build-up and the eventual war in the Persian Gulf a major focus of their organizing. Just as there were liberals and conservatives on both sides of the war issue, there was a split among racists. Some groups were vehement in support of the war effort. The racist Jewish Defense League, for example, picketed and attempted to disrupt an anti-war teach-in in Los Angeles. They were joined by several of their frequent allies from Nemesis, a radical right activist group in L.A. that has targeted Central America solidarity efforts in the past. In San Diego, the head of a pro-troops rally sported a t-shirt showing an Arab being strafed by a jet fighter and the slogan, "I'd fly 10,000 miles to smoke a camel." In Canada, some nazi-skinheads close to the Canadian KKK marched at a pro-war demonstration.

But racist groups were also much in evidence

among war opponents, trying to win new recruits. Such efforts included an anti-intervention demonstration by the Populist Party, (the agglomeration of neo-nazis and tax protesters that ran David Duke for president in 1988). Here in L.A., a Populist Party gathering featured an Arab doctor who had been part of a "peace delegation" to Saddam Hussein led by a North Carolina–based white supremacist, Nord Davis. A national "student peace conference" was held in Chicago on December 15–16, 1990 under the auspices of several front groups for then jailed neo-nazi presidential candidate Lyndon LaRouche.

In Nevada, neo-nazi skinheads with ties to the KKK and Tom Metzger's WAR organization sent upwards of 7,000 letters addressed to "any white service member" to soldiers in the Gulf, urging them not to fight for Israel. Some of the letters, signed by a "racially pure white woman," called on white G.I.s to return home and father white children to insure racial survival. The letters provoked a federal investigation, and declarations by the military that it could do nothing to screen or censor the letters.

White supremacist Tom Metzger used the Gulf issue to fight back from his legal defeat in Portland, Oregon (for inciting nazi skins to kill an Ethiopian refugee). On his telephone hate-lines and in media appearances, such as on "Harvey Levin in the Lion's Den" on Channel 2 KCBS-TV in L.A., Metzger emphasized his opposition—on "white racialist" grounds—to U.S. military action in the Gulf. Referring to Arabs as "sand niggers" and "camel jockeys," his propaganda portrayed the U.S. action as a policy of the "ZOG" (Zionist occupational government, a white supremacist term for the federal government popularized by the clandestine combatants of the Order).

Metzger urged racially conscious white soldiers to get their training in the desert and then return to fight the real war at home for white domination. Metzger, who also opposed U.S. intervention in Vietnam and Central America, says no white soldier should die for "inferior colored people." He criticizes fellow racists whose anti-Jewishness has caused them to ally with Arab groups. "Arabs are also Semites," Metzger reminded his anti-Semitic brethren. "We only fight for Aryans." Nazi boneheads close to Metzger's Canadian affiliate, the Aryan Resistance Movement (ARM), marched in anti-war rallies in Ottawa.

Blaming the war on the Jews may also have motivated the Populist Party, which long received substantial funding and organizational support from Willis Carto, founder of the Liberty Lobby. Echoing some of the views expressed by Metzger and by syndicated columnist Pat Buchanan, the Populists decried the "war party" in Washington as being controlled by Israel. They claimed Bush had planned the war in Israeli interests rather than American ones. They and other racist right groups attempted to use this as a hook to appeal to those who had, from the left, rejected Bush's definition of U.S. interests. Similarly, Metzger's paper was full of cartoons depicting a stereotypical Jew sending "Aryan" U.S. soldiers off to fight the Arabs.

According to Lenny Zeskind, then research director of the Center for Democratic Renewal, a national group that researches the racist right and promotes anti-racist activism, Populist Party candidates in several states opposed the Gulf intervention in the November 1990 elections. The Populists held a demonstration against U.S. intervention in Pittsburgh on November 10, according to Zeskind, which drew about 25 people. Chip Berlet of Political Research Associates, another group that keeps a close watch on the radical right, says that Carto's Liberty Lobby circulated the *Spotlight* and other literature at several anti-war rallies in the east.

The reactionary John Birch Society turned from conducting a national campaign against Nelson Mandela and the ANC to redirect its attention to the Gulf. It organized against the war at Merrimack College and elsewhere in Massachusetts, according to Berlet. The Birchers set up tables at several L.A. demonstrations against the war. They focused their propaganda on opposition to Israel and the U.N. Apparently, it gave the group a new lease on life. Even before Clinton took office, the JBS was enrolling new members and opening new chapters.

Dennis Mahon, the former Imperial Dragon of the paramilitary White Knights of the KKK in Tulsa, Oklahoma led his white-bereted group into the anti-war movement. In the *White Beret,* his newsletter, he encouraged other Klansmen to work with anti-war activists. He said he had "worked with some of the anti-war folks, and let me tell you, their drive and dedication puts most of us to shame. They aren't afraid to get hit on the head by a cop [or] go to jail. I've been very disappointed (in comparison) with the cowardly attributes of many Klan and Identity people in Tulsa. Some of these lefties are discovering the Jew and race problems. They will make excellent Klansmen and women."

Wolves in Peace Clothing

Opposition to the war from the racist right was a factor not only in the U.S. and Canadian cases but in several of the countries in Bush's "coalition." In Germany, Michael Kuehnen, then head of the neo-nazi National Socialists denounced the war and offered to send 500 volunteers to fight along Saddam Hussein (a stance different from the "plague on both your houses" views of Metzger).

In South Africa, Robert von Tonder, head of the white-supremacist Boerstaadt party, sent a message of support to Saddam Hussein, denouncing the war as imperialistic. He compared the U.S. action to the British war against the Boers (Dutch Afrikaaners) in 1899. The leader of another racist group, Coenraad Vermark of the Orde Boerevolk, expressed similar views. This had the odd effect of putting the groups into the same camp with African liberationists such as the P.A.C. who also opposed the U.S. military action, while the apartheid settler government was offering the use of bases in South Africa to support the U.S. Gulf war effort.

Perhaps the largest and most sophisticated campaign by neo-nazi forces in the U.S. against the U.S. presence in Saudi Arabia was mounted by the groups associated with Lyndon LaRouche, the former SDSer turned fascist. LaRouche's organization, which is international in scope, also took part in anti-war mobilizing in Germany and elsewhere in Europe. The LaRouchites stepped up their organizing in L.A., among students and at such events as a city-wide teach-in on the Gulf crisis. LaRouche's newspaper, the *New Federalist,* focused on the war, and issued a supplement headlined "Force Congress to Stop Bush's Mideast War!" which LaRouchites distributed at anti-war rallies. The group actively sought new adherents in the upsurge of spontaneous anti-intervention activism with some limited success.

Many new activists may be unaware of the history of LaRouche and his organization. LaRouche is a notorious homophobe who led efforts to impose a quarantine on people with AIDS through two California ballot initiatives (which were decisively defeated). He is a sophisticated anti-Semite who received funds and an entree to the racist right from Willis Carto of the Liberty Lobby. LaRouche's security was run at one point by Ray Frankhauser, a KKK leader. His followers received paramilitary training from Mitch WerBell, a noted right-wing mercenary. LaRouche had access to top White House officials early in the Reagan administration and shared "intelligence" about progressive groups with contacts on the National Security Council. Earlier, in the '70s, LaRouche's followers became known as "brownshirts" for their strategy of physical attacks on left groups, which LaRouche referred to as "Operation Mop-Up."

Under the auspices of the deceptively named Food for Peace, its farm-organizing front group, and the Schiller Institute, a supposed cultural foundation, the LaRouche network held a so-called "national student peace conference" at a hotel in Chicago, with associated activity at a local campus, on the weekend of December 15–16, 1990. LaRouche forces had organized for the event among students in southern California and around the country, but most participants were actually farmers who have been drawn unwittingly into the Food for Peace operation, and Black people who have been attracted by LaRouche's anti-drug rhetoric and professed support for civil rights. There were only a small number of students, mostly from the midwest.

The LaRouche forces tried to coalesce with a large anti-war mobilization held that same weekend in Chicago, a tactic they also pursued elsewhere. According to Berlet, the Schiller Institute co-sponsored an anti-war rally at the University of Ottawa in Canada with a Middle Eastern student group, and several LaRouchites marched with a banner at the October 20, 1990 anti-war demonstration in New York City. LaRouche's followers also participated in the Cleveland Committee Against the War. At their "anti-war" conference, the LaRouchites featured video-taped addresses and telephone hookups with Helga Zepp-LaRouche (LaRouche's wife) in Europe and with a cultural attache at the Iraqi embassy. A "former" associate of LaRouche's group became one of the principal leaders of the Coalition Against U.S. Military Intervention in the Middle East in Portland, Oregon, editing their newsletter and incorporating a number of articles from LaRouche sources.

The LaRouche groups are particularly dangerous because, despite their fascist orientation, they have been attempting to recruit among Black groups for some time. They cast their opposition to the Gulf intervention and war with an "anti-racist" slant. Their propaganda emphasized the disproportionate non-white make-up of U.S. troops in the desert, and called for an investigation of chattel slavery of Blacks by the royal families of Kuwait and Saudi Arabia. "Economically, the war will mean genocide on a scale unseen in human history, affecting...the Arab world, the Indian sub-continent, Africa and Ibero-America," LaRouche's propaganda proclaims, in an echo of his long-standing view that the Rockefellers and the Queen of England are plotting to eliminate up to 40% of the world's population. The LaRouchites referred to the troops deployed in the Gulf as the "Anglo-American forces."

The LaRouche forces have had some success over the years with their approaches to the Black community, winning some Black religious and political figures to a defense of LaRouche himself as a victim of political persecution by the U.S. government, for example. Several LaRouche gatherings, including a meeting of his International Caucus of Labor Committees in Washington, D.C., have featured speakers from the Nation of Islam (NOI). The editor of the NOI's newspaper, *The Final Call,* spoke at the LaRouche anti-war conference in Chicago. LaRouchites couch their attack on the Anti-Defamation League in anti-racist terms, seeking credibility for some of the more bizarre and anti-Semitic elements of their critique by associating them with legitimate criticisms of the ADL's practices.

The LaRouche forces tried to use their contacts with the NOI to seek entree to Black community organizing against the war in St. Louis. Similarly, they tried to use their ties to Ramsey Clark to legitimize themselves in the anti-war movement. Clark, the former U.S. Attorney General who led one of the major national coalitions against the war, as well as subsequent fact-finding missions and exposés of the brutal consequences of the U.S. war on the Iraqi people, has represented LaRouche's followers in

310

court. He has also spoken at their conferences, and the LaRouchites in L.A. distributed at anti-war rallies in 1990 and 1991 a pamphlet authored by Clark referring to LaRouche as a political prisoner. LaRouche served a federal prison term and was paroled last year. Charges against him included credit card fraud for using phony billings to the accounts of several wealthy old backers to finance his presidential campaign and other activities.

The anti-intervention mobilizing by the LaRouche network represented a major effort to increase their inroads into the Black community and among a new generation of student activists unaware of the group's history of homophobia, anti-Semitism, and violent attacks on the left going back 20 years. LaRouche took a "left" turn in a political career that has zig-zagged across the political map in a quest for power. He may be successful in duping activists who are not familiar with his ties to Willis Carto, his rapprochement with military and intelligence officials in the Reagan White House, and his espousal of anti-gay hysteria in the AIDS crisis. LaRouchites continue this deceptive approach. In 1994, followers of LaRouche attempted to join a coalition opposing the anti-immigrant Proposition 187 on the California ballot, perhaps looking to make inroads into the Latino community.

LaRouche is not the only racist/rightist who enjoyed some success in making inroads on the left through opposition to the Gulf War. Many on the right who opposed the build-up, such as Pat Buchanan, who referred to Jewish supporters of Bush's mobilization as an "amen corner for Israel," folded up their tents and fell in line once the war began. But this was not remarkable, as the reality and rapidity of the war itself, despite its high-tech brutality, deflated much of the anti-war activity that had greeted the build-up and Bush's various dead-lines. Opposition to the Gulf war also apparently gave renewed vigor to the Holocaust revisionists, who subsequently stepped up their advertising and organizing at campuses, promoting the view that the Nazi genocide of the Jews and others is only a hoax perpetrated by the Jews to build support for Israel.

One chilling result of racist mobilizing around both sides of the Gulf war issue was the increase in both anti-Arab and anti-Jewish violence across the country. The legitimization of racism on both the right and the left, as well as the glorification of mili-tarism, led to an unprecedented level of racist politi-cal violence in this country. In Orange County, Arab groups and individuals reported a major increase in harassment and death threats. In San Francisco, the Human Relations Commission conducted hear-ings on this problem.

The Center for Democratic Renewal reported that members of David Duke's National Association for the Advancement of White People in Toledo, Ohio beat up an Arab American businessman. The CDR also reported that Osama Sablami, publisher of the largest Arabic language newspaper in the U.S., received a death threat "if any Americans in Kuwait were harmed." At the same time, some of those who blamed U.S. involvement in the Gulf crisis on Israel were attacking Jewish targets. Several San Francisco Bay Area temples were fire-bombed in attacks attrib-uted to sympathizers of Tom Metzger's WAR organiza-tion. In L.A., three suburban temples were also vandalized with anti-Semitic slogans over the same weekend.

In Los Angeles, fires were set at the businesses of a Lebanese-American and an Iranian-Jewish immigrant. Anti-Arab graffiti was spray-painted on Fouad Halaby's gourmet coffee shop the day before it burned. Detective Mel Arnold of the hate crimes unit of the L.A.P.D. said the incident was being investigated as a likely hate crime related to the war. The suspected arsons were denounced by both Nazih Bayda, regional director of the American-Arab Anti-Discrimination Committee (ADC), and David Lehrer, L.A. head of the Anti-Defamation League of B'nai Brith (ADL).

In two local incidents, arrests were made. Kurt Haber, a 60-year-old Jewish man, was charged with telephoning bomb threats to the headquarters of the ADC inside an Islamic Center, and an Egyptian immigrant was arrested for making a false bomb threat to a non-existent airline flight from the L.A. Airport.

Police never solved the fire-bombing of a Jewish center and synagogue in North Hollywood whose congregation includes Morrocan and Israeli Jews. The temple had links to the Jewish Defense League (JDL) and Meier Kahane's Kach organization, and the complex housed an office of JDL head Irv Rubin. The same night it was struck with several molotov cocktails, an arson fire also broke out at a retail store in another part of L.A. that housed a telephone line for the JDL.

Telephone bomb threats were received in the week after the war began at several Jewish schools and temples around the suburban San Fernando

Valley. Gerald Lebovitz, the principal at one such school, attributed the growing level of anti-Semitic hate crime to tensions fueled by the war, and ordered additional security measures, including a patrol by private guards. On February 1, 1991 the Lomita home of Dr. Shlomo Elspas, head of the Chassidic Jewish Chabad House of the South Bay was vandalized for the ninth time since the Gulf crisis began.

The L.A. police reported stepping up patrols past both Arab and Jewish institutions. Numerous Arab-American business and professional leaders reported receiving threatening calls. The editor of an Iranian-American newspaper in the San Fernando Valley, Iraj Rostami, was attacked by a masked gunman who fired two shots at him in a scuffle before fleeing. Rostami, whose paper *The Iran News*, is printed in Farsi, was treated and released in a local hospital. In San Diego, a mom-and-pop liquor store owned by an Iraqi immigrant family was burned down.

At a Martin Luther King Day candle-light march and rally against hate crimes in North Hollywood, co-sponsored by PART in 1991, Youssef Haddad of the Arab-American Coalition Against the War denounced the violence and threats as an attempt to intimidate the Arab-American community and prevent it from expressing its opposition to the war and exercising its First Amendment rights. Rabbi Steven Jacobs, another speaker, expressed the importance of uniting Arabs and Jews, Muslims and Christians to oppose all such attacks, and to seek peace at home.

The violence wasn't limited to southern California. In Michigan, which also has a large Arab-

American population, the business of a Palestinian-American, Kareem Khoury, was destroyed in an arson fire. Khoury, a U.S. Army veteran, had been outspoken in his opposition to the war. As in the case of the coffee shop in L.A., the store was the target of vandalism shortly before the fire. Khoury's store was splattered with paint, and "USA No. 1!" was spray-painted on the store front the week before the arson. Neighbors, as well as congregants from the Methodist church where Khoury teaches Sunday school, immediately joined in cleaning up the wreckage, and the minister collected more than 600 signatures denouncing the vandalism. In an odd footnote, Khoury himself was later charged with having set the fire, based on the testimony of a disgruntled former employee.

In Lakeland, Florida, an East Indian family received a threatening phone call, telling them to go back to Iraq, or "something like a missile attack" might happen. Shortly thereafter, a pipe bomb was thrown against their garage door. Police quickly arrested a 15-year-old. The high school student had mistakenly believed the family were Iraqi.

In Tulsa, Oklahoma on February 21, 1991 an Iraqi American family was burnt out of their home. According to Abdul Almusanni, the message, "You are dead," was spray-painted on his house. Police investigated the arson attack as a hate crime. Tulsa is the home of several white-supremacist groups including the Oklahoma Whitemen's Association, and was the site of one of Tom Metzger's racist hate lines, over which the WAR leader propagandized against Arabs and Jews in the Gulf war situation.

In San Francisco, Moustafa Awadalla, a Kuwaiti

immigrant, was brutally beaten while delivering a pizza in the Haight Ashbury district, which had also been the scene of organizing by WAR and neo-nazi skinheads associated with it. Awadalla, who required six hours of brain surgery to recover from the beating, believes he was attacked "just for being an Arab."

In Austin, Texas, someone tacked up posters featuring the racist caricature of an Arab man at the University of Texas. They were captioned "Wanted: Dead or Alive—Any Arab." In Boston, Ahmad Tahba, a Palestinian, received death threats and was forced to move from his home. His roommate was told, "Kick the Arab out." In Gaithersburg, Maryland, an Iranian American family was beaten by a road crew. The attackers fractured the father's skull in the beating, and he was partially paralyzed. One of them was quoted as saying, "I want to kill these foreigners to teach them a lesson about complaining in our country." In Lowell, Massachusetts, this type of xenophobic hysteria resulted in totally false charges against an Arab accused by his co-workers of wanting to poison the water supply. In Cambridge, Massachusetts several Kuwaiti students were harassed, resulting in the suspension of those responsible.

In suburban Bloomington, New Jersey, police investigated whether the vandalism of a Jordanian American family's home during the second week of February was a "bias incident." Omar Samman, a U.S. resident for two decades, had reported a threatening phone call received by his family a month before, as the war was imminent. "A man said that if anything happened to our troops in the

Gulf, our family would pay for it," Samman told the press. Intruders slashed several pieces of furniture and broke a large mirror, leaving a yellow ribbon, symbol of support for U.S. military forces in the Gulf, in the living room. Many houses in the neighborhood displayed such ribbons, while the Sammans' did not, but neighbors and families of the children's classmates called with offers of help after the attack.

In Chicago on January 29, 1991 a Jordanian American store-keeper, Omran Jabbar, was beaten with a four-foot sledgehammer handle by a customer, in an attack motivated by the Gulf war. Jabbar suffered a facial fracture and numerous cuts in the severe beating.

Within a month after Operation Desert Storm began, the American Arab Anti-Discrimination Committee received more than 50 reports of such acts of violence, harassment, and intimidation against Arab Americans. These followed on the heels of 47 incidents after Iraqi troops entered Kuwait and Bush declared it "would not stand." Incidents increased from a rate of fewer than one per month early in 1990, to 58 in January 1991 alone. In releasing the figures, the ADC also criticized continuing FBI questioning of Arab Americans. Ghassan Khalek, an employee of the Federal Communications Commission, described the negative effects of having FBI agents arrive at his office and flash their badges to question him, making him appear as a suspect of some sort. "There are people who don't want to hang out with you because they know the FBI is looking for you." But he also told the press conference that at least one co-worker hung a sign on his office door

saying "Arab people are our friends, not our enemies."

Government actions stigmatizing and harassing
U.S. Arabs have not been restricted to the FBI. In
L.A., the state Department of Motor Vehicles
attempted to revoke the personalized license plates
purchased in February 1990 by Dr. Kareem Jaffer
for a 12-year-old BMW he got for his son. The plates
read "4 JIHAD," the teenager's name. A spokesman
for the DMV said the agency had received a complaint about the plates from a motorist and that
since they are "advertising they are for a holy war
against U.S. forces in the Gulf, they would be very
offensive obviously to many people." The agency
sent a letter calling the plates "offensive to good
taste and decency," and asking Jaffer to relinquish
them voluntarily or face legal proceedings to cancel
the plates. But the agency backed down after press
reports disclosed that Jihad was the youth's name.
Dr. Jaffer also pointed out that "holy war" is a
derogatory Western translation of an Arabic term
from the Koran that means "spiritual struggle."

The B'nai Brith Anti-Defamation League (ADL)
reported a record number of attacks against Jews in
1990, with a 71% increase in California alone. Betsy
Rosenthal of the ADL said at the time, "If what has
happened so far this year is any indication of the
ramifications of the Persian Gulf crisis on anti-
Semitic crimes, I would have to anticipate" that
1991 would be even worse.

Infiltration and Espionage

The common oppression suffered at the hands
of racists by Arab and Jewish Americans becomes

ironic in the light of diclosures that prior to and all through this period, the ADL was involved in infiltration of and spying on the American Arab Anti-Discrimination Committee (ADC). David Lehrer of the ADL has attempted to justify this by characterizing the ADC as having been supporters of Khadaffi at an earlier stage, apparently having learned nothing about the way in which U.S. demonization of Arabs and Muslims leads to violence against both Arabs and Jews in this country. For 30 years, the ADL employed (or as they say, contracted the services of) Roy Bullock as a private investigator. In addition to infiltrating neo-nazi and anti-Semitic groups, Bullock kept tabs for the ADL on Arab Americans, Black nationalists, various progressive groups, supporters of the African National Congress, and even journalists and civil libertarians.

Bullock apparently obtained confidential police files from a former CIA agent on the San Francisco police department's "red squad." He may also have had similar files from the L.A.P.D., Portland police, and other departments around the country, although the L.A.P.D. has, as of this writing, refused to cooperate with an investigation by the FBI and the San Francisco District Attorney's office. Some of Bullock's files, in turn, made their way into the ADL's offices, in computerized records labeled "Blacks" and "Pinkos." Bullock and Gerard, his San Francisco P.D. source, repackaged some of this material and sold it to the South African secret police. There is some fear that the material also fell into the hands of the Mossad, the Israeli equivalent of the CIA. At least one of the Arab Americans included in the files was arrested by the Israelis on

319

a visit to occupied Palestinian territories.

An official of an Arab American rights group disclosed that Bullock had infiltrated his organization on behalf of the ADL. Although they had nothing to hide, he said, they became extremely distressed when they learned that Bullock had also gone to white-supremacist meetings (also as a spy for the ADL) and had distributed application blanks for membership in the Arab American group to the neonazis. These kinds of tactics are reminiscent of the dirty tricks of the COINTELPRO period (the FBI infiltration of Black liberation and other left groups). It is not the role of the ADL to spy on or disrupt progressive groups, or to help police departments circumvent hard-won bans on police spying on constitutionally protected political activity. The ADL was able to reach an agreement with the San Francisco D.A. limiting its liability; even the cop who illegally diverted the files was eventually let off when federal agencies refused to allow his prosecution in state court because of national security considerations.

Yet there is no question that infiltration, disruption, and espionage of progressive organizations is continuing today. Whether that activity originates from the repressive forces of the state, from racist right groups seeking recruits or intelligence, or from purported civil rights groups like the ADL, it must be opposed. Self-criticism is an essential component of any strategy by progressive forces to overcome our current weakness. This means that no one, even if they were victims of fascism themselves, can be assumed to be free of similar tendencies, as we can see from the practice of some Jews and some Serbs, for example. We must seek to grow beyond our current small numbers, but we must do so while remaining vigilant about infiltration and provocation in our ranks, and about the debilitating effects of racism within the left. This racism is not simply "exported" by racist right groups that enter our ranks, but arises from the material and ideological conditions of life in the U.S., which continue to be distorted by land theft, slavery, and genocide. Our best defense against such infiltration and disruption is to base our politics on principle and on solidarity with the oppressed. Despite the ultimate rejection by the country of the war-induced hysteria that made Bush seem unbeatable, progressive forces have yet to regain some of the momentum that opposition to the Gulf build-up generated, or to build a powerful anti-racist, anti-sexist movement that can help shape a better future. We will never do so if we allow ourselves to be seduced by the racist right or disrupted by counter-insurgency operatives of whatever stripe.

Afterword

Know the Enemy

A Chinese proverb has it that if you know the enemy, and know yourself, you can fight a thousand battles and never be defeated. More recently, Pogo, a comic strip character who poked fun at McCarthyite politicians and sanctimonious preachers during the '50s, when that was a risky proposition, coined the saying, "We have met the enemy and he is us." Understanding that the enemy is not only external to us, or opposite to us, but that indeed the enemy is within us as well, is vital to anti-racists. We cannot demonize our enemy without dehumanizing ourselves as well.

But having said that, it is still crucial to understand the nature and operation of our enemy, the root sources of the racism we are trying to uproot. If we believe we are dealing only with ignorance, or stupidity, or intolerance (rather than with injustice and self-serving power), we will pursue only well-meaning efforts that will not succeed in dealing with the problem. We will be ill-prepared for the consequences that even these efforts call down on us if the real enemy feels at all threatened. We are up against a system whose survival depends on racism; a sys-

323

tem that produces and reproduces racism in generation after generation, despite any contrary ideals it professes; a system that will in fact take desperate measures to defend, sustain, and perpetuate racism. Because racism is vital to, and inextricable from, the functioning of the system as a whole.

So we need to understand the mechanisms that this racist system uses to propagate itself and to attack or neutralize those it considers its enemies. In the introduction to this volume, I looked at several principles essential to a healthy anti-racist movement: self-respect, self-determination, self-defense, solidarity, spirituality, struggle, self-criticism, and socialism. In closing, I want to examine the nature of the beast, and again, as a mnemonic device, I'm categorizing the most important features of this system and its defense/attack mechanisms with terms beginning with the same letter, C.

This system is, of course, capitalism, the system based on the rule of the dollar over all human endeavors. It functions through commoditization—turning all human relationships, products, and capacities into commodities, artifacts to be bought and sold for a profit. But equally essential to the system as a defining element is colonization, the conquest of land from its original inhabitants, and the expropriation of their labor and resources. Criminalization is another central aspect of the functioning of this system—dissent or resistance is a crime; even work or survival in themselves can be deemed crimes. Finally, when people try to break out of the shackles of commoditization, colonization, and criminalization, the system will resort to its twin tactics of coercion and cooptation, the stick and the carrot, to intimidate or buy off its opposition. This essay will briefly examine each of these five aspects in turn.

Commodities are the building blocks of the system under which we live. "Commodities" does not only mean the kind of trading that goes on at the Chicago Mercantile Exchange, where people gamble on buying or selling pork belly futures, or corn, or orange juice, or precious metals. Commodities are the way every aspect of daily life is organized within the capitalist system, and all human relationships are carried out through and by means of commodity exchanges. Most of us accept this system as fair, just, and natural; accordingly we sell ourselves to the highest bidder, and cannot begin to fathom how this produces so many of the problems we try to overcome. It is this willing participation, in which all our best efforts are used against us, that makes the system so strong.

Money, the measure by which all human activity and all land and natural "resources" are assigned a value so they can be bought and sold, is itself a commodity. Some people make millions of dollars buying and selling money all over the world. As money makes or begets money in this way, all sense of the true, inherent value of human endeavor or planetary existence is lost. What's more, our creative capacities become a commodity, bought and sold on the labor market for wages. Under capitalist slavery, the most brutal and degrading form of exploitation ever devised, human beings themselves became commodities—things to be purchased, used, and discarded. Racism was invented first of all to justify this dehumanization.

But it is almost equally shameful to buy and

sell the land, the air, or the water, all of which our society continues to do. Here in Los Angeles, the "right" to poison the air has become a commodity, in which companies trade authorizations to produce smog. Around the country, homelessness is a manifestation not of personal failings in the homeless, nor some lack of charitability in our national character, but quite simply of the fact that, because land is private property with a dollar value measured in rent, decent housing is a commodity which has been priced out of people's reach. Defying the commodity system by squatting is a crime; even giving away food to people has been criminalized. From Santa Barbara to Santa Ana, cities are making it a crime to live on the streets, in defense of "property values." With the general abolition of chattel slavery, wage slavery continues, in which we sell our creative capacities. If no one cares to buy those capacities, we become criminals.

The global economy is a commodity economy. Not only are goods and products traded, but capital itself flows around the world constantly seeking cheaper labor, constantly driving the cost of labor power down towards or below the cost of reproducing and sustaining human life. Blood and human body parts are commodities today; children are killed for their organs. Procreative capacity is a commodity, as surrogate mothers rent their wombs; top dollar in the international baby market goes, of course, to white babies. And women's bodies in general have long been a prized commodity, bought or rented for sexual exploitation or used to market other commodities with the promise of "sex." The destruction of the environment is rooted in a system that only sees the value of something that can be processed and sold for a profit.

The guiding principle of commodities is always "buy low, sell high," meaning that the competitive advantage always goes to the one who can corner the market, monopolize the source materials, or control the distribution of the product. But, of course, monopoly is the antithesis of competition, a situation in which one "competitor" remains, having swallowed or destroyed the rest. (Yet this doctrine of competition, self-destructive and self-contradictory as it is, has gripped and shaped the psychology of everyone within the confines of the system.)

Of course, there is no price lower than free. Theft, pure and simple, is the impulse of colonization, as it was of slavery: to take what belongs to or is produced by others, especially other cultures or systems, and by absorbing it into our own commodity economy, to assign it a vast commodity exchange value where it had none before. The profit percentage on the sale of a commodity that you obtained with zero cost is of course infinite. Therefore slavery, therefore land theft, therefore the wasting of the land. Marx and other socialists have paid much closer attention to question of labor power as a commodity, and the way this has shaped society and psychology around human alienation, than to the question of the expropriation of land. Yet even Marx acknowledges land and rent as a separate and independent form of capital. In fact, the devastating social, psychological, and cultural effects of colonialism, in which land is taken from those who dwell upon it, and re-conceptualized as a form of capital, are all around us.

327

Much of the world's ecological crisis is due to the vast distortions produced by driving people engaged in collective subsistence agriculture into peonage or the swollen cities, while the land is turned over to unsustainable cash crop monoculture to provide commodities for the world market (cotton, coffee, or cocaine). The cost of this destruction is borne by the colonized, while the proceeds and benefits (until the planet is destroyed) go to the colonizer. Similarly, the advantage of male supremacy to the capitalist is that it allows him to expropriate and profit from women's unpaid, unwaged labor.

As the system has matured, it continues to colonize and re-colonize both other territories and people and also within itself. It has also heightened and intensified colonization by injecting into the colonized lands and people the system of commodity production and exchange. This creates new markets (driving up prices) and incorporates new workers (reducing the costs of labor and of reproducing capital). But just as the worker, whose ability to work is a commodity, can never make enough money to recapture what she produces, the capitalism developed within the colonies is predicated on being subordinate, and can never overcome that condition of subordination or overtake the colonizer.

The state has grown up to enforce and carry out that conquest, colonization, and confiscation domestically and internationally. Those who run the state seek a monopoly on coercive power, the intoxicating and corrupting ability to force people to do what you want. And the essence of this state power is criminalization; defining and carrying out the punishment for disobedience. Criminalization serves

328

several purposes, right up to the present moment. First of all, colonized people are criminalized in their essence. Whoever is not a colonizer and citizen is per se a criminal. Non-payment of taxes and trib- ute—refusing to transfer wealth to the capitalists' government for free—is the first crime. Next is the failure to produce or consume commodities: pover- ty. But behaviors are also criminalized because that makes them more profitable. A black market always allows you to buy cheaper and sell higher. Thus the criminalization of drugs, the criminalization of sex, the criminalization of immigrant labor do not aim at eliminating the market in these commodities, but at regulating and heightening their profitability.

Criminalization also serves two other essential purposes: it marginalizes people; and it drives them into the hands of organized crime, which far from being in contradiction to the system, is dependent on and supportive of it. The psychology of a petty or a major criminal is not opposed to the dollar men- tality of the commodity/colonial system. The contin- uum from crime to business to government is not seamless, but they mesh together fairly well. Just as the slave trade to the American colonies was related to the international trade in rum and tobacco, so today the vast profits of the cocaine and heroin trade flow through the finest banks and savings and loans to be laundered.

Today, criminalization also functions as a method of re-enslavement and re-colonization. The prison industry is a growth mechanism; Governor Pete Wilson of California is apparently relying on it to replace aerospace as the motor of the state's econ- omy. Clinton's crime bill is evidence that this line has now been adopted at a national level, The prisons fill up with people of color, as penal colonies that serve as a cross between slave labor camps and concentration camps. The differing crimes for which men and women are arrested, the differing arrest rates and charges against whites and people of color, draw a searing outline of oppression and stratification in our society.

To protect this system of commodities, colonialism, and crime, the rulers who benefit from it use the twin tactics of coercion and cooptation. Their use of these tactics is grounded in and colored by racism from start to finish. During the era of settlement and slavery in America, for example, the color line between white indentured servants on the one hand, and African slaves and indigenous nations on the other, was enforced and solidified through both punishment of those whites who crossed the line, and inducements for those who didn't. But similar tactics were also used with people of color, though in different measure (more coercion and less cooptation). The loyalty to their masters of those slaves who were prepared to sell out the freedom conspiracies eroded the solidarity of all the slaves, and made possible the execution of the most militant leaders. Native people prepared to turn their lands into "property" for sale to the colonizers received a "fair price," while those who resisted the resulting reservation system were hounded and killed.

These strategies continue to this day. The fierce repression of the Black Panther Party, the Puerto Rican Nationalists, the American Indian Movement, the Brown Berets made the prospects of reintegration into the comforts of the system all the more

330

Afterword: Know the Enemy

attractive to white student radicals in the '60s and
'70s, for instance. The combination of coercion and
cooptation is always designed to make shutting up a
lot more attractive than putting up when the time
comes to make the choice. This is the same strategy
carried out by the tough cop/nice cop interrogation
team, the same false choice presented by conservative and liberal parties that both support the state
and the regime. This is the same approach that has
sustained male supremacy through dichotomizing
women as "madonna or whore"; the same protection
racket that says a woman is either legitimized by
association with a particular male who favors her,
or "fair game" to all men who target her.

Cooptation and coercion never operate sepa-
rately or in a vacuum; one is always the symbiotic
partner of the other in defusing threats to the system. The torturers trained by the CIA in Central and
Latin America learned that only by alleviating the
pain does the torturer break his victim's will and
gain his collaboration. The cooptive offer makes it
harder to withstand the coercion; the threat of coercion makes the appeal of cooptation all the more
attractive. Far from really opposing each other, or
even keeping each other honest, the liberal and conservative variants of capitalism/colonialism in this
way operate smoothly in tandem.

The revolutionary challenge posed by anti-colo-
nial forces to this system and strategy is that of
non-collaboration. For example, his embrace of non-
collaboration, defying both coercion and cooptation
by apartheid-colonialism during a quarter-century
in prison, is what endeared Nelson Mandela to millions. More so even than nonviolence, this replace-

ment of the colonizer's values, goods, and belief system is what fueled Gandhi's struggle for Indian independence. In Puerto Rico, colonized by Columbus half a millenium ago, and still controlled politically, economically, and militarily by the U.S. empire, this strategy, called "retramiento," has enabled the Puerto Rican people to withstand cultural genocide and socio-political annihilation.

This strategy must be embraced not only by the colonized, but by all oppressed and working people, and all people of conscience. We must strive to refuse to participate in our own degradation; seek to restore the dignity and integrity of our cultures and our labor; fight to free the land and restore the natural environment; struggle to free our minds collectively from the shackles of colonialism and competition, so that our bodies will follow. This process of mental and physical decolonization is as essential for the colonizer as for the colonized. It is the only sound basis for anti-racist activism.

Index

Index

Index

Index

Index

Index

Hern, Dr. Warren, 130
Herschensohn, Bruce, 171
Hicks, Joe, 103
High Times, 257
Hill, Paul, 127, 139–140, 141, 153, 157
Hilligoss, Dennis, 252
Hirsch, Michael, 140, 157
Hitler, Adolph, 30, 192
Holocaust, 271, 300, 312
Holy Church of the White Fighting Machine of the Cross, 178
homophobia, 102, 113, 143, 227, 231, 232, 243, 263, 279, 308, 311
   computer-recorded examples of, 120–126
homosexuals
   murder of, 52, 225, 237
   penalties and, 258, 279
House Un-American Activities Committee (HUAC), 186
Houston, TX, 60, 71, 147
   and landfills, 211
Huerta, Dolores, 221
Hulet, Craig, 273, 275–276
Human Life Center, 157
Human Life International (HLI), 157
Hussein, Saddam, 307
Hymers, Robert L., 149, 154

I

IHR. *See* Institute for Historical Review
immigration, 41, 168, 195
Immigration and Naturalization Service (INS), 113–114, 117, 170, 177, 185, 199
Immigration Reform and Control Act (IRCA), 30, 181, 185, 193
InCAR. *See* International Committee Against Racism
INS. See Immigration and Naturalization Service
"Inside the Blue Klux Klan," 82
Institute for Historical Review (IHR), 111, 248, 269, 271, 272
International Caucus of Labor Committees, 310
International Committee Against Racism (InCAR), 266
"Intolerance," 44
Invisible Empire, 71, 72
The Iran News, 314
IRCA. *See* Immigration Reform and Control Act

J

Jabbar, Omran, 317
Jackson, Andrew, 37
Jackson, Barbara, 293–294
Jacobs, Rabbi Steven, 314
Jaffer, Dr. Kareem, 318
Jaffer, Jihad, 318
Japan, 18, 183, 197
JDL. *See* Jewish Defense League
Jeffries, Dr. Leonard, 269
Jennett, Jeff, 78
Jensen, William, 186
Jepsen, Roger, 166
Jewish Defense League (JDL), 86, 239–240, 270, 298, 303
Jewish refugees, 30
Jews
   in Germany, 225–226
   and oppression, 16
   See also Holocaust
Jimenez, Arturo, 59
John Birch Society, 53, 67, 74,

Index

Index

343

Index

Index

Index

Index